The International DIRECTORY of NEWS LIBRARIES

including NEWSPAPER BANNERS

A quick reference of selected worldwide news libraries

Edited by
Andrew V. Ippolito

Fifth Edition

Published by
LDA Publishers
42-36 209 Street Bayside, New York 11361 Toll Free: 800 784 0300
Email : aippol1930@aol.com

In cooperation with
The Special Libraries Association
News Division

Library of Congress Cataloging in Publication Data
026.07
The International Directory of News Libraries, Including Newspaper Banners, Fifth Edition
A quick reference of selected worldwide news libraries. Edited by
Andrew V. Ippolito. Published by LDA Publishers, New York,
in cooperation with the News Division of The Special Libraries Association. 1996

Includes Indexes
1. News Libraries - United States - Directories
2. News Libraries - Canada - Directories
3. News Libraries - International - Directories
4. Newspaper Banners
I. Ippolito, Andrew V. II. Title
ISBN 0-935912-66-5
ISSN 08890919
Price. $149.95

CONTENTS

v. Preface
vi. Acknowledgments
vii. News Division Web Site
vii. News Division Officers
viii. News Division Past Chairs
ix. Awards
x. Guide to NewsLib LISTPROC COMMANDS
xiii Alphabetical Listing of Libraries
1. News Libraries, United States
63. News Libraries, Canada
71. News Libraries, International
89 Archiving Systems
91. News Databases
93. Newspaper Groups
97. Online Databases
103. Special Collections
107. Personnel
113. Banners, United States
135. Banners, Canada
137. Banners, International

Preface

This fifth edition of the "International Directory of News Libraries, including Newspaper Banners", is a global directory of professional contacts in media libraries which provides speedy access to information by listing vox, fax, and now email addresses. Each listing, updated by the librarians themselves, profiles the library and includes which newspapers are willing to allow outside reporters access to the files and which ones perform free search services for other librarians. Each entry features special collections and participation in data networks, news databases, and CD ROM. Personnel listings include memberships in professional media associations. Newspaper banner displays are an exclusive feature of the Directory.

WHAT YOU WILL FIND

The Directory is divided into five sections:

News Libraries/United States
News Libraries/Canada
News Libraries/International
Indexes
Banners

Within each of these sections the listings are arranged by state/province/city. International listings are subdivided by country/city. Look-ups are facilitated by several indexes.

What the Listings Include:

Newspaper Name*
Address
Telephone/Fax/Email Address
Hours /Holiday Open
Year Library was founded
Access Policy for Visiting Reporters
Services to other Librarians
Online Databases*
Web Sites
Internet Services
CD ROM
LAN
WAN
Archiving Systems*
Fee Based Research
News Databases*
Newspaper Groups*
Special Collections*
Personnel Listings*
Personal Email Addresses
* Indexed

ACKNOWLEDGMENTS

Putting together the fifth edition of the **"International Directory of News Libraries, including Banners"**, was an exciting experience, because of the cooperation of so many librarians, some of whom I have never met. They are colleagues on the other end of cyberspace. Without them we would have produced a less complete directory and had much less fun meeting and sharing information on the Internet. So our gratitude and thanks to all those librarians and friends for their interest, suggestions, and encouragement.

Particularly we want to express our deep appreciation for the keen professional talents of **Barbara Semonche** of the University of North Carolina, for her suggestions and the many Internet broadcasts promoting the Directory and for being my confrere; **Cary Kenny,** St. Petersburg Times, for her enthusiastic support and sound recommendations that have found their way into this edition; **Nora Paul,** Poynter Institute, who enhanced the data of the Directory by generously sharing the names of our overseas colleagues; **M.J. Crowley,** Newark Star-Ledger, whose beneficence knows no bounds when it comes to sharing her expertise with colleagues; **Margaret Gale**, British Information Service, a constant source of information and inspiration.

Among News Division members who returned calls and graciously gave advice in designing the questionnaire, offered suggestions and aided in data collection were: **Linda Henderson,** Providence Journal, for her ideas and publicizing the Directory in NewsLIbraryNews (NLN); **Kee Malesky**, National Public Radio; **Charles Campo,** Bangor Dailey News; **Richard Geiger,** San Francisco Chronicle; **Jo Kirks,** Knight-Ridder; **Jennifer Belton,** The Washington Post; **Mary Kate Leming,** Palm Beach Post and **Rosemary Armao,** Investigative Reporters and Editors (IRE).

Email made global involvement a reality. Librarians from around the world contributed to the speedy exchange of data. Among those who responded to our call for help were: **Helen Martin,** Manchester Guardian, who supported the project by being enormously helpful in sending data on United Kingdom libraries and the Association of United Kingdom Media Librarians (AUKML); **Neil Phillips,** British Information Service; **Richard Everett,** Axel Springer Publishing Corporation; **Marianna Englert,** German Society of Documentalists; **Eckard Lange,** Verein Deutsche Archivarc; **Vittorio Caraffa,** La Repubblica; **Gordon Travis,** Tokyo, Japan; **Aase Andreasen,** Politikens, Denmark; **Jirina Matouskova,** Center for Independent Journalism; **Dore Farrell,** The Wall Street Journal Europe; *Margrathe Moss* **Mortensen,** Borsen, Copenhagen; **Daniel Reasor,** International Herald Tribune, Paris; **Stuart Dempster,** Express Newspapers, London and **Sonja Lindegger,** Toronto Globe and Mail.

The News Division Web Site

http://www.nando.net/prof/poynter/nd/ndmenu.html

1996 - 1997 News Division Officers

Chair

Teresa Leonard
919 829 4866
tleonard@nando.net

Chair- Elect

Tom Lutgen
213 237 4758
lutgen@news.latimes.com

Secretary

Jeanette Brown
703 276 5592
jbrown@usatpoc.gannett.com

Treasurer

Jody Habayeb
219 461 8377
jhabayeb@fortwayne.infi.net

Directors

EDUCATION
Ron Larson
608 252 6112
rlarson@bnc.net

PUBLICATIONS
Peter Basofin
916 321 1108
pbasofin@sacbee.com

AWARDS
Charles Campo
207 990 8160

NEWS DIVISION PAST CHAIRS

1923
Joseph F. Kwapil
1925
William A. Alcott
1926
John H. Miller
1927
Agnes Petersen
1928
Maurice Symonds
1929
Joseph F. Kwapil
1930
Ford M. Petit
1931
David G. Rogers
1932
Mildred A. Burke
1933
Alma Jacobus
1934
Blanche Davenport
1935
Ralph J. Shoemaker
1936
Matthew Redding
1937
Mary H. Welch
1938
Frances S. Curtiss
1939
Paul P. Foster
1940
Maurice Symonds
1941
Stephen A. Greene
1942
Albert A. Macon
1943
Charles Stolberg
1945
F. Heaton Shoemaker
1947
Joseph E. Molloy
1948
Agnes Henebry
1950
Milton E. Prensky
1951
Ruth Braun
1952
Chester M. Lewis
1953
Lee Cheney Jessup
1954
Robert A. Diehl
1955
Charles A. Brown
1956
William D. Chase
1957
Helen M. Orcutt
1958
Elliot E. Andrews`
1959
Chester W. Sanger
1960
David A. Rhydwen
1961
Jack K. Burness
1962
Clement Vitek
1963
Elwin S. Greene
1964
Rex Schaeffer
1965
Marian Orgain
1966
Roy T. King
1967
Josephine R. Johnson
1968
Andrew V. Ippolito
1969
John J. Doohan
1970
James S. Scofield
1971
John Frankland
1972
Carol Lindsey
1973
Edward W. Quill
1974
Homer Martin Jr.
1975
Joseph O. Mehr
1976
Allison Oppedahl
1977
Lou Thomas
1978
Kenneth Hayes
1979
Sandra K. Hall
1980
Julia Vance
1981
Shirley Mooney
1982
Harish Trevedi
1983
Barbara Semonche
1984
Kathy Foley
1985
Diane Miller
1986
Carolyn Hardnett
1987
Bob Isaacs
1988
Richard Geiger
1989
Sharon Ostmann
1990
Lany McDonald
1991
Margaret Neu
1992
John Cronin
1993
Donna Scheeder
1994
Mary Kate Leming
1995
Charles Campo

News Division Awards

The News Division Awards are given to individuals in recognition of specific achievement in, or a specific significant contribution to, the field of news librarianship

The Kwapil Award

The Joseph F. Kwapil Memorial Award is the highest recognition of the News Division. It is given for major achievement in the field of news librarianship and for outstanding service to the News Division to a member who has actively participated in the division's programs and projects for a continuous period of ten years or more.

The Henebry Award

The Agnes Henebry Roll of Honor Award is given to a member or former member for service to the division and for participation in division programs and projects.

The Shoemaker Award

The Ralph J. Shoemaker Award is a certificate given to the News Division Chair upon the completion of her or his term of office.

The Vormelker - Thomas Award

The Vormelker - Thomas Student Stipend Award is awarded to a graduate library student.

Guide to NewsLib LISTPROC COMMANDS
(Unix ListProcessor: Listproc)
June 1996

Here are the commands needed to subscribe, unsubscribe, request digest format (and how to cancel the digest format), postpone messages temporarily, receive copies of your own messages, obtain a list of subscribers and how to conceal your email address from the list. ***Remember that listproc commands are CASE SENSITIVE, so follow directions carefully. Also, not all commands go perfectly smoothly even when care is taken.*** That is why lists have listowners to help out! NewsLib's listowner is identified below with contact sources.

Finally, this guide will reveal how to obtain a listing of archive files from NewsLib and then how to retrieve a desired archive file.

*N. B.: ALL of these commands/requests MUST be addressed to the **listproc server**, NOT the list, which is NewsLib. Subscribers post messages to the NewsLib list which is composed of nearly 700 subscribers, BUT they issue NewsLib commands to the listproc server. This is an important distinction. It is the listproc commands that are listed and described below:*

Listproc Email Address: listproc@ripken.oit.unc.edu
NewsLib List Email Address: NewsLib@ripken.oit.unc.edu

Skip the subject line and eliminate any signature lines when sending a command to listproc. In the **message area,** type the appropriate command (in correct upper/lower case) and then send message.

Major commands/requests to listproc@ripken.oit.unc.edu

1. **TO SUBSCRIBE / JOIN NewsLib:**
   Listproc: SUBSCRIBE listname Firstname Lastname
   (e.g., SUBSCRIBE NewsLib Marion Librarian)

1a. **TO POST MESSAGES TO NewsLib:**
   Listproc: Address an email to: **NewsLib@ripken.oit.unc.edu**
   Enter an appropriate message subject heading
   Type your message, sign it and send it

2. **TO LEAVE A LIST:**
   Listproc: UNSUBSCRIBE listname
   (e.g., UNSUBSCRIBE NewsLib)
   Do NOT add your name

3. **TO RECEIVE THE LIST IN DIGEST FORMAT** (mutiple messages compiled into a single mailing, usually daily or weekly):
   Listproc: SET listname MAIL DIGEST
   (e.g., SET NewsLib MAIL DIGEST)

4. **TO CANCEL DIGEST FORMAT** (receive the list as separate mailings):
   Listproc: SET listname MAIL ACK
   (e.g., SET NewsLib MAIL ACK)

5. **TO SUSPEND MAIL TEMPORARILY** (*without* unsubscribing):
   Listproc: SET listname MAIL POSTPONE
   (e.g., SET NewsLib MAIL POSTPONE)

6. **TO RESUME RECEIPT OF MESSAGES:**
   Listproc: SET listname MAIL ACK --or-- SET listname MAIL DIGEST
   (e.g., SET NewsLib MAIL ACK --or-- SET NewsLib MAIL DIGEST)

7. **TO RECEIVE COPIES OF YOUR OWN MESSAGES:**
Listproc: SET listname MAIL ACK
(e.g., SET NewsLib MAIL ACK)

8. **TO *NOT* RECEIVE COPIES OF YOUR OWN MESSAGES:** (NewsLib *default* setting is to *NOT* receive copies of your own messages.)
Listproc: SET listname MAIL NOACK
(e.g., SET NewsLib MAIL NOACK)

9. **TO OBTAIN A LIST OF SUBSCRIBERS:**
Listproc: RECIPIENTS listname
(e.g., RECIPIENTS NewsLib)

10. **TO HIDE YOUR EMAIL ADDRESS, FROM THE LIST OF NewsLib SUBSCRIBERS:**
Listproc: SET listname CONCEAL YES
(e.g., SET NewsLib CONCEAL YES)
TO REVERSE THIS COMMAND, USE:
SET listname CONCEAL NO
(e.g., SET NewsLib CONCEAL NO)

11. **TO OBTAIN A LISTING OF ARCHIVE FILES FOR NewsLib:** (3-step process)
Listproc: INDEX listname
(e.g., INDEX NewsLib)
Then send the message

Shortly you will receive a LONG list of NewsLib messages.
Note the date and style of the ones of interest.

Next send an email to listproc with this request
(e.g., GET NewsLib jul95)
Then send the message

Note the date and style of the ones of interest
Next send an email to listproc with this request
(e.g., GET NewsLib.newslib950722)
Note: that stands for 1995 (Month) 07 (day) 22
Then send the message

Finally, a full-text copy of the messages you want will arrive in your email box

12. **TO SEARCH THE ARCHIVES FOR KEYWORDS:**
Note: This search engine is not always effective

Listproc: SEARCH listname "keywords"
Boolean searches are possible using the symbols "&" (and), "l" (or), and "~" (not).
e.g.: To search for "Datatimes" or "Nexis" in NewsLib, use the command SEARCH NewsLib "Datatimes l Nexis"
Next follow the sequence above for retrieving desired messages.

Barbara F. Semonche, Library Director
(Listowner: NewsLib, NCSLA)
UNC - CH School of Journalism and Mass Communication
Howell Hall, CB# 3365
Chapel Hill, NC 27599-3365
Telephone: 919 962 1204; Fax 919 962 0620
Email: semonch@gibbs.oit.unc.edu
Home Page: http://sunsite.unc.edu/journalism/

Alphabetical Listing of Libraries

667 Aalborg Stiftstidende
668 Aalborg TVR
84 ABC News Research Center
- Washington Bureau Library
341 ABC News Research Center
502 Abilene Reporter—News
661 Ace Ltd.
- Information Services
635 The Adelaide Advertiser
81 The Advocate
224 The Advocate
750 Aftenposten
706 Agence France—Press (AFP)
85 Agence France—Presse
637 The Age/Sunday Age
542 Air Force Times
86 Akron Beacon Journal
- Washington Bureau of KR Inc.
420 Akron Beacon Journal
10 Alabama Advertiser
441 Albany Democrat—Herald
157 Albany Herald
320 Albuquerque Journal/ Tribune
542 Alexandria Journal
257 The Alpena News
450 Altoona Mirror
503 Amarillo Daily News / Globe Times
503 Amarillo Globe Times
255 American Antiquarian Society
- Library
87 American Association of Retired Persons
- Research and Information Library
261 American Automobile Manufacturers Association
342 American Banker / Bond Buyer
343 American Civil Liberties Union Library (ACLU)
- Press Office
432 Amos Press, Inc.
- Corporate Library
12 Anchorage Daily News
478 Anderson Independent—Mail
833 Anglia Television
258 Ann Arbor News
88 ANSA
- Italian News Agency
722 - Italian News Agency Library
566 Appleton Post-Crescent
669 Arhus Stifstidende
16 Arizona Daily Star
15 The Arizona Republic / The Phoenix Gazette
18 Arkansas Democrat—Gazette
542 Arlington Journal
542 Army Times
727 Asahi Shimbun
728 Asahi Shimbun
306 Asbury Park Press
401 Asheville Citizen—Times
89 The Associated Press
344 Associated Press
- News Research Center
345 - Photo Archive
729 - Library
792 - News Library
726 Association of Japanese Libraries
793 Association of UK Media Librarians
158 Athens Daily News / Banner—Herald
486 Athens Daily Post—Athenian
159 Atlanta Constitution
159 Atlanta Journal and Atlanta Constitution
743 Auckland Star Limited
504 Austin American—Statesman
641 Australian Broadcasting Corporation
712 Axel—Springer Publishing Corp.
704 Badisches Tagblatt
720 Bahai World Centre
- Library
20 Bakersfield Californian
233 Baltimore Sun
229 Bangor Daily News
224 Baton Rouge Advocate
259 Battle Creek Enquirer
260 The Bay City Times
794 BBC
- News/Research Library
795 - Photograph Library
797 - Information Research Library
346 BBC Radio (London)
- New York Office
782 BBC Scotland
773 BBC Wales
796 BBC World Service
172 The Beacon—News
505 Beaumont Enterprise
451 Beaver County Times
173 The Belleville News Democrat
544 Bellingham Herald
442 Bend Bulletin
749 Bergens Tidende
251 Berkshire Eagle
705 Berliner Zeitung
672 Berlingske Tidende
673 Berlingske Tidende—Nordfoto
685 Bibliotekarforbundet
506 Big Spring Herald
692 Billedarkivet
282 Biloxi Daily Herald
327 Binghamton Press
1 Birmingham News
769 Birmingham Post and Mail
2 Birmingham Post-Herald
417 The Bismarck Tribune
434 The Blade
90 Block Communications
674 Boersen
675 Born & Unge BUPL
676 Borsens Nyhedsmagasin
236 Boston Globe
237 Boston Herald
737 Brabant Pers bv
137 The Bradenton Herald
590 The Brandon Sun
21 Brawley News
507 Brazosport Facts
545 Bremerton Sun
73 Bristol Press
723 British Council
798 British Film Institute
347 British Information Services
- Library
799 British Library
- Newspaper Library
328 Brooklyn Public Library
- Business Library
329 - Periodicals Room
330 - Social Science Division
230 Brunswick Times Record
460 Bucks County Courier Times
331 Buffalo News
800 Builder Group
91 Bureau of National Affairs
- Library
317 Burlington County Times
531 Burlington Free Press
348 Business Week
801 Cable News Network
783 Caledonian Newspapers
581 Calgary Herald
582 Calgary Sun
42 California State Library
- Periodicals Section
477 The Call
587 Canadian Broadcasting Corp.
- TV News Library
610 Canadian Broadcasting Corp.
611 - News Library
612 - Radio Archives
613 - Reference Library
614 The Canadian Press
244 Cape Cod Times

232 The Capital
325 The Capital
92 Capital News Service
321 Carlsbad Current—Argus
235 Carroll County Times
580 Casper Star-Tribune
93 Catholic News Service
- Information Services
94 CBS News
349 - Reference Library
217 Cedar Falls Courier
761 Center for Independent Journalism
- Freedom Forum Library
770 Central Broadcasting
469 Centre Daily Times
700 CFPJ
560 Charleston Daily Mail
561 Charleston Gazette and Sunday Gazette-Mail
404 Charlotte Observer
487 Chattanooga Free Press
488 Chattanooga Times
176 Chicago Sun—Times
177 Chicago Tribune
746 Christchurch Star
238 The Christian Science Monitor
546 The Chronicle
597 The Chronicle—Herald / Mail Star
201 Chronicle—Tribune
738 CHW/FJC
624 CIDA
- Center for International Training
422 The Cincinnati Enquirer
423 The Cincinnati Post
400 Citizen Register / Westchester Rockland Newspapers
284 The Clarion Ledger
489 Clarksville Leaf—Chronicle
490 Cleveland Daily Banner
27 CNN
- Los Angeles Bureau Library
160 - Library
350 - New York Bureau Library
288 Columbia Daily Tribune
289 Columbia Missourian
351 Columbia University
- Journalism Library
425 The Columbus Dispatch
162 Columbus (GA) Enquirer
162 Columbus Ledger—Enquirer
495 The Commercial Appeal
178 Commercial—News
303 Concord Monitor
352 Conde Nast Publications Inc.
- Library
802 Confederation of British Industries
- Information Center
95 Congressional Research Service
72 Connecticut Post
62 Contra Costa Times
96 Copley News Service
716 The Cork Examiner / Evening Echo
508 Corpus Christi Caller—Times
615 Corriere Canadese
353 Council on Foreign Relations
- Library
497 Country Music Foundation
- Library and Media Center
479 Courier
636 The Courier Mail
308 Courier—News
776 Coventry Newspapers
534 Covington Virginian
97 Cox Newspapers
570 La Crosse Tribune
616 CTV Television Network
- Research Library
780 D C Thompson & Co. Ltd.
751 Dagbladet
715 Dagbladid-Visir
400 Daily Argus / Westchester Rockland Newspapers
64 Daily Camera/Sunday Camera
354 Daily Challenge
435 The Daily Chief—Union
407 The Daily Courier
247 Daily Evening Item
803 Daily Express / Sunday Express
355 Daily Express / Sunday Express (London)
- New York Office
593 The Daily Gleaner
250 Daily Hampshire Gazette
226 Daily Iberian
400 Daily Item / Westchester Rockland Newspapers
804 Daily Mail
356 Daily Mail (London)
- New York Office
805 Daily Mirror / Sunday Mirror
63 The Daily News
548 The Daily News
589 Daily News
598 The Daily News
28 Daily News of Los Angeles
400 Daily News / Westchester Rockland Newspapers
463 Daily News—Philadelphia
210 The Daily Nonpareil
439 Daily Oklahoman / Oklahoma City Times
264 The Daily Press
312 Daily Record
202 Daily Reporter
389 The Daily Star
806 Daily Telegraph / Sunday Telegraph
400 Daily Times / Westchester Rockland Newspapers
509 Dallas Morning News
677 Danmarks Biblioteksskole
670 Danmarks Journalisthojskole
686 Danmarks Radio
693 Danmarks Radio
79 Day
426 Dayton Daily News
139 Daytona Beach News and Journal
139 Daytona Journal
4 The Decatur Daily
510 Del Rio News—Herald
466 Delaware County Daily Times
392 Democrat and Chronicle / Times—Union
511 Denison Herald
512 Denton Record—Chronicle
66 Denver Post
779 Derby Evening Telegraph
648 La Derniere Heure / Les Sports
212 Des Moines Register
529 Deseret News
678 Det Fri Aktuelt
262 Detroit Free Press
263 Detroit News
625 Le Devoir
181 The Dispatch
747 The Dominion / Dominion Sunday Times
- Library
98 Dowrey Washington News Bureau
452 Doylestown Intelligencer/ Record
687 DR—Radio
- Library
276 Duluth News—Tribune
245 Eagle—Tribune
807 Economist
357 Economist (London)
- New York Bureau
663 Editora Abril SA
583 The Edmonton Journal
584 Edmonton Sun
584 Edmonton Sun
513 El Paso Herald—Post
514 El Paso Times
427 Elyria Chronicle—Telegram
240 Enterprise
454 Erie Daily Times/Morning News and Weekender/ Times News
454 Erie Weekender
599 ETV Television Network
- News Research Library
649 European Commission
709 European Institute for the Media
707 The European Stars and Stripes
190 The Evansville Courier
191 Evansville Press
772 Evening Argus
716 Evening Echo
831 Evening Gazette
832 Evening Gazette
717 Evening Herald
748 Evening Post
718 Evening Press
804 Evening Standard
808 Evening Standard
596 Evening Telegram
595 Evening Times—Globe—Telegraph—Journal
459 Express

Alphabetical Listing of Libraries

809 Express Newspapers
- Picture Library
841 Express & Star Ltd.
453 Express Times
679 Fagbladet Journalisten
13 Fairbanks Daily News Miner
642 Fairfax Editorial Library
542 Fairfax Journal
406 Fayetteville Observer—Times
542 Federal Times
701 Le Figaro Magazine
617 The Financial Post
810 Financial Times
647 De Financiele Economische Tijd
333 Finger Lakes Times
- Library
699 Finnish Broadcasting Co.
- Library - Information Services
265 Flint Journal
481 Florence Morning News
5 Florence Times Daily
143 Florida Times-Union
358 Forbes Inc.
359 Ford Foundation
- Library
29 Foreign Press Center
99 Foreign Press Center
360 Foreign Press Center
68 Fort Collins Coloradoan
140 Fort Lauderdale News
141 Fort Myers News-Press
515 Fort Worth Star—Telegram
418 The Forum
744 Fourth Estate Periodicals Ltd.
711 Frankfurter Allgemeine Zeitung
277 Free Press
36 Freedom Forum
- Pacific Coast Center
138 - Florida Office
361 - Media Studies Center
393 - Rochester Office
498 - First Amendment Center
714 - Asian Center
765 - European Center
532 Freedom Forum World Center
462 Freedonia Gazette
23 Fresno Bee
690 Fyens Stiftstidende—arkivet
6 Gadsden Times
142 Gainesville Sun
516 Galveston Daily News
100 Gannett News Service
400 Gannett Suburban Newspapers
408 The Gastonia Gazette
645 Gazet van Antwerpen
209 The Gazette
65 Gazette Telegraph
739 de Gelderlander
215 Globe-Gazette / Sunday Globe
319 Gloucester County Times
763 Goteborgs—Posten
419 Grand Forks Herald
266 The Grand Rapids Press
444 Grants Pass Daily Courier
568 Green Bay Press-Gazette
409 Greensboro News & Record
409 Greensboro Record
482 Greenville News
811 The Guardian/Observer
710 Handelsblatt
291 Hannibal Courier-Post
456 Harrisburg News
456 Harrisburg Patriot and Evening News / Sunday Patriot
101 Harte—Hanks Newspapers
75 Hartford Courant
239 Harvard University
- Business School / Baker Library
283 Hattiesburg American
25 Hayward Daily Review
102 Hearst Newspapers & Hearst Feature Service
77 The Herald
547 The Herald
784 Herald
179 Herald and Review
638 Herald and Weekly Times
241 Herald News
400 Herald Statesman / Westchester Rockland Newspapers
188 Herald—Bulletin
405 Herald—Sun
688 Herning Folkeblad
660 Het Belang van Limburg
650 Het Laatste Nieuws
658 Het Volk
410 High Point Enterprise
322 Hobbs Daily News-Sun
309 The Home News & Tribune
167 Honolulu Advertiser
168 Honolulu Star—Bulletin
517 Houston Chronicle
787 Huddersfield Newspapers
788 Hull Daily Mail
562 Huntington Herald-Dispatch
7 The Huntsville News
8 The Huntsville Times
626 Hydro—Quebec
- Autochtones Et Collectivites
169 Idaho Statesman
812 IISS
186 Illinois Register
813 Illustrated London News
- Picture Library
698 Ilta-Sanomat
708 Inca-Fiej Research Association
218 Independence Daily Reporter
814 The Independent
815 Independent Television Commission
196 Indianapolis News
196 Indianapolis Star / Indianapolis News
680 Information
463 Inquirer—Philadelphia
362 International Herald Tribune
- New York Contact
702 International Herald Tribune
290 Investigative Reporters and Editors (IRE)
- Resource Center
816 IPC Magazines
717 Irish Independent / Evening Herald
768 Irish News
718 Irish Press / Evening Press
719 Irish Times
103 ITAR—TASS News Agency
363 - New York Bureau
335 The Ithaca Journal
267 Jackson Citizen Patriot
491 The Jackson Sun
519 Jacksonville Daily Progress
311 Jersey Journal
459 Jersey Shore Express
721 Jerusalem Post
643 John Fairfax Group
- Library
364 John Fairfax U.S. Limited
492 Johnson City Press
457 Johnstown Tribune—Democrat
180 Joliet Herald-News
292 Joplin Globe
199 Journal & Courier
400 Journal News / Westchester Rockland Newspapers
365 Journal of Commerce
182 Journal Star
543 Journal—American
192 The Journal—Gazette
338 The Journal—Register
574 Journal—Times
681 Jyllands—Posten
696 Jyllands—Posten-arkivet
753 KACST
- Library
268 Kalamazoo Gazette
293 Kansas City Star
293 Kansas City Star
569 Kenosha News
221 The Kentucky Post
493 Kingsport Times—News
601 Kitchener—Waterloo Record
463 Knight Ridder Video (KR Video)
104 Knight—Ridder Newspapers
494 Knoxville News—Sentinel
197 Kokomo Tribune
695 Kommunernes Gensidige Forsikringsselskab
682 Kristeligt Dagblad
199 Lafayette-West Lafayette Courier
225 Lake Charles American Press
458 Lancaster Intelligencer Journal
458 Lancaster New Era / Intelligencer Journal / Sunday News
458 Lancaster Sunday News
269 Lansing State Journal
323 Las Cruces Sun—News
301 Las Vegas Sun / Las Vegas Review—Journal

437 Lawton Constitution/The Sunday Constitution
437 Lawton Sunday Constitution
633 The Leader Post
567 Leader Telegram
144 The Ledger
790 Leicester Mercury
460 Levittown—Bristol—Longhorne Bucks County Courier Times
170 Lewiston Tribune
222 Lexington Herald—Leader
754 Lianhe Wanabao
755 Lianhe Zaobao
664 Lidove noviny, a.s.
- Documentation Department
299 Lincoln Journal Star
299 Lincoln Star
791 Liverpool Daily Post
602 London Free Press
817 London News Network
818 London Weekend Television Limited
- Information Research Unit
26 Long Beach Press—Telegram
69 Longmont Daily Times—Call
324 Los Alamos National Laboratory
30 Los Angeles Police Department
31 Los Angeles Times
366 Louis Harris and Associates, Inc.
- Information Services
223 Louisville Courier—Journal and Louisville Times
223 Louisville Times
70 Loveland Daily Reporter-Herald
520 Lubbock Avalanche Journal
535 Lynchburg Daily Advance
618 Maclean's Magazine
270 Macomb Daily
164 The Macon Telegraph
200 Madison Courier
804 Mail on Sunday
445 Mail Tribune
231 Maine Sunday Telegram
829 Manchester Evening News
683 Manedsbladet Press
429 Mansfield News Journal
165 Marietta Daily Journal
32 Marin Independent Journal
214 Marshalltown Times—Republican
536 Martinsville Bulletin
105 McClatchy Newspapers of California
367 The McGraw Hill Companies
- Standard & Poor's TM/Central Inquiry
106 Media General News Service Inc.
840 Media in Wessex
107 Medill News Service
33 Merced Sun-Star
14 Mesa Tribune
146 Miami Herald
203 Michigan City News-Dispatch
242 Middlesex News
339 Middletown Record
339 Middletown Times Herald—Record/Sunday Record
771 Midland Independent Newspapers
572 Milwaukee Journal Sentinel
572 Milwaukee Sentinel
280 Minnesota Public Radio
- Research
285 The Mississippi Press
298 Missoulian
- Newsroom Library
665 Mlada fronta Dnes
- Documentation Department
9 Mobile Press Register
34 Modesto Bee
594 Moncton Times—Transcript
703 Le Monde
35 The Monterey County Herald
10 Montgomery Advertiser
542 Montgomery Journal
627 Montreal Gazette
418 Moorhead (MN) Forum
651 De Morgen
697 Morgenavisen Jyllands Posten
449 The Morning Call
819 Morning Star
271 Morning Sun
496 Morristown Citizen Tribune
204 Muncie Evening Press
204 Muncie Star and Evening Press
272 Muskegon Chronicle
438 Muskogee Daily Phoenix and Times—Democrat
148 Naples Daily News
757 Narodna Obroda
- Documentation Department
499 Nashville Banner
108 National Association of Broadcasters
- Library
109 National Broadcasting Co.
- Library
368 - Reference Library
145 National Enquirer
110 National Geographic Society
111 National Press Club and News Information Center
112 National Public Radio
- Broadcast Library
113 - Reference Library
542 Navy Times
766 Neue Zurcher Zeitung
- Redaktionsinformatikerin
461 New Castle News
304 New Hampshire Sunday News
78 New Haven Journal
78 New Haven Register
734 New Straits Times Press Berhad
- Resource Center-RIS Department
369 New York Daily News
370 New York Magazine
- Information Services
371 New York Post
372 New York Public Library
- Newspaper Library
373 - Telephone Reference
374 New York Times
114 New York Times Regional Newspaper Group
745 New Zealand Herald
115 Newhouse News Service
537 Newport News Daily Press
537 Newport News Times Herald
307 The News
585 News
535 The News and Daily Advance
83 The News Journal
412 The News & Observer
187 The News Sun
555 The News Tribune
337 Newsday, Inc.
175 The News—Gazette
428 The News—Herald
296 The News—Leader
539 Newspaper Association of America (NAA)
652 Newspaper De Morgen
- Documentation
234 The Newspaper Guild
193 The News—Sentinel
74 The News—Times
276 News-Tribune
375 Newsweek Magazine
603 Niagara Falls Review
386 Niagara Gazette
646 Nieuwe Gazet
653 De Nieuwe Gida
730 Nihon Keizai Shimbun
731 Nikket BP Inc.
726 Nippon Toshokan Kyokai (Association of Japanese Libraries)
538 Norfolk Ledger-Star
604 The North Bay Nugget
777 North of England Newspapers
286 Northeast Mississippi Daily Journal
778 The Northern Echo
116 Northwest Newspapers
430 Northwest—Signal
80 Norwich Bulletin
740 NOS—Journaal
- Documentation Department
632 Le Nouvelliste
758 Novy Cas
- Documentation Department
604 Nugget
37 The Oakland Tribune
398 Observer—Dispatch
- News Department
439 Oklahoma City Times
388 Olean Times—Herald

Alphabetical Listing of Libraries

549 The Olympian
300 Omaha World—Herald
619 Ontario Legislative Library
- Information and Reference Servcies
38 The Orange County Register
446 The Oregonian
149 The Orlando Sentinel
573 Oshkosh Northwestern
605 Ottawa Citizen
606 Ottawa Sun
117 Ottaway Newspapers
156 The Palm Beach Post
174 The Pantagraph
376 Parade Publications, Inc.
563 Parkersburg News and Sentinel
550 Pasco Herald
252 The Patriot Ledger
48 PC World
- Editorial Library
551 Peninsula Daily News
150 Pensacola News—Journal
377 People Magazine
- Research Operations
205 Peru Daily Tribune
463 Philadelphia Inquirer
463 Philadelphia Newspapers
463 Philadelphia Online
15 Phoenix Gazette
19 Pine Bluff Commercial
464 Pittsburgh Post—Gazette
424 The Plain Dealer
470 Pocono Record
684 Politiken Newspapers
- Library
521 Port Arthur News
198 The La Porte Herald—Argus
231 Portland Press Herald/ Maine Sunday Telegram
305 Portsmouth Herald
835 Portsmouth Publishing and Printing
479 Post and Courier
279 Post—Bulletin
336 Post—Journal
194 Post—Tribune
465 Pottsville Republican
391 Poughkeepsie Journal
151 Poynter Institute for Media Studies
- Patterson Library
759 Praca
- Documentation Department
760 Pravda
- Newsroom and Information Services
327 Press & Sun—Bulletin
607 La Presse
- Ottawa Bureau
628 La Presse
41 The Press—Enterprise
476 Providence Evening Bulletin
476 Providence Journal-Bulletin
476 Providence Journal—Bulletin / Sunday Journal
476 Providence Sunday Journal
588 The Province / Vancouver Sun
71 Pueblo Chieftain
71 Pueblo Star Journal
314 PW Communications
211 Quad—City Times
640 Queensland Newspapers
183 The Quincy Herald—Whig
724 RAI Radiotelevisione Italiana
412 Raleigh News and Observer
485 Rapid City Journal
390 Reader's Digest Association Inc.
- Editorial and Research Libraries
629 Reader's Digest Magazines Ltd.
467 Reading Eagle
467 Reading Times / Eagle
57 Record
310 The Record
397 - Editorial Library
76 Record Journal
40 Record Searchlight
- Library
243 Recorder
586 Red Deer Advocate
735 Reforma / El Norte / InfoSel
- Servicios de Informacion
443 The Register—Guard
302 Reno Gazette—Journal
400 Reporter Dispatch / Westchester Rockland Newspapers
421 Repository
725 La Repubblica
189 The Republic
334 Reuters
118 Reuters Information Services
820 Reuters News Service
540 Richmond News Leader
540 Richmond Times—Dispatch
541 The Roanoke Times
392 Rochester Chronicle
392 Rochester Times-Union
184 Rock Island Argus
185 Rockford Register Star
387 The Rockland Journal—News
67 Rocky Mountain News
447 Roseburg News—Review
662 Royal Gazette
- Library
821 Royal Institute of International Affairs
657 RTBF Charleroi
774 S4C
43 Sacramento Bee
44 Sacramento Union
274 Saginaw News
294 St. Louis Post—Dispatch
281 St. Paul Pioneer Press
152 St. Petersburg Times
448 Salem Statesman—Journal
414 The Salisbury Post
530 Salt Lake Tribune
522 San Angelo Standard—Times
523 San Antonio Express—News
523 San Antonio News
45 San Bernardino County Sun
46 San Diego Daily Transcript
47 San Diego Union—Tribune
49 San Francisco Chronicle
50 San Francisco Examiner
51 San Gabriel Valley Daily Tribune
52 San Jose Mercury News
53 San Pedro News—Pilot
431 Sandusky Register
732 Sankei Shimbun
54 Santa Barbara News—Press
55 Santa Cruz Sentinel
56 Santa Rosa Press Democrat
153 Sarasota Herald—Tribune
394 The Saratogian
634 Saskatoon Star—Phoenix
609 Sault Star
166 Savannah Evening Press
166 Savannah Morning News and Evening Press
119 Schlein News Bureau
378 Scholastic Inc.
781 Scotsman
785 Scottish Daily Record
468 Scranton Times
120 Scripps Howard News Service
121 Scripps League Newspapers (SLN)
552 Seattle Post—Intelligencer
553 Seattle Times
295 The Sedalia Democrat
736 Servicios de Informacion
575 Sheboygan Press
216 Sioux City Journal
630 Societe Radio-Canada
- Library
654 Le Soir
379 Il Sole—24 Ore / EMC
- New York Contact
631 Le Soleil
206 South Bend Tribune
839 South Wales Evening Post
608 Southam News
- Library
287 Southeast Missourian
837 Southern Newspapers
3 Southern Progress Corporation
484 Spartanburg Herald—Journal
600 The Spectator
554 Spokesman—Review
830 Sport Newspapers
380 Sports Illustrated
297 Springfield News—Leader
- News Information Center
433 Springfield News—Sun
659 De Standaard
400 Standard Star / Westchester Rockland Newspapers
528 Standard—Examiner
248 Standard—Times
822 The Star
278 Star Tribune Newspaper of the Twin Cities
400 Star / Westchester Rockland Newspapers

332 Star—Gazette
313 Star—Ledger
39 Star—News
480 The State
186 The State Journal Register
413 State Library of North Carolina
- Information Services Section
381 Staten Island Advance
756 Straits Times and Business Times
713 Suddeutsche Zeitung
282 The Sun Herald
483 The Sun News
823 The Sun / News of the World
246 The Sun / The Sunday Sun
803 Sunday Express
805 Sunday Mirror
82 Sunday Republican
253 Sunday Republican
415 Sunday Star—News
256 Sunday Telegram
806 Sunday Telegraph
825 Sunday Times
838 Sunderland Echo
411 The Sun—Journal
140 Sun—Sentinel
576 Superior Evening Telegram
764 Swedish Broadcasting Corporation
644 Sydney Morning Herald
395 Syracuse Herald American Post Standard
395 Syracuse Herald Journal / Post—Standard / Herald American Post Standard
395 Syracuse Post Standard
396 Syracuse University
- Newhouse School of Public Communications
518 Taft Broadcasting
- US National Aeronautical Space Administration
154 Tallahassee Democrat
155 Tampa Tribune
471 Tarentum Valley News Dispatch
742 Telegraaph Dagblad
256 Telegram & Gazette, Sunday Telegram
171 The Telegraph
213 Telegraph Herald
- Library Services
524 Temple Daily Telegram
500 The Tennessean
525 Texarkana Gazette
382 Thirteen/WNET
122 Thomson Newspapers Inc.
824 Time Out Magazine
383 Time Warner
- Research Library
826 Time—Life News Service
163 The Times
195 The Times
228 The Times
315 The Times
273 Times Herald
340 Times Herald—Record
- Information Retrieval Department
542 Times Journal Co.
472 The Times Leader
762 Times Media Ltd.
825 The Times / Sunday Times
22 Times—Advocate
402 Times—News
227 The Times—Picayune
207 Times—Union
326 Times—Union / Sunday Times Union
219 The Topeka Capital—Journal
620 Toronto Globe and Mail
621 Toronto Star
622 Toronto Sun
58 Torrance Daily Breeze
249 The Transcript
275 Traverse City Record-Eagle
316 Trentonian
436 Tribune Chronicle
455 Tribune—Review
550 Tri—City Herald
741 TROS Broadcasting
17 Tucson Citizen
440 Tulsa World
59 Turlock Journal
161 Turner Broadcasting System Inc.
- Photo-Video Services
11 Tuscaloosa News
691 TV2
- Library
694 TV—ARC Tekst
689 TV/Midt-Vest
666 TV/Nord
671 TV-P
- Library
655 TVV/Humo/Telemoustique/L'Instant/Gael
304 Union Leader and New Hampshire Sunday News
253 Union—News / Sunday Republican
123 United States Information Agency
- TV News Library
827 United States Information Service
124 US Information Agency
- Information Bureau
125 - TV News Library
126 US Library of Congress
- Congressional Reference Division
127 - Congressional Research Service
128 - Congressional Research Service LM-215
129 - Congressional Research Service
130 - Copyright Office
131 U.S. News & World Report
132 US Smithsonian Institution
- Library
844 University of Bournemouth
- Dorset House Library
836 University of Central Lancashire
- Centre for Resource & Information Management
403 University of North Carolina
- School of Journalism
786 University of Strathclyde
- Department of Information & Science
767 University of Wales
- Department of Information & Library Studies
533 USA Today
60 Vallejo Times Herald
471 Valley News Dispatch
556 Vancouver Columbian Newspaper
588 Vancouver Sun
501 Vanderbilt University
- Television News Archive
61 Ventura County Star
752 Verdens Gang
384 The Village Voice
- Editorial Library
538 Virginian—Pilot and Ledger—Star
828 VNU Business Publications
526 Waco Tribune—Herald
254 Wakefield Daily Item
385 Wall Street Journal
656 Wall Street Journal Europe
557 Walla Walla Union-Bulletin
24 Walt Disney Imagineering
- Information Resource Center
133 Washington Bureau News Service
134 The Washington Post
- News Research Center
135 The Washington Times
208 The Washington Times—Herald
82 Waterbury Republican—American / The Sunday Republican
217 Waterloo—Cedar Falls Courier
399 Watertown Daily Times
577 Waukesha Freeman
578 Wausau Daily Herald
564 Welch Daily News
558 Wenatchee World
639 The West Australian
199 West Lafayette Journal and Courier
156 West Palm Beach Evening Times
775 Western Mail & Echo Ltd.
834 Western Morning/Evening News Co.
565 Wheeling Intelligencer and News Register
565 Wheeling News Register
220 The Wichita Eagle
527 Wichita Falls Times Record News
527 Wichita Record News
473 Wilkes-Barre Citizens' Voice
472 Wilkes-Barre Times Leader

Alphabetical Listing of Libraries

415 Wilmington Morning Star/ Sunday Star—News
623 Windsor Star
591 Winnipeg Free Press
592 The Winnipeg Sun
416 Winston—Salem Journal
579 Wisconsin Rapids Daily Tribune
571 Wisconsin State Journal
842 Wolverhampton Express & Star
318 Woodbridge News Tribune
147 WPLG TV Broadcast 10
136 WTTG Fox Television
559 Yakima Herald-Republic
733 Yomiuri Shimbun
843 York & County Press
474 York Daily Record
475 The York Dispatch & York Sunday News
789 Yorkshire Post

NEWS LIBRARIES UNITED STATES

1 **Alabama (Birmingham)**
BIRMINGHAM NEWS
2200 North 4th Ave, Birmingham, AL 35202
205-325-2409; FAX 205-325-2495

Newspaper Group: Newhouse Newspapers
Access: Not open to the public.
Personnel
Librarian — Ann Hobbs

2 **Alabama (Birmingham)**
BIRMINGHAM POST-HERALD
PO Box 2553, Birmingham, AL 35202 — See Banner
205-325-2492

Newspaper Group: Scripps-Howard
Access: Not open to public.
Personnel
Librarian — Kay Melcher

3 **Alabama (Birmingham)**
SOUTHERN PROGRESS CORPORATION
2100 Lakeshore Dr (PO Box 2581), Birmingham, AL 35202
205-877-6327; FAX 205-877-6807

Hours: Mon—Fri 8—4:30
Access: Not open to other media.
Services to Other News Libraries: Telephone reference if time permits. Sends copies of clips.
Online Databases: DIALOG; Datatimes.
Personnel
Director — Ann Nathews, (6327; anathews@aol.com)
Asst Director — Jason Burnett, (6731), SLA
Library Assts — Ruthanne Noll, (6388)
Lisa Broglie, (6388), SLA

4 **Alabama (Decatur)**
THE DECATUR DAILY
201 First Avenue SE (PO Box 2213), Decatur, AL 35609 — See Banner
205-353-4612; FAX 205-340-2366

Newspaper founded: 1912; library founded: 1973.
Hours: Mon—Fri 8am-5pm
Services to Other News Libraries: Will send copies of clips; free.
Resources: Photo files, reference books, maps, pamphlets. Clippings.
Personnel
Librarian — Franklin Harris

5 **Alabama (Florence)**
FLORENCE TIMES DAILY
219 West Tennesee St, Florence, AL 35630 — See Banner
205-766-8405; FAX 205-740-4717

Newspaper founded: 1867.
Newspaper Group: New York Times Co.
Hours: Mon—Fri 8am—5pm
Services to Other News Libraries: Telephone reference. Will FAX clippings.
Resources: Photo files, reference books. Microforms: roll, fiche. Clippings.
Special Collections: Tennessee Valley Authority Government documents (selected periodicals).
Personnel
Director — Valeria Scherer

6 **Alabama (Gadsden)**
GADSDEN TIMES
401 Locust St (PO Box 188), Gadsden, AL 35999
205-549-2000; FAX 205-549-2105

Personnel
Librarians — Diane Dixon, (2049)
Angel Pruitt

7 **Alabama (Huntsville)**
THE HUNTSVILLE NEWS

Note: Closed.

8 **Alabama (Huntsville)**
THE HUNTSVILLE TIMES
2317 S Memorial Pkwy, Huntsville, AL 35801 — See Banner
205-532-4000; FAX 205-532-4420

Newspaper founded: 1910; library founded: 1986.
Newspaper Group: Newhouse Newspapers
Hours: Mon—Fri 9—5
Services to Other News Libraries: Telephone reference. Sends copies of clips. Fee: $45/hr. Accepts requests through a newspaper library only.
Access: Other special libraries.
Resources: Photo files, reference books, maps, pamphlet file. Microforms: roll. Clippings.
Fee-Based Research: Information Service. Fee: $7.50/article ($5/students); $1 long distance FAX charge. Copies. Contact Kay Davis (4220).
News Databases: SII.
Archival Systems: LASR.
Special Collections: Space related materials and Wernher von Braun team members.
Personnel
Asst Director — Emily McKay, (4414; mckay@traveller.com)
Librarians — Rebecca L. Moore, (4414; rlmoore@aol.com), SLA

9 **Alabama (Mobile)**
MOBILE PRESS REGISTER
304 Government St (PO Box 2488), Mobile, AL 36630
334-433-1551; FAX 334-434-8662

Newspaper Group: Newhouse Newspapers
Access: Reporters by appointment.
News Databases: SII.
Online Databases: Datatimes.
Personnel
Librarian — Debra Stearns, (434-8635)

10 **Alabama (Montgomery)**
MONTGOMERY ADVERTISER
200 Washington Ave, Montgomery, AL 36104
334-262-1611; FAX 334-261-1505

Newspaper Group: Gannett Newspapers
Email: 75151.2602@Compuserve.com; adver@mindspring.com.

MONTGOMERY ADVERTISER (cont'd)

Access: Open to other media; reporters with prior approval. Not open to public.
Archival Systems: PhotoView; NewsView.
LAN: Yes.
Fee-Based Research: Fee: $35/hour. Copies: $.50 per page; prepaid.
Online Databases: NEXIS.
Personnel
Librarian — Peggy Ross

11 **Alabama (Tuscaloosa)**
TUSCALOOSA NEWS
2001 Sixth St (PO Drawer 1), Tuscaloosa, AL 35402
205-345-0505; FAX 205-349-0802

Hours: Mon—Fri 8—5.
Access: Open to other media by appointment.
Personnel
Librarian — Rachel Durrett, (251)

12 **Alaska (Anchorage)**
ANCHORAGE DAILY NEWS
1001 Northway Dr (PO Box 14-9001), Anchorage, AK 99519-9001 — See Banner
907-257-4593; FAX 907-258-2157

Newspaper founded: 1946; library founded: 1964.
Newspaper Group: McClatchy Newspapers
Hours: Mon—Fri 8am—5pm
Home Page (URL): http://www.adn.com.
Online Databases: Internet; DIALOG; Dow Jones; Datatimes.
News Databases: SAVE.
Services to Other News Libraries: Will do telephone reference (contact: Sharon Palmisano). Will send copies of clippings; Fee: $25. Will express mail clips. Fee: negotiable.
Resources: Photo files, negatives, reference books, maps, pamphlet files. Microforms: roll, fiche. Newspaper index, clippings.
Personnel
Librarians — Sharon Palmisano, (Spalmisano@POP.ADN.COM), SLA
Michael Robinson, (Mrobinson@POP.ADN.COM)

13 **Alaska (Fairbanks)**
FAIRBANKS DAILY NEWS MINER
Box 710, Fairbanks, AK 99707
907-456-6661; FAX 907-452-7917

Newspaper Group: Media News Group
Hours: Mon—Fri 8—5:30
Access: Yes. Sends clips.
Personnel
Librarian — Mary Beth Smetzer, (204)

14 **Arizona (Mesa)**
MESA TRIBUNE
120 West 1st Ave, Mesa, AZ 85202
602-898-6548; FAX 602-898-6362

Newspaper founded: 1913; library founded 1950.
Newspaper Group: Cox Enterprises
News Databases: ATEX.
Services to Other News Libraries: Telephone reference. Sends copies of clips. Express mail.
Resources: Photo files, negatives, reference books, pamphlet file. Microforms: roll, fiche. Clippings.
Personnel
Librarian — Sandra Alteri

15 **Arizona (Phoenix)**
THE ARIZONA REPUBLIC / THE PHOENIX GAZETTE
120 E Van Buren, Phoenix, AZ 85004 — See Banner
602-271-8115 / Reference 602-238-4446; FAX 602-271-8914; Email: PNILIB@INDIRECT.COM

Newspaper founded: 1880; library founded: 1947.
Newspaper Group: Central Newspapers, Inc.
Hours: Mon—Fri 8am—8pm; Sat 8—5; Sun 7am—7pm.
Holidays Open: All holidays.
Archival Systems: AP Preserver; SAVE.
CD ROM: Yes.
Home Page (URL): http://www.azcentral.com.
Fee-Based Research: Research Fee: $60/hour. Copies: $2/article. FAX: $.50/page. Microform Copies: $2/article. Contact: Peg Prendergast.
Online Databases: DIALOG; AOL; DataQuick; CDB Infotek; Dow Jones; Burrelle's; Datatimes; NEXIS; LEXIS; NewsNet.
News Databases: SAVE.
Front End System: SII.

CD ROM: Disclosure; Magazine Article Summaries; US Census; Facts on File; Companies International; US Business Reporter.
Services to Other News Libraries: Telephone reference. Send or FAX copies of clips.
Access: Other media—call for appointment. Public Service line M-F 9am—11am (8017).
Resources: Photo files. Negatives. Reference books. Maps. Pamphlet file. Microforms: roll, jackets. Clippings. Periodicals.
Special Collections: Arizona information and History
Personnel
Manager — Paula Stevens, (8115), SLA
Reference Librarians — Donna Colletta, (8144), SLA
Joanne Dawson, (8144), SLA
Heather Goebel, (8140), SLA
Photo Librarian — John Stanley, (8555)
Photo Reprints — Nancy Van Leeuwen, (8025)
Public Service Line — Peg Prendergast, (8017)

16 **Arizona (Tucson)**
ARIZONA DAILY STAR
4850 S Park Ave (PO Box 26807), Tucson, AZ 85726 — See Banner
520-573-4160; FAX 520-573-4190

Newspaper Group: Pulitzer Publishing Co.
Home Page (URL): http://www.azstarnet.com.
Access: Yes. Sends clips.
Online Databases: Datatimes; NewsBank.
Fee-Based Research: Research fee: $50/hour. Copies: $1/article. FAX: $3/search. Microform copies: $1/page. Prepaid.
Personnel
Librarian — Elaine Y. Raines, (Eraines@azstarnet.com), SLA

17 **Arizona (Tucson)**
TUCSON CITIZEN
4850 S Park, Tucson, AZ 85714 — See Banner
520-573-4560 / Reference 520-573-4570; FAX 520-573-4569

Newspaper founded: 1870. Library Founded: 1956.
Newspaper Group: Gannett Newspapers
Hours: Mon-Fri 6am—6pm
Services to Other News Libraries: Telephone reference. Sends copies of clips. Will FAX clippings.
Resources: Photo files, negatives, reference books, maps, pamphlet file. Microforms: roll, jacket. Clippings.
Access: Open to other libraries.
Online Databases: Datatimes.

TUCSON CITIZEN (cont'd)

Special Collections: Clippings File 1956—Nov 1993.
Personnel
Director — Charlotte Kenan, SLA
Asst Librarian — Jeannie Jett

18 **Arkansas (Little Rock)**
ARKANSAS DEMOCRAT—GAZETTE
Capitol Ave and Scott (PO Box 2221), Little Rock, AR 72203 — See Banner
501-378-3851; FAX 501-378-3489

Hours: Mon—Fri 9—5
Online Databases: LEXIS/NEXIS.
News Databases: NewsView.
Services to Other News Libraries: Telephone reference. Sends copies of clips—variable fee. Will FAX clippings.
Resources: Photofiles, negatives, maps, pamphlet file. Microforms. Newspaper index, clippings.
Personnel
Manager — Alfred M. Thomas, SLA
Librarian — Monte Bemis, (3498)

19 **Arkansas (Pine Bluff)**
PINE BLUFF COMMERCIAL
300 Beech St, Pine Bluff, AR 71601
501-534-3400; FAX 501-543-1455

Newspaper Group: Donrey Media Group
Personnel
Librarian — Vickie Owen, (456)

20 **California (Bakersfield)**
BAKERSFIELD CALIFORNIAN
1707 'Eye' St (PO Box 440), Bakersfield, CA 93301 — See Banner
805-395-7473; FAX 805-395-7519

Newspaper founded: 1866; library founded: 1984.
Hours: Mon—Fri 8—6
Access: Members of other media, other special libraries staff.
Services to Other News Libraries: Telephone reference (Tues—Fri 1—5). Will FAX clips at no charge.
Home Page (URL): http://www.bakersfield.com.
Resources: Clipping files, reference books, photos, microfilm/microfiche index.
Personnel
Director — Sandra Molen, SLA
Staff — Sharon Beauers

21 **California (Brawley)**
BRAWLEY NEWS

Newspaper closed.

22 **California (Escondido)**
TIMES—ADVOCATE
207 E Pennsylvania, Escondido, CA 92025 — See Banner
619-745-6611 ext 427; FAX 619-745-3769

Newspaper founded: 1886.
Newspaper Group: Tribune Company Owned Newspapers
Hours: Mon—Fri 8am—5pm
Services to Other News Libraries: Telephone reference. Sends copies of clips, express mail clips. Variable fee, prefer written request, shipping cost must be reimbursed. Contact: Patricia Hansen.
Resources: Photo files, reference books, maps, pamphlet files. Microforms: roll, fiche. Clippings.
Access: Other media by appointment. Requirements: non-competitive, non-advocacy. Other special libraries. Closed to the public.
Personnel
Director — Patricia Hansen

23 **California (Fresno)**
FRESNO BEE
1626 E St, Fresno, CA 93786
209-441-6111; FAX 209-441-6070; Email: 102556.124@compuserve.com

Newspaper Group: McClatchy Newspapers
Hours: Mon—Sat 7—6
Access: Open to other media; not open to other special libraries.
News Databases: LASR.
Online Databases: DIALOG; Datatimes; NEXIS.
Personnel
Head Librarian — Mabel Wilson, SLA
Staff — Vera Matthews
Nancy Ramirez

24 **California (Glendale)**
WALT DISNEY IMAGINEERING—
Information Resource Center
1401 Flower St (PO Box 25020), Glendale, CA 91221-5020
818-544-7845

Personnel
Librarian — Saundra L. Murray, (Saundra_Murray@CC.WDI.DISNEY.COM), SLA

25 **California (Hayward)**
HAYWARD DAILY REVIEW
116 W Winton Ave, Hayward, CA 94540 — See Banner
510-783-6111; FAX 510-293-2319

Newspaper founded: 1944; library founded: 1952.
Newspaper Group: Alameda Newspapers Group
Hours: Mon—Fri 8am—12n
Access: Yes.
Services to Other News Libraries: Telephone reference. Sends copies of clips, fee: $1 per page plus postage. Personal letter stating request required. No microfilm copies, clips only.
Resources: Photo files, negatives, reference books, maps, clippings.

26 **California (Long Beach)**
LONG BEACH PRESS—TELEGRAM
604 Pine Ave, Long Beach, CA 90844 — See Banner
310-435-1161; FAX 310-437-7892

Newspaper Group: Knight-Ridder Newspapers Inc.
Hours: Mon—Fri 10—6
Access: Over phone. Sends clips. Open to other media by appointment.
News Databases: SAVE.
Personnel
Librarian — Robert Andrew

27 **California (Los Angeles)**
CNN—
Los Angeles Bureau Library
6430 Sunset Blvd Suite 60, Los Angeles, CA 90028
213-460-5075; FAX 213-460-5081

Personnel
Contact — Karen Rosen, SLA

28 **California (Los Angeles)**
DAILY NEWS OF LOS ANGELES
21221 Oxnard St (PO Box 4200), Woodland Hills, CA 91367 — See Banner
818-713-3000; FAX 818-713-3037

Newspaper Founded: 1911; library founded: 1970.
Newspaper Group: Tower Media
Hours: 7am—11pm
CD ROM: NEC; Hitachi. Databases: DIALOG; L.A. Times; ProQuest; N.Y. Times.
Online Databases: DIALOG; SAVE; Datatimes; LEXIS; NEXIS.

DAILY NEWS OF LOS ANGELES (cont'd)

News Databases: SAVE.
Electronic Clipping Files: VU/TEXT
Services to Other News Libraries: Telephone reference. Contact Deborah Reifman (3656). Sends copies of clips. Contact: Margaret Douglas (3658).
Access: Other media, other special libraries. Must inquire by phone or mail.
Resources: Photo files, reference books, maps. Microforms: roll. Newspaper index, clippings. Periodicals, movie press kits, graphics.
Personnel

Director	Margaret Douglas, (3656), SLA
Librarians	Miriam Velasquez, (3789)
	Vicki Gallay, (3789)
	Daniel Edelson, (3789)
	Kent Coloma

29 **California (Los Angeles)**
FOREIGN PRESS CENTER
11000 Wilshire Blvd, Federal Bldg Room C-200, Los Angeles, CA 90024
310-575-7693; FAX 310-473-1876

30 **California (Los Angeles)**
LOS ANGELES POLICE DEPARTMENT
150 N Los Angeles St, Los Angeles, CA 90012
213-485-3586

Apply to the LAPD for a press pass.

31 **California (Los Angeles)**
LOS ANGELES TIMES
Times Mirror Square, Los Angeles, CA 90053
213-237-7181; FAX 213-237-4641

Newspaper founded: 1881. Library founded: 1905.
Newspaper Group: Times Mirror Co.
Hours: Mon—Fri 8am—11pm; Sat 11am—4pm; Sun 2pm—11pm
Archival Systems: BRS.
LAN: Yes.
Online Databases: DIALOG; Dow Jones; Datatimes; MEDLARS; LEXIS/NEXIS; OCLC; Data Resources, Inc.; CQ Washington Alert.
News Databases: SAVE.
CD ROM: Yes.
Fee-Based Research: Research Fee: $80/hour. Copies; FAX; Microform Copies. Prepay.
Home Page (URL): http://www.latimes.com.
Services to Other News Libraries: Telephone reference (237-7181).
Resources: Photo files, negatives, reference books, maps, pamphlet file,. Microforms: roll, fiche. Clippings.
Access: Must be reciprocal.
Personnel

Director	Thomas M. Lutgen, (4758; tom.lutgen@latimes.com), SLA
Deputy Director	Dorothy Ingebretsen, (3351), SLA
Admin Aide	William Lawrence, (7796)
Research Head	Cary Schneider, SLA
Database Maint	Judith Weigel, (3361)
Graphics Head	Mildred Simpson, (7767), SLA

32 **California (Marin County—San Rafael)**
MARIN INDEPENDENT JOURNAL
150 Alameda del Prado, Novato, CA 94949 See Banner
415-883-8600; FAX 415-883-6924

Newspaper founded: 1861; library founded: 1957.
Newspaper Group: Gannett Newspapers
Hours: Mon—Fri 10am—7pm
Online Databases: NEXIS.
Resources: Photo files. Negatives. Reference books. Maps. Pamphlet file. Microforms: roll. Newspaper index, clippings. Index at Marin County Free Library, Civic Center Branch.
Services to Other News Libraries: Telephone reference. Will FAX clippings.
Access: Other media, special libraries by mail only.
Special Collections: Historical files of local interest, including San Quentin Prison and the Golden Gate Bridge.
Personnel

Head	Carol Farrand, (382-7236)

33 **California (Merced)**
MERCED SUN-STAR
3033 North G St (PO Box 739), Merced, CA 95341
209-722-1511; FAX 209-384-2226

Hours: 8am—1pm
Access: Reporters—Yes. Sends clips.
Personnel

Librairan	Rosie Rocha, (457)

34 **California (Modesto)**
MODESTO BEE
1325 H St (PO Box 3928), Modesto, CA 95352
209-578-2370; FAX 209-578-2207

Newspaper Group: McClatchy Newspapers
Hours: 8am—9pm.
Access: Yes. Sends clips.
News Databases: SAVE.
Online Databases: AOL; CompuServe; AZNET.
Special Collections: Graphic Collection: Cumulus Image Archive.
Personnel

Librarian	Kate Roberts

35 **California (Monterey)**
THE MONTEREY COUNTY HERALD
8 Upper Ragsdale Dr (PO Box 271), Monterey, CA 93942-0271
408-646-4336; FAX 408-372-8401; Email: herald@ix.netcom.com

Newspaper Group: Scripps-Howard
Access: Not open to public or other libraries.
Personnel

Librarian/Director	Elizabeth Roberts

36 **California (Oakland)**
FREEDOM FORUM—
Pacific Coast Center
Jack London Sq, 70 Washington St, Suite 210, Oakland, CA 94607
510-287-9960; FAX 510-287-9980

37 **California (Oakland)**
THE OAKLAND TRIBUNE
PO Box 28884, Oakland, CA 94604
510-208-6420; FAX 510-208-6477

Year founded: 1874.
Newspaper Group: Alameda Newspapers Group
Hours: Mon—Fri 8am—8pm; Sat 8—4.
Access: Other library/media by appointment. Closed to general public.
Services to Other News Libraries: Telephone reference. Sends copies of clips. Will FAX clips.
Resources: Photo files. Reference books, maps, pamphlet file. Microforms: roll. Newspaper index, clippings.
Online Databases: Datatimes.
Personnel

Librarian	Steven A. Lavoie, SLA

38 **California (Orange County)**
THE ORANGE COUNTY REGISTER
625 N. Grand Ave, Santa Ana, CA 92701 See Banner
714-835-1234; FAX 714-542-5037

Newspaper founded: 1905; library founded: 1962.
Newspaper Group: Freedom Newspapers
Hours: Mon—Fri 7am—10pm; Sat, Sun 9am—10pm
Home Page (URL): http://acregister.com.
Services to Other News Libraries: Telephone reference. Contact: Sharon Ostmann. Limited research and copying at discretion of director. Database available through Datatimes.
Access: Other media and special libraries: only phone requests at discretion of director.
CD ROM: Yes.
Fee-Based Research: Research Fee: $60/hour. Copies: $5/article. FAX: $5/search. Microform Copies: $5/article. Prepaid. Contact Patrick Chelling or Chris Andres (565-6077).
Online Databases: DIALOG; Dow Jones; LEXIS; Datatimes; NEXIS; LegiTech; DataQuick; DAMAR; IRSC; CDB Infotek.
News Databases: Datatimes; NewsBank.
Electronic Clipping Files: Datatimes NewsBank
Resources: Photo files, negatives, reference books, maps, Pamphlet file. Microforms: roll, fiche. Clippings, all on fiche.
Personnel

Director	Sharon Ostmann, (953-4937; sharon_ostmann@link.freedom.com or ostmann@cerfnet), SLA
Photo Res	Pam Eisenberg, (953-4985; pamy@ocr1.freedom.com), SLA
Researchers	Scott Wilson, (953-2254; swilson@link.freedom.com)
	Penny Love, (953-7859; love@ocr1.freedom.com; love@cerf.net), SLA
	Jan Rose, (953-2255)
	Mike Rosentreter, (953-2251)
Research Assistants	Gayle Carter, (564-7027)
	Wen Gao, (953-7797)
	Lois Stuart, (565-6007; LoJoS2RT@aol.com)

39 **California (Pasadena)**
STAR—NEWS
911 E Colorado Blvd, Pasadena, CA 91109
818-578-6300; FAX 818-792-9413

Newspaper Group: Thompson Newspapers
Access: Not open to other media. Will answer phone questions.
Personnel

Librarian	Linda Hammes, (4446)

40 **California (Redding)**
RECORD SEARCHLIGHT—Library
1101 Twin View Blvd, Redding, CA 96003
916-225-8297; FAX 916-225-8212

Personnel

Librarian	Connie Locker, SLA

41 **California (Riverside)**
THE PRESS—ENTERPRISE
3512 14th St, Riverside, CA 92502
909-684-1200; FAX 909-782-7572

Access: Open to other media by appointment. Sends clippings.
Online Databases: Datatimes; NEXIS.
Personnel

Library Director	Jacqueline S. Chamberlain, (782-7579; JChamberlain@PE.Com), SLA
Asst Library Director	Nadine S. Kapper, SLA

42 **California (Sacramento)**
CALIFORNIA STATE LIBRARY—Periodicals Section
PO Box 942837, Sacramento, CA 94237
916-445-2585

43 **California (Sacramento)**
SACRAMENTO BEE
2100 Q St, Sacramento, CA 95816
916-321-1108; FAX 916-326-5585; Email: sacbee@netcom.com

Newspaper founded: 1857.
Newspaper Group: McClatchy Newspapers
Sacramento Bee available on DIALOG, DataTimes, NEXIS and Legitech.

Services to the Pubic: Call BeeSearch (916-326-5566) Tue—Thur 10—4. Articles cost $5 plus tax.

Services to Other News Libraries: Larger organizations are expected to retrieve Bee Stories on commercial databases (DIALOG, DataTimes, NEXIS). For older material, the Bee Library will help reporters/editors from other media if they make request through their own news library. Will help journalists from smaller organizations directly. Hours: Mon—Fri 7am—7pm.
Archival Systems: LASR.
Fee-Based Research: Research Fee: $50/hour. Copies: $5/article. FAX: $2/search. Microform copies: $10/article. Prepaid. Contact Bee Search (326-5566).
Resources: Photo files, newspaper clippings, microfilm/fiche, reference books, maps.
CD ROM: Newsbank; DataQuick; PhoneDisc.
Archival Systems: AXS.
LAN: Apple.
Online Databases: DIALOG; Datatimes; NEXIS; LEXIS; SAVE; DataQuick and others.
News Databases: SII.
Personnel

Librarian	Pete Basofin, (pbasofin@sacbee.com), SLA
Research Libn	Rebecca Boyd, (bboyd@sacbee.com), SLA

44 **California (Sacramento)**
SACRAMENTO UNION

Closed.

45 **California (San Bernardino)**
SAN BERNARDINO COUNTY SUN
399 North D St, San Bernardino, CA 92401 See Banner
909-889-9666; FAX 909-885-8741

Newspaper founded: 1894; Library founded: 1973.
Newspaper Group: Gannett Newspapers
Hours: Mon—Fri 8—5
Services to Other News Libraries: Telephone reference. Sends copies of clips. Express mails clips. Telefacsimile clips.
Resources: Photo files, negatives, reference books, maps, pamphlet file. Microform: roll. Clippings.
Personnel

Librarian	Anita Kaschube, SLA
Asst Librarian	Peggy Hardy

46 **California (San Diego)**
SAN DIEGO DAILY TRANSCRIPT
2131 3rd Ave (PO Box 85469), San Diego, CA 92101 See Banner
619-232-4381; FAX 619-239-5716

Newspaper founded: 1886; library founded: 1973.
Hours: Mon—Fri 9:30am—5pm
Services to Other News Libraries: Telephone reference. Will FAX clippings.
Resources: Limited photo files. Reference books, maps, pamphlet file. Newspaper index, clippings.

47 **California (San Diego)**
SAN DIEGO UNION—TRIBUNE
350 Camino de la Reina (PO Box 191), San Diego, CA 92108 See Banner
619-299-3131

Newspaper founded: 1869; library founded: 1945.
Newspaper Group: Copley Newspapers
Hours: Mon—Fri 9am—10pm; Sat, Sun 5pm—9pm
Online Databases: DIALOG; NEXIS; Datatimes; Dow Jones; NewsBank.
News Databases: IDI/Basis.
Services to Other News Libraries: Telephone reference. Will send copies of clips in reasonable amount.
Access: By appointment only.
Archival Systems: Basis.
CD ROM: Yes.
LAN: Yes.
WAN: Yes.
Fee-Based Research: Research Fee: $50/hour. Contact Anne Magill (293-1414).
Resources: Photo files, negatives, reference books, maps, pamphlet files. Microforms: roll, fiche, jackets. Newspaper index, clippings.

Personnel

Library Mgr	Sharon Stewart Reeves, (1410; Sharon.Reeves@SDUniontrib.Com), SLA
Research Supv	Anne Magill, (1414; Anne.Magill@SDUniontrib.Com), SLA

48 **California (San Francisco)**
PC WORLD—
Editorial Library
501 Second St #600, San Francisco, CA 94107
415-978-3211; FAX 415-442-1891

Personnel

Librarian	Stella W. Chan, (stella_chan@PCWorld.com)

49 **California (San Francisco)**
SAN FRANCISCO CHRONICLE
901 Mission St, San Francisco, CA 94103 See Banner
415-777-7230; FAX 415-896-0668

Newspaper founded: 1865; library founded: pre 1879.
Hours: Sun—Thur 24 hours; Fri 7am—12m; Sat 7am—5pm
Home Page (URL): http://www.sfgate.com.
CD ROM: NYT; LAT; SF.
Archival Systems: AXS.
LAN: Yes.
Archival Systems: AP Preserver; Basis.
Online Databases: DIALOG; Dow Jones; LegiTech; Datatimes; LEXIS; NEXIS; DataQuick; Information America; Dun & Bradstreet; CDB Infotek; Washington Alert.
News Databases: Datatimes.
Electronic Clipping Files: Datatimes/BASIS
Services to Other News Libraries: Telephone reference; will send copies of clips (usually no charge);
Access: Reporters by appointment and must show credentials; other media by phone only.
Resources: Photo files, maps, negatives, pamphlet file. Microforms: roll, jackets. Newspaper index, clippings. Reference books. CD-ROM.

Personnel

Director	Richard Geiger, (geigerr@sfgate.com), SLA
Asst Head Librarian	June Dellapa, SLA
Librarians	Johnny Miller
	Bill Van Niekerken, SLA
	Kathleen Rhodes
	Barbara Jo Littlefield
	Scott Errihard
	Charles Malarkey
	Niamh O'Sullivan
	Otis Stillwell
	Rotimi Burns
	Lynette Francis
	Gerald Jampol
	Mary Jo Webb

50 **California (San Francisco)**
SAN FRANCISCO EXAMINER
110 Fifth St (PO Box 7260), San Francisco, CA 94102 See Banner
415-777-7845; FAX 415-512-9486

Newspaper founded: 1865; library founded: 1920.
Newspaper Group: Hearst Newspapers
Hours: Mon—Fri 7am—8pm; Sat 8am—6pm; Sun 6am—12:30pm
Email: 71564.153; schwabeh@sfgate.com.
Online Databases: DIALOG; Information America; Dun & Bradstreet; IRSC; Information America; NEXIS; Datatimes.
News Databases: SII; DIALOG; Datatimes; NEXIS.
Archival Systems: Fetch.
Services to Other News Libraries: Telephone reference. Contact: Judy Canter. Will send copies of clippings; no fee to other newspapers. Will FAX/mail clips.
Resources: Photo files, negatives, reference books, maps, pamphlet files. Microforms: roll, fiche, jackets. Clippings.
Special Collections: San Francisco History; California History.

Personnel

Director	Judy Canter, (canterj@sfgate.com), SLA
Asst Chief Librarian	Michael Tuller, (7844), SLA
Librarians	Melvin Patterson
	Arthur Hagen
	C.L. Moss, (mossy@sfgate.com)
	Marvin Gilbreath
	Melissa Hom, (homm@sfgate.com), SLA
	Lois Jermyn
	Rebecca David

51 **California (San Gabriel Valley)**
SAN GABRIEL VALLEY DAILY TRIBUNE
PO Box 1259, Covina, CA 91722
818-962-8811

Newspaper Group: Thomson Newspapers
Services to Other News Libraries: Open to visiting reporters.
Access: Permission needed.

Personnel

Librarians	C.C. Gomez
	Rene Johnson

52 **California (San Jose)**
SAN JOSE MERCURY NEWS
750 Ridder Park Dr, San Jose, CA 95190 See Banner
408-920-5000 / reference 408-920-5346; FAX 408-271-3799

Newspaper founded: 1851; library founded: 1929.

SAN JOSE MERCURY NEWS (cont'd)

Newspaper Group: Knight-Ridder Newspapers Inc.
Hours: Mon—Fri 6am—11pm; Sat, Sun 8—4
Holidays Open: 9—5.
Access: To other media and special libraries. Will send copies.
Email: merclib@aol.com; sjmsearch@aol.com.
Home Page (URL): http://www.sjmercury.com; http://www.sjmercury.com/library.
CD ROM: BIP+; Facts on File; Mercury News; Insight; 40 other titles.
Online Databases: CompuServe; DIALOG; NEXIS; Datatimes.
LAN: SII; MAC Ethernet; PC Network.
News Databases: SAVE.
Archival Systems: SAVE; Fetch.
LAN: Yes.
WAN: Yes.
Services to Other News Libraries: Telephone reference, will send copies of clippings. Fee if more than 3 copies.
Fee-Based Research: Research fee: $45/hour. Copies. FAX: $9.95/search. Microform copies: $9.95/article. Prepay. Contact: Sharon Vaughn (920-5999).
Resources: Photo files, reference books, maps, pamphlet files. Microforms: roll, fiche. Clippings.

Personnel

Director	Gary Lance, (5345; glancer@aol.com), SLA
Asst Head	Debbie Bolvin, (5346; dbolvin@aol.com)
Librarians	Lorene Laffranchi
	Marcia Gordon, (marciagord@aol.com), SLA
	Diana Stickler
	Janis Gott
	Morna Baird, SLA
News Search Libn	Sharon Vaughn, (SJMSearch@aol.com)
Library Techs	Mark Spain
	Joe Reifer
Clerk	Jessica Savin

53 **California (San Pedro)**
SAN PEDRO NEWS—PILOT
362 Seventh St (PO Box 191), San Pedro, CA 90733
310-832-0221

Newspaper Group: Copley Newspapers
Hours: 8—5

Personnel

Librarian	Midori Yasuda

54 **California (Santa Barbara)**
SANTA BARBARA NEWS—PRESS
De la Guerra Pl, Santa Barbara, CA 93102 — See Banner
805-564-5200

Newspaper founded: 1901; library founded: 1940's.
Hours: Mon—Fri 1pm—4pm
Services to Other News Libraries: Telephone reference; will send copies of clippings. Fee: 3/$1.00. Requirements: limited request.
Access: To other non-competitive media; other special libraries.
Resources: Photo files, negatives, reference books, maps, pamphlets. Microforms: roll, fiche. Newspaper index, clippings.
Special Collections: Historical society publications; Santa Barbara magazines; Local history books.

Personnel

Director	Sue De Lapa, (332)
Library Clerk	Fran Wasielewski, (331)

55 **California (Santa Cruz)**
SANTA CRUZ SENTINEL
207 Church St (PO Box 638), Santa Cruz, CA 95061 — See Banner
408-423-4242; Email: Sented@Cruzio.com

Newspaper founded 1856 (weekly in 1884); library founded: 1965.
Newspaper Group: Ottaway Newspapers, Inc.
Hours: Mon—Fri 8:30am—3:45pm
Services to Other News Libraries: Telephone reference. Will FAX clippings. Requirements: non-reporters, with some exceptions.
Access: No access to other media or special libraries.
Resources: Photo files, negatives, reference books, maps, pamphlet files. Newspaper index, clippings.
Special Collections: Historical files on the county.

Personnel

Director	Christine Watson, SLA

56 **California (Santa Rosa)**
SANTA ROSA PRESS DEMOCRAT
427 Mendocino Ave, Santa Rosa, CA 95402
707-546-2020; FAX 707-546-2437

Personnel

Library Director	Alison J. Head, (Ahead@eds.Calstate.Edu), SLA

57 **California (Stockton)**
RECORD
530 E. Market, Stockton, CA 95201 — See Banner
209-943-6397; FAX 209-546-8288; Email: 102347.1215@Compuserve.Com

Newspaper founded: 1895; library founded: 1952.
Newspaper Group: Omaha World Herald
Hours: Mon—Fri 9am—6pm
Access: Not open to other media.

Personnel

Director	Thai Strom, (8290), SLA

58 **California (Torrance)**
TORRANCE DAILY BREEZE
5215 Torrance Blvd, Torrance, CA 90509 — See Banner
310-540-5511 / reference ext 376; FAX 310-540-6272

Newspaper founded: 1894; library founded: 1965.
Newspaper Group: Copley Newspapers
Hours: Mon—Fri 8:30am—5pm
Online Databases: NEXIS; Datatimes; DIALOG.
News Databases: BASIS.
Services to Other News Libraries: Telephone reference (ext 376). Sends copies of clippings. Fee: $1.00/page. Requirements: for stories after March 1, 1984, printouts sent. Will not FAX clips.
Resources: Photo files, negatives, reference books, maps, pamphlet files, clippings.
Special Collections: Local history materials.

Personnel

Director	Samuel J. Gnerre, (376), SLA
Asst Librarian	Steve Takata

59 **California (Turlock)**
TURLOCK JOURNAL
138 S Center St (PO Box 800), Turlock, CA 95380 — See Banner
209-634-9141; FAX 209-632-8813

Newspaper founded: 1904.
Newspaper Group: Freedom Newspapers
Days Not Published: New Year's Day, Independence Day, Labor Day, Veteran's Day, Thanksgiving, Christmas.
Special Collections: Turlock Daily Journal bound edition 1904—.

60 **California (Vallejo)**
VALLEJO TIMES HERALD
440 Curtola Pkwy (PO Box 3188), Vallejo, CA 94590
707-644-1141; FAX 707-643-4322

Newspaper Group: Donrey Media Group
Personnel
Librarian Connie Ramos

61 **California (Ventura)**
VENTURA COUNTY STAR
5250 Ralston St, Ventura, CA 93003
805-650-2900; FAX 805-650-2944

Year founded: 1875.
Newspaper Group: John P. Scripps Newspapers Group
Hours: Mon—Fri 8am—5pm
Access: Other media on approval of librarian.
Resources: Reference books, maps, pamphlet file. Microforms: roll. Newspaper index, clippings.
Services to Other News Libraries: Will do limited searches.
Personnel
Director Wanda Woessner, (5803)

62 **California (Walnut Creek)**
CONTRA COSTA TIMES
2640 Shadelands Dr (PO Box 5088), Walnut Creek, CA 94596 See Banner
510-943-8190; FAX 510-943-8362

Newspaper founded: 1913; library founded: 1978.
Newspaper Group: Knight-Ridder Newspapers Inc.
Hours: Mon—Fri 8:30am—8:30pm
Access: Open to public via telephone only.
Services to Other News Libraries: Telephone reference. Sends copies of clips. No fee. Will FAX clips.
News Databases: NewsView; PhotoView.
Archival Systems: NewsView.
LAN: Yes.
WAN: Yes.
Online Databases: DIALOG; Datatimes; NEXIS.
Resources: Photo files, reference books, maps, pamphlet files. Microforms: roll, fiche. Clippings, slides, periodicals, digital photos.
Archival Systems: AP Preserver.
Fee-Based Research: Research Fee: $75/hour. Copies: $1/article. FAX: $1/page. Microform Copies: $1/article. Prepay or invoice. Contact Mona Hatfield (943-8190).
Personnel
Manager Mona Hatfield, (mgh@well.com), SLA
Librarians Laura Perkins
Monica Ballard

63 **California (Whittier)**
THE DAILY NEWS
7612 Green Leaf Ave, Whittier, CA 90608
310-698-2571; FAX 310-698-0450

Newspaper Group: Thomson Newspapers
Personnel
Librarian Kathy Lindsey

64 **Colorado (Boulder)**
DAILY CAMERA/SUNDAY CAMERA
1048 Pearl St, Boulder, CO 80302 See Banner
303-442-1202; FAX 303-449-9358

Newspaper founded: 1891; library founded: 1930.
Newspaper Group: Knight-Ridder Newspapers Inc.
Hours: Mon—Fri 9am—5pm
Access: Open to visiting reporters by appointment.
Services to Other News Libraries: Telephone reference. Sends copies of clippings; no fee. Will FAX clips.
News Databases: SAVE.
Resources: Photo files, reference books. Clippings.
Personnel
Librarian Charlotte Smokler, (303)

65 **Colorado (Colorado Springs)**
GAZETTE TELEGRAPH
30 S. Prospect St, Colorado Springs, CO 80901 See Banner
719-632-5511; FAX 719-636-0202; Email: GTNews@USA.NET

Newspaper founded: 1871.
Newspaper Group: Freedom Newspapers
Hours: Mon—Fri 9am—5:30pm; Sat, Sun open to reporters only.
Services to Other News Libraries: Telephone reference. Will FAX clippings.
Access: Not open to other media.
Resources: Photo files, reference books, maps, pamphlet files. Microforms. Newspaper index, clippings.
News Databases: Datatimes.
Online Databases: Datatimes; DIALOG; Internet; LEXIS/NEXIS.
Personnel
Senior Res Analyst Pulaski O. Davis, (183), SLA
Researcher Victor Greto, (182)
Photo Librarian Tess Richardson, (126)

66 **Colorado (Denver)**
DENVER POST
1560 Broadway, Denver, CO 80202 See Banner
303-820-1444; FAX 303-820-1406

Newspaper Group: Media News Group
Hours: Mon—Fri 9am—11:30pm
Email: Library@Denverpost.com.
Access: Open to other libraries. Sends copies of clips.
Services to Other News Libraries: Answers questions from news libraries.
Online Databases: NEXIS; Datatimes; Newsbank (on CD).
Resources: Newspaper index 1895—present.
Fee-Based Research: $5/call (900-225-5552).
Personnel
Librarian Victoria L. Makings, SLA
Asst Librarian Karen Klute

67 **Colorado (Denver)**
ROCKY MOUNTAIN NEWS
400 W. Colfax (PO Box 719), Denver, CO 80204 See Banner
303-892-5417; FAX 303-892-2577; Email: library@denver-rmn.com

Newspaper founded: 1859; library founded: 1951.
Newspaper Group: Scripps-Howard
Hours: Mon—Fri 9am—7pm; Sat 9am—6pm; Sun 12n—6pm. Public hours: NewsQuest (892-2300) leave message for call back.
Access: Other media, by appt only. Open to other special libraries.
Services to Other News Libraries: Telephone reference; FAX/Mail copies of clippings.
Home Page (URL): http://www.denver-rmn.com.
Resources: Photo files, reference books, maps, pamphlet files. Microforms. VU/TEXT access to Scripps Howard databases; clips and photo files 1930's—1989; Local maps; reference books.
Online Databases: SAVE; DIALOG; LEXIS/NEXIS; Datatimes; Dow Jones.
Fee-Based Research: Research fee: $40/hour; Copies: $5/article; FAX; Microform Copies: $10/article; Credit card or invoice. Contact: Janet Boss (892-2746).

ROCKY MOUNTAIN NEWS (cont'd)

Special Collections: Historic houses in Denver.
Personnel

Director	Janet Boss, (2746; Boss@denver-rmn.com), SLA
Asst Director	Carol L. Kasel, (5417; Kasel@denver-rmn.com), SLA
Photo Librarian	Paula Ehresman, (2586; Ehresman@denver-rmn.com), SLA

68 **Colorado (Fort Collins)**
FORT COLLINS COLORADOAN
1212 Riverside Ave (PO Box 1577), Ft Collins, CO 80522 — See Banner
970-493-6397; FAX 970-224-7899

Newspaper founded: 1873.
Newspaper Group: Gannett Newspapers
Hours: Mon—Fri 8—5
Services to Other News Libraries: Telephone reference. Will FAX clippings.
Access: Open to other media by appointment.
Resources: Photo files, reference books, maps, pamphlet files. Microforms: fiche. Clippings. Newspaper Index from 1977.
Personnel
Director — Kathleen M. Lewis, (224-7751)

69 **Colorado (Longmont)**
LONGMONT DAILY TIMES—CALL
350 Terry, Longmont, CO 80501
303-776-2244 ext 22; FAX 303-678-8615

Newspaper Group: Lehman Newspapers
Hours: Mon—Fri 8—5
Services to Other News Libraries: Telephone requests. Sends copies of clippings.
News Databases: Stauffer Gold.
Personnel
Librarian — Shirley Jean Silvers, (222)

70 **Colorado (Loveland)**
LOVELAND DAILY REPORTER-HERALD
201 E 5th St, Loveland, CO 80537 — See Banner
970-669-5050

Newspaper founded: 1880; library founded: 1960.
Newspaper Group: Lehman Newspapers
Hours: Mon—Fri 9am—4pm
Services to Other News Libraries: Telephone reference. Contact: Dorothy Karlin. Sends copies of clippings. Fee: postage.
Access: Open to other media during business hours.
Resources: Photo files, negatives. Microforms: roll. Newspaper index, clippings.
Personnel
Director — Juanita Cisneros, (ext 357), SLA

71 **Colorado (Pueblo)**
PUEBLO CHIEFTAIN
825 W 6th, Pueblo, CO 81003
719-544-3520

Hours: Mon—Fri 10am—6pm
Services to Other News Libraries: Sends copies of clippings.
Access: Open to public; open to other libraries, reporters by appointment.
Personnel
Librarian — Helene Spitzer, (491)

72 **Connecticut (Bridgeport)**
CONNECTICUT POST
410 State St, Bridgeport, CT 06604
203-333-0161; FAX 203-367-8158

Personnel
Librarian — Marva dHamilton, (330-6240)

73 **Connecticut (Bristol)**
BRISTOL PRESS
99 Main St, Bristol, CT 06010
860-584-0501; FAX 860-585-9283

Personnel
Librarian — Virginia Rogers

74 **Connecticut (Danbury)**
THE NEWS—TIMES
333 Main St, Danbury, CT 06810 — See Banner
203-744-5100 / Reference ext 349; FAX 203-792-8730

Newspaper founded: 1883; library founded: 1970.
Newspaper Group: Ottaway Newspapers, Inc.
Hours: Mon—Fri 8am—3pm
Services to Other News Libraries: Telephone reference. Will FAX clips.
Resources: Photo files, reference books, maps, pamphlets file. Microforms: roll. Newspaper clippings.
Access: Other media, other special libraries.
Personnel
Director — Donald K. Erickson, (349), SLA

75 **Connecticut (Hartford)**
HARTFORD COURANT
285 Broad St, Hartford, CT 06115 — See Banner
860-241-6664; FAX 860-520-6906

Library founded: 1950.
Newspaper Group: Times Mirror Co.
Hours: Mon—Fri 8:30am—11pm; Sat, Sun 2:30pm—11pm
Access: Open to public by appt only.
Services to Other News Libraries: Telephone reference. No research.
Online Databases: Datatimes; NEXIS.
Special Collections: Hartford Courant on microfilm from 1764.
Personnel
Librarian — Kathleen McKula, SLA

76 **Connecticut (Meriden - Wallingford)**
RECORD JOURNAL
11 Crown St, Meriden, CT 06450 — See Banner
203-235-1661; FAX 203-639-0210

Access: Open to other media by appointment.
Personnel
Librarian — Lynne Turdin

77 **Connecticut (New Britain)**
THE HERALD
One Herald Sq, New Britain, CT 06050 — See Banner
860-225-4601; FAX 860-225-2611

Year founded: 1880.
Hours: Mon—Fri 7:30am—3:30pm
Access: Open to the public; open to other libraries and media. Will FAX clippings.
Resources: Photo files. Reference books. Microforms: roll. Newspaper index.
Special Collections: Bound volumes to 1885; New Britain history (books, clippings).
Personnel
Librarian — Virginia Blanchfield, (302)

78 **Connecticut (New Haven)**
NEW HAVEN REGISTER
40 Sargent Drive, New Haven, CT 06511
203-789-5200; FAX 203-865-7894

Library founded: 1935.
Personnel
Librarian — Wilbur Mesing

79 **Connecticut (New London)**
DAY
47 Eugene O'Neill Dr, New London, CT 06320 See Banner
860-442-2200

Newspaper founded: 1881; library founded: Newspaper Index 1929; clippings: 1977.
Hours: Mon—Fri 8—2
Services to Other News Libraries: Telephone reference. Will not send copies of clips.
Access: Open for in-house research to other media and special libraries.
Resources: Photo files, negatives, reference books. Microforms: roll.
Personnel
Director Tami Jo Ferdula, (385)

80 **Connecticut (Norwich)**
NORWICH BULLETIN
66 Franklin St, Norwich, CT 06360
860-887-9211 ext 287; FAX 860-887-9666

Year founded: 1791.
Newspaper Group: Gannett Newspapers
Hours: Mon—Fri 7am—12m
Access: Open to public, other libraries and media by appointment only.
Services to Other News Libraries: Telephone reference. Sends copies of clips.
Resources: Photo files. Microforms: rolls. Newspaper index, clippings.
Special Collections: Bound volumes available to the public from 1920—1982. Microfilm from Oct. 1982 to present. Extensive collection from 1791—1920 not available for public use.
Personnel
Librarian Barbara Hanes

81 **Connecticut (Stamford)**
THE ADVOCATE
75 Tresser Blvd (Box 9307), Stamford, CT 06904-9307 See Banner
203-964-2200; FAX 203-964-2345

Newspaper founded: 1829; Library founded: 1930's.
Newspaper Group: Times Mirror Co.
Hours: Mon—Fri 11am—11pm; Sat 12n—8pm
Services to Other News Libraries: Limited telephone reference.
Resources: Photo files, negatives, reference books, maps, pamphlet file. Microforms: roll. Clippings.
Special Collections: Antique newspapers, photos.
Personnel
Librarian Leigh Michels, (3709), SLA

82 **Connecticut (Waterbury)**
WATERBURY REPUBLICAN—AMERICAN / THE SUNDAY REPUBLICAN
389 Meadow St (PO Box 2090), Waterbury, CT 06722 See Banner
203-574-3636; FAX 203-596-9277

Newspaper founded: 1844 (American), 1881 (Republican).
Hours: Mon—Fri 2pm—5pm; 6pm—9pm.
Services to Other News Libraries: Telephone reference. Will FAX clippings.
Access: Open to other media and other special libraries.
Resources: Photo files, reference books, maps, pamphlet files. Microforms: roll, fiche. Newspaper index, clippings.
Personnel
Librarian Anita Bologna, (347)

83 **Delaware (Wilmington)**
THE NEWS JOURNAL
950 Basin Rd, New Castle, DE 19720
302-324-2500; FAX 302-324-5509

Year founded: 1871; library founded: 1954.
Newspaper Group: Gannett Newspapers
Hours: Mon—Fri 8am—9pm
Services to Other News Libraries: Telephone reference. Will FAX clips. Call or make request in writing.
Access: Other media, special libraries. Call for appointment.
Resources: Photo files. Reference books, maps, pamphlet file. Microforms: rolls, fiche, jackets. Clippings.
Special Collections: Wilmington City directories, 1900—.
Personnel
Director Charlotte J. Walker, (2896), SLA
Librarians Anne Haslam, (2898)
Cecilia James, (2897)

84 **District of Columbia**
ABC NEWS RESEARCH CENTER—Washington Bureau Library
1717 DeSales St NW, Washington, DC 20036
202-222-7048; FAX 202-222-7153

Personnel
Librarian Melinda S. Carlson, SLA

85 **District of Columbia**
AGENCE FRANCE—PRESSE
1015 1st ST #500, Washington, DC 20005
202-289-0700; FAX 202-414-0548

Personnel
Librarian Colette Projent, (414-0576)

86 **District of Columbia**
AKRON BEACON JOURNAL—Washington Bureau of KR Inc.
700 National Press Bldg, Washington, DC 20045 See Banner
202-383-6070; FAX 202-628-4175

Personnel
Librarian Jo Kirks, (6070), SLA

87 **District of Columbia**
AMERICAN ASSOCIATION OF RETIRED PERSONS—Research and Information Library
601 E Street NW, Room A2-213, Washington, DC 20049
202-434-6247; FAX 202-434-6480

Personnel
Librarian Mary Katherine Hartz, (MHARTZ@AARP.ORG)

88 **District of Columbia**
ANSA—Italian News Agency
1285 National Press Bldg, Washington, DC 20045
202-628-3317/18; FAX 202-638-1792

89 **District of Columbia**
THE ASSOCIATED PRESS
2021 K St. NW #606, Washington, DC 20006
202-776-9400; FAX 202-776-9570/1

Personnel
Head Librarian Vicki Belcher, (VBelcher@AP.Org)
Librarian David Goodfriend, (DGoodfriend@AP.Org)

90 **District of Columbia**
BLOCK COMMUNICATIONS
955 National Press Bldg, Washington, DC 20045
202-662-7070; FAX 202-662-7328

91 **District of Columbia**
BUREAU OF NATIONAL AFFAIRS—Library
1231 25 St NW, Room N200, Washington, DC 20037-1197
202-452-6380; FAX 202-452-4084

Access: Open to other media by appointment.
Personnel

Director	Marilyn M. Bromley, (mbromley@bna.com), SLA
Sen Reference Librarian	Catherine Kitchell, (ekitchell@bna.com), SLA

92 **District of Columbia**
CAPITAL NEWS SERVICE
770 National Press Bldg, Washington, DC 20045
202-628-1677; FAX 202-628-1676

93 **District of Columbia**
CATHOLIC NEWS SERVICE—Information Services
3211 Fourth St NE, Washington, DC 20017
202-541-3254

Personnel

Librarian	Anne Leveque, SLA

94 **District of Columbia**
CBS NEWS
2020 M St NW, Washington, DC 20036
202-457-4468; FAX 202-457-4326

Personnel

Director	Alexandra Cosgrove, (bce@cbsnews.com), SLA

95 **District of Columbia**
CONGRESSIONAL RESEARCH SERVICE
Library of Congress, Washington, DC 20540
202-707-5700

Hours: Mon—Fri 8:30am—9:30pm; Weekends 8:30—5pm
Online Databases: NEXIS; DIALOG; SCIPIO.
Access: Open to the media.
Personnel

Director	Daniel P. Mulhollan

96 **District of Columbia**
COPLEY NEWS SERVICE
1100 National Press Building, Washington, DC 20045
202-737-6960

97 **District of Columbia**
COX NEWSPAPERS
2000 Pennsylvania Ave NW #10000, Washington, DC 20006
202-331-0900; FAX 202-331-1055

98 **District of Columbia**
DOWREY WASHINGTON NEWS BUREAU
937 National Press Building, Washington, DC 20045
202-783-1760; FAX 202-783-1955

99 **District of Columbia**
FOREIGN PRESS CENTER
The White House, Office of the Press Secretary, Washington, DC 20500
202-456-2100

White House Press Pass - before applying for a pass, you must obtain a press pass from one of the four press galleries of the US Congress. Write a letter requesting an application form to the Office of the Press Secretary.

100 **District of Columbia**
GANNETT NEWS SERVICE
1000 Wilson Blvd, Arlington, VA 22229-0001
703-276-5588

Personnel

Librarians	Goni Blodgett
	Theresa Campbell

101 **District of Columbia**
HARTE—HANKS NEWSPAPERS
958 National Press Building, Washington, DC 20045
202-628-1585

102 **District of Columbia**
HEARST NEWSPAPERS & HEARST FEATURE SERVICE
1701 Pennsylvania Ave NW, Washington, DC 20006
202-298-6920; FAX 202-333-1184

103 **District of Columbia**
ITAR—TASS NEWS AGENCY
1004 National Press Bldg., Washington, DC 20045
202-662-7080; FAX 202-393-6495

Email: Borsc@aol.com.

104 **District of Columbia**
KNIGHT—RIDDER NEWSPAPERS
790 National Press Bldg, Washington, DC 20045
202-383-6080; FAX 202-628-4175

Personnel

Librarian	Jo Kirks, (6070), SLA

105 **District of Columbia**
MCCLATCHY NEWSPAPERS OF CALIFORNIA
624 National Press Building, Washington, DC 20045
202-662-8740; FAX 202-662-8738

106 **District of Columbia**
MEDIA GENERAL NEWS SERVICE INC.
1214 National Press Building, Washington, DC 20045
202-662-7660

107 **District of Columbia**
MEDILL NEWS SERVICE
1325 G Street NW #730, Washington, DC 20005-3104
202-347-8700; FAX 202-662-1804

108 **District of Columbia**
NATIONAL ASSOCIATION OF BROADCASTERS—Library
1771 N St NW, Washington, DC 20036
202-429-5490; FAX 202-775-3520

Hours: Mon—Fri 11—4
Access: Open to the public and other libraries by appointment only. Telephone reference. ILL with local trade associations and law firms only.

NATIONAL ASSOCIATION OF BROADCASTERS (cont'd)

Online Databases: DIALOG; NewsNet; SAVE; Datatimes.

Personnel

VP	Susan M. Hill, (5488; SHill@Capcon.Net), SLA

109 **District of Columbia**
NATIONAL BROADCASTING CO.—Library
4001 Nebraska Ave NW, Washington, DC 20016
202-885-4853; FAX 202-686-8815

Personnel

Contact	Charlotte Kohrs, (CKohrs@NBC.COM)

110 **District of Columbia**
NATIONAL GEOGRAPHIC SOCIETY
17th and M Sts NW, Washington, DC 20036
202-857-7787; FAX 202-429-5731; Email: natgeol@capcon.net

Hours: Mon—Fri 8:30am—5pm
Access: ILL within METRO Washington area. Tours available by calling director. Open to the public; Telephone reference.
Online Databases: DIALOG; NEXIS; OCLC; Datatimes.
CD ROM: Yes.
Special Collections: National Geographic Research Collection; Exploration and Travel.

Personnel

Director	Susan Fifer Canby, SLA
Asst Directors	Ann Benson, (7789)
	Ellen Briscoe, (7050), SLA

111 **District of Columbia**
NATIONAL PRESS CLUB AND NEWS INFORMATION CENTER
529 14 St NW, Washington, DC 20045
202-662-7523; FAX 202-879-6725

Hours: Mon—Thur 9—7; Fri 9—6
Access: Open to other media by appointment.
Online Databases: LEXIS/NEXIS; DIALOG; Datatimes; CQ Washington Alert.
Special Collections: Photographs; Archives of the National Press Club; Audio tapes of luncheon speakers; Cartoon Art.

Personnel

Director	Barbara P. Vandergrift, (barbvand@dgs.dgsys.com), SLA

112 **District of Columbia**
NATIONAL PUBLIC RADIO—Broadcast Library
635 Massachusetts Ave NW, Washington, DC 20001
202-414-2060

Hours: Mon—Fri 7:30am—8pm; Sat, Sun 8—5
Home Page (URL): http://www.npr.org.
Services to Other News Libraries: Telephone reference. Will FAX available transcripts. Requests from public handled by Audience Svcs Dept (414-3232).
Online Databases: DIALOG; Dow Jones; NEXIS; Datatimes.
CD ROM: Yes.
LAN: Yes.
Special Collections: Television Journalism.

Personnel

Broadcast Libns	Katherine Plumb, (2064; kplumb@npr.org)
	Beth Howard, (2061; bhoward@npr.org)
	Tom Tuszynski, (2065; ttuszynski@npr.org)
	Denise Chen, (2062; dchen@npr.org)
	Robert Goldstein, (2066; rgoldstein@npr.org)

113 **District of Columbia**
NATIONAL PUBLIC RADIO—Reference Library
635 Massachusetts Ave NW, Washington, DC 20001
202-414-2350; FAX 202-414-3056

Hours: Mon—Fri 7:30am—8pm; Sat, Sun 8—5
Services to Other News Libraries: Telephone reference. Will FAX available transcripts. Requests from public will be handled by Audience Svcs Dept (414-3232).
Online Databases: DIALOG; Dow Jones; Datatimes; NEXIS.
CD ROM: Yes.
LAN: Yes.

Personnel

Library Mgr	Rob Robinson, (2355)
Reference Libns	Kee Malesky, (2356; kmalesky@npr.org)
	Alphonse Vinh, (2352; avinh@npr.org)

114 **District of Columbia**
NEW YORK TIMES REGIONAL NEWSPAPER GROUP
1627 I St NW, #700, Washington, DC 20006
202-862-0333; FAX 202-862-0382

Hours: Mon—Fri 10—6
Access: Open to other media by appointment.
Online Databases: LEXIS/NEXIS; DIALOG; Datatimes; Dow Jones.

Personnel

Research Spec	Barclay Walsh, (BWALS@NYTIMES.COM), SLA
Research	Marjorie Goldborough, (0334; Magold@pipeline.com), SLA

115 **District of Columbia**
NEWHOUSE NEWS SERVICE
2000 Pennsylvania Ave NW #3900, Washington, DC 20006
202-785-0101; FAX 202-383-7820

Personnel

Librarian	Donna Walters

116 **District of Columbia**
NORTHWEST NEWSPAPERS
316 Third St NE, Washington, DC 20002
202-546-2547

117 **District of Columbia**
OTTAWAY NEWSPAPERS
1025 Connecticut Ave NW #310, Washington, DC 20036
202-828-3390; FAX 202-828-3490

118 **District of Columbia**
REUTERS INFORMATION SERVICES
1333 H St NW, 5th Fl, Washington, DC 20005
202-898-8300; FAX 202-898-8383

Personnel

Director of Research	Colleen Williams, (310-5478)

119 District of Columbia
SCHLEIN NEWS BUREAU
308 E Capitol St NE #9, Washington, DC 20003
202-544-5893

120 District of Columbia
SCRIPPS HOWARD NEWS SERVICE
1090 Vermont Ave NW #1000, Washington, DC 20005
202-408-1484

121 District of Columbia
SCRIPPS LEAGUE NEWSPAPERS (SLN)
PO Box 1109, Herndon, VA 22070
703-713-1920; FAX 703-713-1939

122 District of Columbia
THOMSON NEWSPAPERS INC.
1331 Pennsylvania Ave NW #524, Washington, DC 20004
202-628-2157; FAX 202-347-5017

123 District of Columbia
UNITED STATES INFORMATION AGENCY
TV News Library
601 D St NW, Room 2100, Washington, DC 20547
202-501-6481

Personnel
Contact — Pamela J. Lenz-Commerford, SLA

124 District of Columbia
US INFORMATION AGENCY—
Information Bureau
301 Fourth St SW #135, Washington, DC 20547
202-619-4870; FAX 202-619-4879

Personnel
Librarian — Eileen G. Deegan, (Deegan@USIA.GOV)

125 District of Columbia
US INFORMATION AGENCY—
TV News Library
601 D St NW Room 2100, Washington, DC 20547
202-501-6481

Hours: Mon—Fri 7—4
Online Databases: LEXIS/NEXIS.
Personnel
Director — Pamela J. Lenz-Commerford, (PLenz@USIA.GOV), SLA

126 District of Columbia
US LIBRARY OF CONGRESS—
Congressional Reference Division
1st and Independence Aves SE, Room LM219, Washington, DC 20540
202-707-8939; FAX 202-707-1833

Personnel
Librarian — Donna W. Scheeder, (scheeder@CRS.loc.gov)

127 District of Columbia
US LIBRARY OF CONGRESS—
Congressional Research Service
1st and Independence Aves SE,
202-707-6459

Personnel
Contacts — Karin H. Calvert, (KCALVERT@CRS.LOC.GOV), SLA
Robert H. Howe, (8713), SLA

128 District of Columbia
US LIBRARY OF CONGRESS—
Congressional Research Service LM-215
4938 47th St NW, Washington, DC 20016
202-707-8999; FAX 202-707-3662

Personnel
Contact — Margaret A. Garvin, (PGARVIN@CRS.LOC.GOV), SLA

129 District of Columbia
US LIBRARY OF CONGRESS—
Congressional Research Service
101 Independence Ave LM 203, Washington, DC 20540
202-707-8912; FAX 202-707-2615

Personnel
Contact — Regina M. Hamilton, (RHAMILTON@CRS.LOC.GOV), SLA

130 District of Columbia
US LIBRARY OF CONGRESS—
Copyright Office
Washington, DC 20559
202-707-6779; FAX 202-707-4435

Personnel
Librarian — William E. Laing, (LAING@MAILLOC.GOV), SLA

131 District of Columbia
U.S. NEWS & WORLD REPORT
2400 N St NW, Washington, DC 20037-1196 — See Banner
202-955-2348 / Reference 202-955-2350; FAX 202-955-2506

Year founded: 1933; library founded: 1933.
Hours: Mon, Tues 8am—6pm; Wed—Fri 8am—10pm
Access: Other media—US News material only; other special libraries. Telephone reference.
Services to Other News Libraries: Telephone reference. Sends copies of clips—US News material only. Express mails clips—requester cost. Telefacsimile clips.
Home Page (URL): http://www.usnews.com.
Resources: Photo files, negatives. Reference books, maps. pamphlet file. Microforms: roll, fiche. Newspaper clippings, Index.
CD ROM: UMI General Periodicals; US Code: PhoneDisc; Census.
LAN: Yes.
Fee-Based Research: Citations provided free.
News Databases: ATEX; BiblioTech.
Online Databases: NEXIS; BRS; DIALOG; Dow Jones DataStar; Datatimes; Military Database; CQ Washington Alert; Baseline.
Electronic Clipping Files: NEXIS; Datatimes; EBSO; Newsbank; H.W. Wilson; IAC.
Special Collections: Large vertical file and govt documents collection, especially congressional hearings, prints and reports. Corporate and federal agency annual reports. Clippings from major US newspapers through 1994.
Personnel
Director — Kathleen Trimble, (2693), SLA
Asst Director — Kate Forsyth, (2139)
Database Admin/Index Ed — Lisa Costello, (2224), SLA
ILL — Anne Brockett, (2012)
Photos — Xi Van Fleet, (2332)

132 **District of Columbia**
US SMITHSONIAN INSTITUTION—Library
10th & Constitution Ave NW, Washington, DC 20560
202-357-2139; FAX 202-786-2443; Email: Libemoll@SIVM.SI.EDU

Online Databases: DIALOG; First Search; EPIC; Citadel.
Personnel
Director of Libraries — Barbara Smith, (2240)
Branch Libn — Martin Smith

133 **District of Columbia**
WASHINGTON BUREAU NEWS SERVICE
5810 Runford Dr, New Carrollton, MD 20784
301-577-8361 / 301-459-9860; FAX 301-577-3689

134 **District of Columbia**
THE WASHINGTON POST—News Research Center
1150 15th St NW, Washington, DC 20071 See Banner
202-334-7341; FAX 202-334-5575

Year founded: 1933; News library founded: 1933.
Hours: Mon—Fri 6am—12m; Reference 10am—12:30pm
Access: Other media/special libraries—10am—2pm (M-F) by appointment only.
Archival Systems: Merlin; Basis; NewsView.
Online Databases: Lusknet; DIALOG; Dow Jones; SAVE; Datatimes; LEXIS/NEXIS; Info Globe; Canadian Press; USNI Military Database; Federal Election Commission (FEC); CQ Washington Alert; Dow Jones; AMA Net; PostHaste; Maryland Legislature; Profile; Virginia Legislature.
News Databases: BASIS.
Electronic Clipping Files: The Washington Post Online is available from: DIALOG, Datatimes, NEXIS, CompuServe, Profile, Legislate
Services to Other News Libraries: Telephone requests. FAX and mail Post stories.
Resources: Photo files, reference books, maps, pamphlet files. Microforms. Newspaper index 1972—to date. PostHaste: The Washington Post Online clips.
Special Collections: Watergate; US Politics; Congress Presidency; Iran-Contragate; Richard M. Nixon.
Personnel
Director — Jennifer Belton, (6762; Belton@Wash), SLA
Research Manager — Margot Williems, SLA
Database Coordinator — Cassandra Davis, SLA

135 **District of Columbia**
THE WASHINGTON TIMES
3600 New York Ave NE, Washington, DC 20002 See Banner
202-636-3016/ Reference 202-636-3093 (Access, Media, government, and SLA only)

Newspaper founded: 1982; Library founded: 1982.
Hours: Sun—Fri 8am—12m; Sat 12n—8pm
Access: Open to other media, government and SLA, other special libraries.
Services to Other News Libraries: Telephone reference. Sends copies of clips. Express mails clips with your FedEx or FAX. Telefacsimile clips.
Resources: Photo files, reference books, maps. Microforms: roll, fiche. Newspaper index, clippings.
Online Databases: LEXIS/NEXIS; Datatimes; DIALOG.
Personnel
Librarian — Joseph Szadkowski, SLA

136 **District of Columbia**
WTTG FOX TELEVISION
5151 Wisconsin Ave NW, Washington, DC 20016
202-244-5151; FAX 202-895-3133

Personnel
Contact — Sandra Caster, SLA

137 **Florida (Bradenton)**
THE BRADENTON HERALD
102 Manatee Ave W (PO Box 921), Bradenton, FL 34206 See Banner
813-748-0411; FAX 813-745-7097

Newspaper founded: 1922.
Newspaper Group: Knight-Ridder Newspapers Inc.
Hours: Mon—Fri 8am—5pm (no holidays)
Email: BHIP.INFI.NET.
Online Databases: DIALOG; CompuServe.
News Databases: SAVE; SAVE.
Services to Other News Libraries: Telephone reference. Contact: M.K. Shealy. Sends copies of clips. Fee—$2 per article. Will not express mail clips.
Access: Open to the public; open to other special libraries.
Resources: Photo files, negatives, reference books. maps, pamphlet file. Microforms: roll. Clippings.
Archival Systems: MacArchive; Fetch.
Special Collections: Historical photos.
Personnel
Director — M.K. Shealy, (4054), SLA

138 **Florida (Cocoa Beach)**
FREEDOM FORUM—Florida Office
300-A S Atlantic Ave, Cocoa Beach, FL 32931
407-783-3335; FAX 407-783-9041

139 **Florida (Daytona Beach)**
DAYTONA BEACH NEWS AND JOURNAL
901 Sixth St, Daytona Beach, FL 32015
904-252-1511; FAX 904-252-8470

Access: Reporters by appointment.
Online Databases: CompuServe; AOL.
Personnel
Librarian — Cheryl Sheppard

140 **Florida (Fort Lauderdale)**
SUN—SENTINEL
200 E Las Olas Blvd, Fort Lauderdale, FL 33301 See Banner
954-356-4000 / Reference ext 4740; FAX 954-356-4748

Newspaper founded: 1911; library founded: 1949.
Newspaper Group: Tribune Company Owned Newspapers
Hours: Mon—Fri 9am—9pm; Sat, Sun 1pm—9pm
Access: Not open to the public; open to other special libraries.
Services to Other News Libraries: Telephone reference. Contact: Michael Meiners. Sends copies of clips; express mail clips. Contact: Magaly Morales. No fee.
CD ROM: Newsbank; Local Property Records; Criminal/Civil Courts.
LAN: Ethernet.
Online Databases: Datatimes; DIALOG; NEXIS; CompuServe.
News Databases: SAVE.
Electronic Clipping Files: SAVE

SUN—SENTINEL (cont'd)

Resources: Photo files, reference books, maps, pamphlet files. Microforms: roll, fiche. Clippings.
Personnel
Research Manager — Bob Isaacs, (4741; ISAACS@SUNSENT.com), SLA
Research Supv — Michael Meiners, (4743; MEINERS@SUNSENT.com)
Database Supv — Dean Perry, (4752; PERRY@SUNSENT.com), SLA
Digital Photo Arch — Robert Cauvel, (4744; FLCAUVEL@SUNSENT.com)

141 Florida (Fort Myers)
FORT MYERS NEWS-PRESS
2442 Dr. Martin Luther King Jr. Blvd, Ft Myers, FL 33901 — See Banner
941-335-0200; FAX 941-332-7581

Newspaper Group: Gannett Newspapers
Hours: 7am—7pm
Access: Reporters by appointment.
Electronic Clipping Files: PaperDesk Archive
CD ROM: Yes.
Personnel
Director — Peter W. Ford, (PFord@Reganet.Com)
Research Editor — (8546)

142 Florida (Gainesville)
GAINESVILLE SUN
2700 SW 13th St, Gainesville, FL 32608 — See Banner
352-374-5074; FAX 352-338-3128

Newspaper founded: 1876; library founded: 1965.
Newspaper Group: New York Times Co.
Hours: 9—5
Services to Other News Libraries: Telephone reference. Contact: Robert Ivey. Sends/Faxes copies of clips. No express mail clips.
Access: Local TV media are restricted from using the library; open to other media and other special libraries.
Resources: Photo files, reference books, maps, pamphlet files. Microforms: roll. Newspaper index, clippings.
Archival Systems: KARDEX; PageSpeed.
Personnel
News Researcher — Shauna Bergwall, (338-3109; ShaunaB@aol.com), SLA

143 Florida (Jacksonville)
FLORIDA TIMES-UNION
1 Riverside Ave, Jacksonville, FL 32231 — See Banner
904-359-4111 / reference ext 4466; FAX 904-359-4478

Newspaper founded: 1864; library founded: 1967.
Newspaper Group: Morris Communications Corp.
Hours: Mon—Fri 7:30am—9pm
News Databases: Datatimes.
Services to Other News Libraries: Telephone reference. Contact: Maryann Sterzel. Sends copies of clips. Fee: $1/copy. Requirements: at the request of reporters or editors.
Access: Not open to the public or other special libraries.
Resources: Photo files, reference books, maps, pamphlet files. Microforms: roll. Clippings.
Personnel
Director — Maryann P. Sterzel, (4458), SLA

144 Florida (Lakeland)
THE LEDGER
PO Box 408, Lakeland, FL 33802 — See Banner
813-687-7000 / reference ext 7843; FAX 813-687-7090

Newspaper Group: New York Times Co.
Hours: Mon—Fri 8:30am—4:30pm
Services to Other News Libraries: Telephone reference. Sends copies of clips. Fee: $1.50/sheet. Requirements: know date or subject detail. Contact: Lorelei Thiele.
Resources: Photo files, reference books. Microforms: roll. Clippings.
Personnel
Librarian — Sandy Kline, (7843; SandraSueK@aol.com), SLA

145 Florida (Lantana)
NATIONAL ENQUIRER
600 SE Coast Ave, Lantana, FL 33464
407-586-1111 ext 282; FAX 407-540-1090

Library founded: 1976.
Hours: Mon—Fri 9am—5:30pm
Access: Not open to the public or other libraries; Reporters by appointment.
Online Databases: SAVE.
Resources: Clippings.
Special Collections: International and national directories.
Personnel
Photo Library — Thelma Bravon, (212-988-3320)
Librarian — Martha Moffett, (2309)

146 Florida (Miami)
MIAMI HERALD
1 Herald Pl, Miami, FL 33101 — See Banner
305-376-3434; FAX 305-995-8183

Newspaper founded: 1904; Library founded: 1955.
Newspaper Group: Knight-Ridder Newspapers Inc.
Hours: Mon—Sat 10am—9pm
Online Databases: BRS; SAVE; Dow Jones; DIALOG; LEXIS/NEXIS; Datatimes; Wilsonline.
News Databases: QL Systems.
Services to Other News Libraries: Telephone reference after clearance from Editor. Sends copies of clips.
Access: Open to other media after clearance from Editor; open to other special libraries through mail requests only.
Resources: Photo files, negatives (for color pictures), reference books, maps, pamphlet files. Microforms: roll, fiche, jackets. Clippings.
Personnel
Editor/Info Svc — Bill Whiting, (2101; WWhiting@aol.com), SLA
Library Mgr — Gaye Nemeti, (3403), SLA
Res Mgr — Elizabeth Donovan, (3404; EDonovan@delphi.com), SLA

147 Florida (Miami)
WPLG TV BROADCAST 10
3800 Biscayne Blvd, Miami, FL 33137
305-325-2467; FAX 305-325-2467

Founded: 1956. Library founded: 1978.
Hours: Mon—Fri 9—6
Access: Open to other television media.
News Databases: Newstar.
Online Databases: DIALOG; CompuServe; DBT.
CD ROM: Yes.
Personnel
Director — Joseph F. Wright, (467), SLA

148 Florida (Naples)
NAPLES DAILY NEWS
1075 Central Ave, Naples, FL 33940 — See Banner
813-262-3161 / reference 813-263-4796

Newspaper founded: 1923; library founded: 1970?

NAPLES DAILY NEWS (cont'd)

Hours: Mon—Fri 8am—5pm
Services to Other News Libraries: Telephone reference. Contact: Gerald Johnson. Sends copies of clips. No fee. Will not express mail clips.
Access: Open to other media by appointment. Open to other special libraries.
Resources: Photo files, negatives, reference books, maps, pamphlet files. Microforms: roll. Clippings.
Personnel
Director — Gerald Johnson, (4796), SLA

149 **Florida (Orlando)**
THE ORLANDO SENTINEL
633 N Orange Ave, Orlando, FL 32801 — See Banner
407-420-5000; FAX 407-420-5350

Year founded: 1877; library founded: 1948.
Hours: 8am—11pm
Online Databases: SAVE (VU/TEXT); NEXIS; Datatimes; CompuServe; DIALOG.
News Databases: DIALOG; Datatimes; SAVE.
Services to Other News Libraries: Telephone reference. Sends (fee)/Faxes copies of clips with supervisor approval. Express mails clips—requires requestor's Federal Express number
Access: Other media, other special libraries by appointment.
Resources: Photo files. Reference books. Maps. Microforms: roll, fiche. Clippings.
Personnel

Director	Judy L. Grimsley, (5511; JGrimsle@Tribune.Com), SLA
Info Systems Spec	Jill Simser, (5510)
Reference Librarian	Ric Russo, (5510)
Research Librarian	Susan Thompson, (5510)

150 **Florida (Pensacola)**
PENSACOLA NEWS—JOURNAL
One News-Journal Pl, Pensacola, FL 32501
904-435-8699; FAX 904-435-8633

Newspaper Group: Gannett Newspapers
Access: Open to visiting reporters.
Personnel
Librarian — Christine McDowell

151 **Florida (St. Petersburg)**
POYNTER INSTITUTE FOR MEDIA STUDIES—
Patterson Library
801 Third St S, St. Petersburg, FL 33701
813-821-9494; FAX 813-821-0583

Home Page (URL): http://www.nando.net/prof/poynter/home.html.
Personnel
Librarian — Nora M. Paul, (npaul@delphi.com; NPAUL@POYNTER.ORG), SLA

152 **Florida (St. Petersburg)**
ST. PETERSBURG TIMES
490 First Ave South (Box 1121), St. Petersburg, FL 33701 — See Banner
813-893-8111 / Reference ext 7096 / 1-800-333-7505; FAX 813-893-8107

Hours: Mon—Fri 11:30am—8pm
Access: Open to other media and other special libraries—requests cleared on an ad hoc basis.
Services to Other News Libraries: Telephone reference. Sends copies of clips—no fee. Express mails clips. Telefacsimile clips; call first.
Email: 76117,1133; (all staff addresses are first initial,last name.
Home Page (URL): http://www.sptimes.com.
CD ROM: DDA Phonedisc Reverse; Newsbank (Tampa Tribune, St. Petersburg Times); Oxford English Dictionary; Information Finder by World Book; Florida Census Summary Tape Files; Florida Statutes; US Code; others.
Archival Systems: AP Preserver.
Online Databases: LEXIS/NEXIS; CQ Washington Alert; CompuServe; DIALOG; Datatimes and many others.
Fee-Based Research: Research fee: $75/hour; Copies: $2/article; FAX $1/page; Microform Copies: $3/article. Invoice; prepay; credit card. Contact: Caroline Ziadie (893-8911).
News Databases: LASR(Systems Integrators Inc.).
Resources: Photo files, negatives, reference books, maps, pamphlet files. Microforms: roll, fiche. Clippings, charts, graphs.
Special Collections: Library consists of a graphic library and a news research library; Large book collection of Florida material, historic oversize aerial photos of local area, historic photos of downtown St. Petersburg, clippings from 1950's to 1986 of Evening Independent which folded in November, 1986, and microfilm of Evening Independent back to 1907.
Personnel

Library Director	Cary Kenney, (8108; ckenney@sptimes.com), SLA
Deputy Librarian	Barbara Hijek, (3372)
Graphics Lib Coord	Claire Giglio, (8154)
Researchers	Carolyn Hardnett, (7096)
	Kitty Bennett, (7096)
	John Martin, (7096)
Database Editors	Laurie Anderson, (2391), SLA
	Suzanne Palmer, (2388)
	Eileen Maloney, (8286)
	Sue Usberghi, (2389)
	Deborah Peters, (2390)

153 **Florida (Sarasota)**
SARASOTA HERALD—TRIBUNE
801 S Tamiami Trail, Sarasota, FL 34237
941-957-5219; FAX 941-957-5276; Email: SarasotaHT@Delphi.Com

Newspaper Group: New York Times Co.
Hours: Mon—Fri 8—6
Personnel
News Res Mgr — Janice Gehle, SLA

154 **Florida (Tallahassee)**
TALLAHASSEE DEMOCRAT
277 N Magnolia Dr (PO Box 990), Tallahassee, FL 32302
904-599-2100; FAX 904-599-2295

Newspaper Group: Knight-Ridder Newspapers Inc.
Personnel
Library Administrator — Debra Galloway, (debgal@reenet.seri.fsu.edu), SLA

155 **Florida (Tampa)**
TAMPA TRIBUNE
202 Parker St, Tampa, FL 33606
813-259-7711 / Reference ext 7665; FAX 813-259-7676; Email: TampaTribune@delphi.com

Year founded: 1895; Library founded: 1940.
Newspaper Group: Media General, Inc.
Hours: 7am—11pm
News Databases: LASR.
Services to Other News Libraries: Telephone reference. Sends copies of clips, no fee. Express mail charged to requesting library.
Access: Open to other special libraries, public and other media by appointment
Resources: Photo files, photo file index, color transparencies, reference books, maps, charts, pamphlet files. Microforms: roll, fiche. Clippings.

TAMPA TRIBUNE (cont'd)

Online Databases: DIALOG; CompuServe; NEXIS.
Special Collections: Oversized aerial photos of Tampa Bay area; Historic photos of Tampa; Clippings and microfilm of The Tampa Times which closed August 1982.
Personnel

Library Director	Jerry Chambers, (7672), SLA
Library Mgr	Alyce Diamandis, (7379), SLA
Librarian	Sherry Suits, (7535)

156 **Florida (West Palm Beach)**
THE PALM BEACH POST
2751 S Dixie Hwy, West Palm Beach, FL 33405
407-820-4495; FAX 407-837-8409; Email: Library@pbpost.com

Newspaper founded: 1916.
Newspaper Group: Cox Enterprises
Hours: Mon—Fri 5:30am—12m; Sat 10am—6pm; Sun 9am—10pm
Access: To other media, by permission of chief librarian. Assist public through Post Facts.
Services to Other News Libraries: Telephone reference. Sends copies of clips.
Home Page (URL): http://pbpost.com/storm96 and http://pbpost.com/pbbiz/top50.
Online Databases: AirPac; CDB Infotek; AOL; Database Technologies; Dow Jones; Information America; ISC; PACER; WDIA; WESTLAW; Internet; DIALOG; Datatimes; LEXIS/NEXIS; CompuServe.
News Databases: SAVE; MacArchive.
LAN: Ethernet.
Resources: Photo files, reference books, maps, pamphlet files. Microforms: roll, fiche, jackets. Clippings. Miami News Collection.
Fee-Based Research: Research—fee; Copies; FAX; Microform Copies. Contact: Jackie Zaborski (820-4002).
Archival Systems: SAVE; Fetch.
Special Collections: Miami News Archives.
Personnel

Manager/Oper	Sammy Alzofon, SLA
Systems/Training	Barbara G. Shapiro, SLA
Photo Mgr	Manny Gonzalez
Database Ed/Print Coll	Xiao Kai Chen, SLA
Database Ed/New Ventures	Holly Diaz
AME/Info Svcs	Mary Kate Leming, SLA
Library Clerk	Marion Sessoms
PostFacts Mgr	Jackie Zaborski, SLA
Researcher	Derek Willis, SLA
Database Editor	Mary Dixon
Library Mgr/Research	Michelle Quigley, SLA

157 **Georgia (Albany)**
ALBANY HERALD
126 N Washington St (PO Box 48), Albany, GA 31702-0048 See Banner
912-888-9300 / library 912-888-9371, 9361; FAX 912-888-9357

Newspaper founded: 1891.
Newspaper Group: Gray Communications Systems Inc.
Hours: Mon—Fri 8:30—5:30
Services to Other News Libraries: Telephone reference. Contact: Susan Frier. Sends copies of clips.
Resources: Photo files, negatives, reference books, maps. Newspaper index, clippings.
Personnel

Librarian	Susan Frier

158 **Georgia (Athens)**
ATHENS DAILY NEWS / BANNER—HERALD
1 Press Pl, Athens, GA 30601
706-549-0123; FAX 706-208-2246; Email: 76735.26@compuserve.com

Access: Open to other media by appointment.
Personnel

Librarian	Beth Hedrich

159 **Georgia (Atlanta)**
ATLANTA JOURNAL AND ATLANTA CONSTITUTION
72 Marietta St, Atlanta, GA 30303 See Banner
404-526-5151; FAX 404-526-5840; Email: ajc8@ping.com

Newspaper founded: 1883 (Journal); 1868 (Constitution). Library founded: 1940
Newspaper Group: Cox Enterprises
Hours: 6am—12m
Archival Systems: ImageSpeed; Fetch.
Fee-Based Research: Research Fee: $60/hour. Copies: $5/Article. Credit card or invoice. Contact: AJC Newsearch (526-5668).
Online Databases: DIALOG; Dow Jones; NEXIS; Datatimes; Information America.
News Databases: Documaster; Image Speed.
Services to Other News Libraries: Telephone reference. Sends copies of clips; no fee. Express mail clips. Requirements: charge to requesting library.
Access: Open to other media; must have valid press card; must not be working on competing story. Open to other special libraries and academic researchers.
Resources: Photo files, reference books, maps, pamphlet files. Microforms: roll, fiche, jackets. Newspaper index and clippings.
Personnel

Director/News Res Svcs	Virginia Everett, (5213), SLA
Deputy Director	Kathleen Flynn, (5424)
Reference Supv	Richard Hallman, SLA
Reference Librarians	Dorothy Shea
	Kathryn Hulshof
	John Jackson
Systems Supv	Vivian Flagg-Davis, SLA
Tech Training Coord/Sys	Lauren Colburn
Photo Librarians	Kathy Drewkes
	Kevin Gnewikow
	Valerie Lyons, SLA

160 **Georgia (Atlanta)**
CNN—
Library
One CNN Center, Atlanta, GA 30303
404-827-1125; FAX 404-827-5283

Home Page (URL): http://www.CNN.Com.
Personnel

Librarian	Debra K. Bade, (DebraBade@Turner.Com), SLA
News Archives Mgr	Dina S. Gunderson, (1330), SLA

161 **Georgia (Atlanta)**
TURNER BROADCASTING SYSTEM INC.—
Photo-Video Services
One CNN Ctr 9S, Atlanta, GA 30303
404-827-4258; FAX: 404-827-4258

Personnel

Librarian	Lee Eltzroth, (LEE.ELTZROTH@TURNER.COM)

162 **Georgia (Columbus)**
COLUMBUS LEDGER—ENQUIRER
17 W 12th St, Columbus, GA 31994
706-324-5526; FAX 706-576-6236

Newspaper Group: Knight-Ridder Newspapers Inc.
Access: Open to librarians/reporters by appointment.
Personnel

News Info Supv	Valerie McNeill, (576-6263)
Librarian	Patricia F. Thrower

163 **Georgia (Gainesville)**
THE TIMES
345 Green St NW (PO Box 838), Gainesville, GA 30503
770-532-1234; FAX 770-532-0457

Newspaper Group: Gannett Newspapers
Hours: 7—5:30
Personnel
Librarian Linda Bulloch

164 **Georgia (Macon)**
THE MACON TELEGRAPH
120 Broadway (PO Box 4167), Macon, GA 31213
912-744-4200; FAX 912-744-4385

Newspaper Group: Knight-Ridder Newspapers Inc.
Access: Open to librarians and other media by appointment.
Personnel
Librarian Harriet Comer, (4328)

165 **Georgia (Marietta)**
MARIETTA DAILY JOURNAL
580 Fairground St, Marietta, GA 30060
404-428-9411; FAX 404-422-9533

166 **Georgia (Savannah)**
SAVANNAH MORNING NEWS AND EVENING PRESS
105-111 W Bay St (PO Box 1088), Savannah, GA 31402
912-652-0319; FAX 912-234-6522; Email: Research@sava.gulfnet.com

Newspaper Group: Southeastern Newspapers Corp.
Fee-Based Research: Research fee; Copies.
Personnel
Head/News Research Julia C. Muller
Assistant Sara Wright

167 **Hawaii (Honolulu)**
HONOLULU ADVERTISER
605 Kapiolani Blvd (PO Box 3100), Honolulu, HI 96801
808-525-8000

Newspaper Group: Gannett Newspapers
Hours: Mon—Fri 7am—9:30pm; Sat 7am—8pm; Sun 1pm—9pm
Online Databases: NEXIS.
Resources: Photo files, reference books, maps, pamphlet file. Microforms: roll, fiche, jackets. Newspaper index, clippings.
Special Collections: Hawaiiana.
Personnel
Director Beatrice Kaya, (7669), SLA
Asst Librarian Margaret Iwamoto, (7670)

168 **Hawaii (Honolulu)**
HONOLULU STAR—BULLETIN
PO Box 3080, Honolulu, HI 96802
808-525-8000

Library founded: 1930.
Newspaper Group: Liberty Newspapers L.P.
Hours: Mon—Fri 7am—9:30pm; Sat 7am—8pm; Sun 1pm—9pm
Resources: Photo files, reference books, maps, pamphlets. Microforms: roll, fiche, jackets. Newspaper index, clippings.
Online Databases: NEXIS.
Special Collections: Hawaiiana.
Personnel
Librarian Beatrice Kaya, (7669), SLA
Asst Librarian Margaret Iwamoto, (7670)

169 **Idaho (Boise)**
IDAHO STATESMAN
1200 N Curtis Rd (PO Box 40), Boise, ID 83707 See Banner
208-377-6200; FAX 208-377-6449

Newspaper founded: 1864; library founded: 1972.
Newspaper Group: Gannett Newspapers
Hours: Mon-Fri 8:30am—5pm
Online Databases: DIALOG; Datatimes; NEXIS.
Services to Other News Libraries: Limited telephone reference. Sends copies of clips.
Access: To other media and other special libraries by appointment only.
Resources: Photo files, reference books, maps, pamphlet files. Microforms: roll, fiche, jackets. Clippings.
Personnel
Director Althea Orvis, (6435)

170 **Idaho (Lewiston)**
LEWISTON TRIBUNE
505 C St, Lewiston, ID 83501
208-743-9411; FAX 208-746-1185

Library founded: 1952.
Hours: Mon—Fri 8—5
CD ROM: Pioneer; NEC.
Archival Systems: PhotoView.
LAN: Netware.
Archival Systems: PhotoView; NewsView.
News Databases: NewsView.
Online Databases: NEXIS.
Personnel
Librarian Phyllis Collins

171 **Illinois (Alton)**
THE TELEGRAPH
111 E Broadway (PO Box 278), Alton, IL 62002 See Banner
618-463-2500; FAX 618-463-9829

Hours: Mon—Fri 8am—3:30pm
Services to Other News Libraries: Telephone reference. Sends copies of clips. Fee: 50c/copy. Requirements: paid in advance. No express mail clips.
Access: Not open to other media or other special libraries.
Resources: Photo files, reference books, maps, pamphlet files. Microforms: roll. Clippings.
Special Collections: Robert Wadlow; Elijah Lovejoy; Piasa Bird.
Personnel
Librarian Charlotte Stetson

172 **Illinois (Aurora)**
THE BEACON—NEWS
101 S River, Aurora, IL 60506 See Banner
708-844-5844; FAX 708-844-1043

Newspaper founded: 1846; library founded: 1977?
Newspaper Group: Copley Newspapers
Hours: Mon—Fri 8am—4:30pm; Sat: No librarian on duty.
News Databases: SII.
Services to Other News Libraries: Telephone reference. Sends copies of clips. No fee. Will not express mail clips. No microfilm search.
Access: Not open to other media or other special libraries.
Resources: Photo files, Reference Books, maps, pamphlet files. Clippings. Microforms: roll. Newspaper index.
Online Databases: Copley Database.
Personnel
Director Patricia Hard, (5884)

173 **Illinois (Belleville)**
THE BELLEVILLE NEWS DEMOCRAT
120 S Illinois (PO Box 427), Belleville, IL 62222 See Banner
618-234-1000; FAX 618-234-9597

Newspaper founded: 1858; library founded: 1981.
Newspaper Group: Capital Cities Communications Inc.
Hours: Sun—Sat 8am—5:30pm
Access: Open to other media by appointment.
Services to Other News Libraries: Telephone reference. Sends copies of clips. Requirements: Limited Requests.
Resources: Photo files, reference books, maps. Microforms: roll. Clippings.
Personnel

Librarian	Deborah Miller, (513)

174 **Illinois (Bloomington)**
THE PANTAGRAPH
301 W. Washington, Bloomington, IL 61701 See Banner
309-829-9411; FAX 309-829-7000

Newspaper founded: 1837; library founded: 1929.
Newspaper Group: Chronicle Publishing Co.
Hours: Mon—Fri 8am—9pm
Services to Other News Libraries: Telephone reference. Contact: Diane Logsdon. Sends copies of clips.
Access: Not open to other media; open to other special libraries.
Email: pantlib@pantagraph.com.
Resources: Photo files, negatives, reference books, maps, pamphlet files. Microforms: roll, fiche, jackets. Clippings.
News Databases: Datatimes.
Online Databases: Datatimes.
Personnel

Director	Diane Logsdon, (247), SLA
Assistant	Carlene Mathis-Kull
Clerk	Mildred Buckles

175 **Illinois (Champaign-Urbana)**
THE NEWS—GAZETTE
Box 677 (15 Main Street), Champaign, IL 61824 See Banner
217-351-5228; FAX 217-351-5374

Newspaper founded: 1852; library founded: 1946.
Hours: Mon—Fri 8am—4:30pm
Services to Other News Libraries: Telephone reference. Contact: Carolyn J. Vance. Sends copies of clips. Requirements: limit: 3 copies. Express mail clips if client pays fee and staff time permits.
Access: Open to other media and other special libraries by appointment.
Resources: Clippings, reference books, maps, pamphlet files. Microforms: roll. Photo files.
Personnel

Chief Librarian	Carolyn J. Vance, (cjvance@prairienet.org), SLA
Library Asst	Judith L. Huss, (5210)

176 **Illinois (Chicago)**
CHICAGO SUN—TIMES
401 N. Wabash Ave, Chicago, IL 60611 See Banner
312-321-3000; FAX 312-321-3228

Newspaper Group: Chicago Sun—Times, Inc.
Hours: Mon—Fri 7:30am—midnight; Sat—Sun lpm—9pm
Online Databases: DIALOG; SAVE; Datatimes; NEXIS.
Electronic Clipping Files: Info Globe
Services to Other News Libraries: Telephone reference. 312-321-2593. Sends copies of clips. Private researcher fee for large projects. Charge for express mail.
Access: Not open to other media. (Other media: contact Public Service Bureau 312-321-2039). Not open to other special libraries.
Resources: Photo files, negatives, reference books, maps, pamphlet files. Microforms: roll, fiche. Newspaper index, clippings.
Personnel

Director	Terry Marie Golembiewski, (3008), SLA

177 **Illinois (Chicago)**
CHICAGO TRIBUNE
435 N Michigan Ave, Chicago, IL 60611 See Banner
312-222-3466, 3871, 4416 / reference 312-222-3466; FAX 312-321-0420

Newspaper founded: 1847.
Newspaper Group: Tribune Company Owned Newspapers
Hours: 24 hrs/day
Services to Other News Libraries: Telephone reference. Sends copies of clips. No fee. Requirements: Brief, explicit, dates. Express mail clips.
Access: Open to other media outside of metropolitan Chicago. Requirements: brief, explicit dates. Open to other special libraries on limited basis, only to non-profit organizations.
Archival Systems: AP Preserver; SAVE.
CD ROM: Yes.
LAN: Yes.
WAN: Yes.
Online Databases: DIALOG; Dow Jones; SAVE; Info Globe; Datatimes; Federal Election Commission; Pacer (Federal Courts); Chicago Law Bulletin; CDB Infotek; Internet; Agri Data Network; LEXIS/NEXIS NewsNet.
News Databases: SAVE.
Resources: All news on line since January 1, 1985. Photo files, negatives, reference books, maps, pamphlet files. Microforms: roll, fiche, jackets. Newspaper index, clippings.
Special Collections: Chicago History and Biography; Freedom of Information; World War I history; Paul Gapp Library of Architecture and Urban Affairs; Native Americans.
Personnel

Director	John Jansson, (3466;, SLA
Mgr Research	Victoria Boylan, (3871), SLA
Mgr Data Base	Richard Rott, (4419), SLA
Mgr Photos	Mary Wilson, (4416), SLA

178 **Illinois (Danville)**
COMMERCIAL—NEWS
17 W North, Danville, IL 61832
217-446-1000; FAX 217-446-6648

Newspaper Group: Gannett Newspapers
Access: Open to other media by appointment.
Personnel

Librarian	Janet Leisch

179 **Illinois (Decatur)**
HERALD AND REVIEW
601 E William (PO Box 311), Decatur, IL 62525 See Banner
217-429-5151; FAX 217-446-6913

Founded: 1873; library founded: 1888.
Newspaper Group: Lee Newspapers
Hours: Mon—Sat 7am—11:30pm; Sun 3pm—11:30pm
Services to Other News Libraries: Telephone reference. Contact: Vickie Sangster. Sends copies of clips. Fee: $1/page if date of article is known. $20/hr for research.

HERALD AND REVIEW (cont'd)

Access: Open by appointment only.
Resources: Photo files, negatives, reference books, maps, pamphlet files. Microforms: roll. Newspaper index, clippings, PMT files.
Personnel
Librarian — Lisa Morrison, (0979)

180 **Illinois (Joliet)**
JOLIET HERALD-NEWS
300 Caterpillar Dr, Joliet, IL 60436
815-729-6161; FAX 815-729-6059

Newspaper Group: Copley Newspapers
Personnel
Librarian — Patra Murphy

181 **Illinois (Moline)**
THE DISPATCH
1720 5th Ave, Moline, IL 61265 — See Banner
309-764-4344; FAX 309-757-4992

Newspaper founded: 1878.
Newspaper Group: Small Newspapers
Hours: Mon—Fri 8am—4pm
Days Not Published: New Year's Day, Memorial Day, Independence Day, Labor Day, Thanksgivingand Christmas.
Access: Open to visiting reporters. Open to the public.
Services to Other News Libraries: Clip searches—$30/hour plus copy cost.
Resources: Photo files, maps. Newspaper index, clippings.
Personnel
Director — JoAnn Parmley, (247)

182 **Illinois (Peoria)**
JOURNAL STAR
1 News Plaza, Peoria, IL 61643
309-686-3108; FAX 309-686-3296

Established 1855.
Newspaper Group: PJS Enterprises
Days Not Published: Christmas Day.
Online Databases: Datatimes.
Personnel
Librarian — Judy Howard, SLA

183 **Illinois (Quincy)**
THE QUINCY HERALD—WHIG
130-38 S 5th (PO Box 909), Quincy, IL 62306
217-223-5100; FAX 217-221-3395

Days Not Published: New Year's Day, May 30, Independence Day, Labor Day, Thanksgiving.
Personnel
Librarian — Judy Nelson, (375)

184 **Illinois (Rock Island)**
ROCK ISLAND ARGUS
1724 4th Ave, Rock Island, IL 61201
309-786-6441; FAX 309-757-4992/309-786-7639

Newspaper founded: 1851.
Hours: Mon—Fri 6:30am—3pm
Days Not Published: New Years Day, Memorial Day, Independence Day, Labor Day, Thanksgiving, and Christmas.
Services to Other News Libraries: Telephone reference. Contact person: JoAnn Parmley. Sends copies of clips. Fee: $5.00.
Resources: Photo files. Microforms: roll. Clippings.
Personnel
Librarian — JoAnn Parmley, (1991)

185 **Illinois (Rockford)**
ROCKFORD REGISTER STAR
99 E State St, Rockford, IL 61105
815-987-1200; FAX 815-987-1365

Newspaper Group: Gannett Newspapers
Access: Open to visiting reporters by appointment.
Personnel
Info Librarian — Clarence Kamler, (1349)
Svc Director — Jan Stilson

186 **Illinois (Springfield)**
THE STATE JOURNAL REGISTER
1 Copley Plaza (PO Box 219), Springfield, IL 62705 — See Banner
217-788-1504; FAX 217-788-1551

Established: 1831.
Newspaper Group: Copley Newspapers
Hours: 7:30am—4:30pm
Access: Open to the public and other libraries.
News Databases: BASIS.
Fee-Based Research: Research Fee.
Services to Other News Libraries: Telephone reference. Sends copies of clips.
Resources: Photo files, negatives, reference books, maps, pamphlet files. Microforms: roll, fiche. Newspaper index.
Online Databases: Datatimes; NEXIS.
Personnel
Librarian — Sandra L. Vance, SLA

187 **Illinois (Waukegan)**
THE NEWS SUN
100 Madison St, Waukegan, IL 60085 — See Banner
708-336-7000 / reference ext 369; FAX 708-249-7246

Newspaper founded: 1892; library founded: 1940?
Newspaper Group: Copley Newspapers
Hours: Mon—Fri 7am—3:45pm
Days Not Published: New Years Day, Memorial Day, Labor Day, Christmas.
News Databases: BASIS.
Services to Other News Libraries: Telephone reference. Contact: Barbara Apple. Will not send copies of clips.
Access: Open to other media if not available elsewhere. Open to other special libraries.
Resources: Photo files, reference books, maps, pamphlet files. Microforms: roll, fiche. Newspaper index, clippings.
Personnel
Chief Librarian — Barbara Apple, (369)

188 **Indiana (Anderson)**
HERALD—BULLETIN
1133 Jackson St, Anderson, IN 46016 — See Banner
317-622-1212; FAX 317-646-6541

Newspaper founded: Bulletin 1885; Herald 1868.
Hours: Mon—Fri 7am—3pm
Services to Other News Libraries: Telephone reference. Sends copies of clips.
Resources: Photo files, reference books, pamphlet file. Clippings.
News Databases: Stauffer Gold.
Personnel
Director — Anita Heiny, (209)

189 **Indiana (Columbus)**
THE REPUBLIC
333 2nd St, Columbus, IN 47201
812-372-7811; FAX 812-379-5608

Newspaper Group: Home News Enterprises
Days Not Published: New Year's Day, Memorial Day, Independence Day, Labor Day, Thanksgiving, Christmas.
Access: By appointment.
Personnel
Librarian — Jane Peabody, (5633)

190 **Indiana (Evansville)**
THE EVANSVILLE COURIER
300 E Walnut St (PO Box 268), Evansville, IN 47702-0268
812-464-7442; FAX 812-422-8196

Established: 1845.
Newspaper Group: Scripps-Howard
Home Page (URL): http://www.evansville.net.
Online Databases: Datatimes.
Personnel
Librarian — Roseann Derk, (7440), SLA

191 **Indiana (Evansville)**
EVANSVILLE PRESS
300 E Walnut St (PO Box 454), Evansville, IN 47703-0454 — See Banner
812-424-7711 / 1-800-677-7737; FAX 812-464-7641

Year established: 1906.
Access: Not open to other media.
Personnel
Librarian — Ellen Sprepski, (7616)

192 **Indiana (Fort Wayne)**
THE JOURNAL—GAZETTE
600 W Main St, Fort Wayne, IN 46802 — See Banner
219-461-8377; FAX 219-461-8648

Newspaper founded: 1899; Library founded: 1976.
Hours: Mon—Fri 8am—5pm
Services to Other News Libraries: Telephone reference. Sends copies of clips. Fee: $1/clip. Requirement: payment in advance. No express mail clips.
Access: Open to other media. Competing media will be aided with fee; small search with permission of editor. Open to other special libraries.
Resources: Photo files, reference books, maps, pamphlet files. Microforms: roll, jackets. Clippings.
News Databases: Information International Inc.
Personnel
Director — Jody S. Habayeb, (JHabayeb@Mail.Ewi.Com)
Librarians — Michelle Shepherd; Cindy Kump

193 **Indiana (Fort Wayne)**
THE NEWS—SENTINEL
600 W Main St, Fort Wayne, IN 46802 — See Banner
219-461-8468; FAX 219-461-8817

Year established: Sentinel—1833; News—1874; News-Sentinel—1918.
Newspaper Group: Knight-Ridder Newspapers Inc.
Hours: 8—5
Days Not Published: Sundays, Christmas Day.
Archival Systems: SAVE.
Online Databases: SAVE.
Services to Other News Libraries: Telephone reference. Contact: Laura Weston. Sends copies of clips by FAX.
Resources: Photo files, reference books, maps, pamphlet files. Microforms: roll. Newspaper index, clippings.
Special Collections: Local History; Dan Quayle History.
Personnel
Library Manager — Laura L. Weston, (weston@plink.geis.com), SLA

194 **Indiana (Gary)**
POST—TRIBUNE
1065 Broadway, Gary, IN 46402 — See Banner
219-881-3134; FAX 219-881-3232

Newspaper founded: 1908; library founded: 1936.
Newspaper Group: Knight-Ridder Newspapers Inc.
Hours: Mon—Fri 8am—9:30pm
Online Databases: SAVE; AOL; NEXIS.
News Databases: SAVE.
Archival Systems: SAVE.
Fee-Based Research: Research Fee: $35/hour. Copies: $3/article; FAX: (Limited) $1/page. Prepay.
Services to Other News Libraries: Limited telephone reference. Sends limited copies of clips. Request must come through requestor's library. Fee: $3/clip, plus minimum reference service fee. Will be handled only if time/personnel permits, extra charge for telefacsimile clips.
Access: Open to staff only. Other media on time available basis with permission of Executive Editor, EME or Chief Librarian. Requirements: prior appointment, outside 75 mile radius, brief, explicit request. Access fee may apply.
Special Collections: Gary History.
Personnel
News Info Mgr — Louise K. Tucker, SLA
Staff — Valerie Johnson; Carol Chisholm

195 **Indiana (Hammond)**
THE TIMES
417 Fayette St, Hammond, IN 46325 — See Banner
219-933-3357; FAX 219-933-3249

Newspaper founded: 1906; library founded: 1960.
Newspaper Group: Howard Publications
Days Not Published: New Year's Day, Christmas.
Access: Open to other media by appt only. Open to other special libraries.
Resources: Photo files, negatives. Microforms: roll. Clippings.
Personnel
Librarian — Karen Matuska, (Matuska@Houpubs.com)

196 **Indiana (Indianapolis)**
INDIANAPOLIS STAR / INDIANAPOLIS NEWS
307 N Pennsylvania St, Indianapolis, IN 46204
317-633-1240; FAX 317-630-9540; Email: Library@Starnews.com

Year founded: Star—1903; News—1869.
Newspaper Group: Central Newspapers, Inc.
Access: Open to visiting reporters.
News Databases: Datatimes.
Online Databases: Datatimes; NEXIS.
Special Collections: Indiana Lore and History.
Personnel
Librarian — Sandra E. Fitzgerald, (9293), SLA

197 **Indiana (Kokomo)**
KOKOMO TRIBUNE
300 N Union, Kokomo, IN 46901 — See Banner
317-459-3121; FAX 317-456-3815; Email: Ktonline@aol.com

Year established: 1850.
Newspaper Group: Thomson Newspapers
Special Collections: Indiana, Howard County, Cass County, Tipton County, and Miami County History.
Personnel
Librarian — Elizabeth Rother, (252)

198 **Indiana (La Porte)**
THE LA PORTE HERALD—ARGUS
701 State St, La Porte, IN 46350
219-362-2161; FAX 219-362-2166

Year established: 1880.
Newspaper Group: Small Newspapers
Hours: 7am—3pm
Personnel
Librarian — Mark Kreag

199 **Indiana (Lafayette)**
JOURNAL & COURIER
217 N 6th St, Lafayette, IN 47901
317-423-5511; FAX 317-420-5246

Year established: 1829.
Newspaper Group: Gannett Newspapers
Home Page (URL): http://www.jconline.com/jconline.
CD ROM: Yes.
LAN: Yes.
Fee-Based Research: Copies; FAXing.
Personnel
Librarian — Rita L. Owens, (owens@jandc.man.com)

200 **Indiana (Madison)**
MADISON COURIER
310 Courier Sq, Madison, IN 47250
812-265-3641

Personnel
Librarian — Darla Stodghill

201 **Indiana (Marion)**
CHRONICLE—TRIBUNE
610 S Adams, Marion, IN 46952
317-664-5111; FAX 317-664-6292

Year established: 1930.
Newspaper Group: Gannett Newspapers
Hours: 9—5
Access: Open to visiting reporters.
Personnel
Librarian — Wende Wright

202 **Indiana (Martinsville)**
DAILY REPORTER
60 S. Jefferson St (PO Box 1636), Martinsville, IN 46151 — See Banner
317-342-3311 / Reference 317-342-6384; FAX 317-342-1446

Newspaper founded: 1889.
Hours: Mon—Fri 8am—5pm; Sat 8am—12n
Days Not Published: Sunday, Christmas
Services to Other News Libraries: Telephone reference. Sends copies of clips at cost. Contact: Robin Surfact.
Access: Open to other media; open to other special libraries.
Online Databases: Datatimes.
Resources: Photo files, negatives. Microforms: roll. Newspaper index.

203 **Indiana (Michigan City)**
MICHIGAN CITY NEWS-DISPATCH
121 W Michigan Blvd, Michigan City, IN 46360 — See Banner
219-874-7211; FAX 219-872-8511

Newspaper founded: 1881.
Newspaper Group: Nixon Newspapers
Hours: Mon—Fri 7:30am—5pm
Days Not Published: New Year's Day, Memorial Day, Labor Day, Christmas, Sunday.
Services to Other News Libraries: Telephone reference. Contact: Jan Hager. Sends copies of clips/no fee.
Access: Not open to public or other special libraries.
Resources: Photo files, negatives, reference books, maps. Clippings.
Personnel
Director — Marybeth Peterka

204 **Indiana (Muncie)**
MUNCIE STAR AND EVENING PRESS
125 S High, Muncie, IN 47302
317-747-5767

Year established: 1899.
Newspaper Group: Central Newspapers, Inc.
Personnel
Librarian — Breena Wysong

205 **Indiana (Peru)**
PERU DAILY TRIBUNE
26 W Third St, Peru, IN 46970
317-473-6641; FAX 317-472-4438

Newspaper Group: Nixon Newspapers
Days Not Published: New Year's Day, Memorial Day, Independence Day, Labor Day, Thanksgiving, Christmas.
Personnel
Librarian — Faye White

206 **Indiana (South Bend—Mishawaka)**
SOUTH BEND TRIBUNE
225 W Colfax, South Bend, IN 46626 — See Banner
219-235-6161 / reference ext 237; FAX 219-236-1765

Newspaper founded: 1872; library founded: 1930s.
Newspaper Group: Sherry Communications
Hours: Mon—Fri 7:30am—4:30pm
Days Not Published: Independence Day, Labor Day, Christmas
Services to Other News Libraries: Telephone reference.
Access: Open to other media with special request.
Resources: Photo files, negatives, reference books. maps. Microforms: roll, jackets. Newspaper index, clippings.
Personnel
Librarian — Rusty Grauel, (347)
Assistant — Kathy Ginter, (347)

207 **Indiana (Warsaw)**
TIMES—UNION
Times Bldg (PO Box 1448), Warsaw, IN 46580
219-267-3111; FAX 219-287-7784

Year established: Times—1856; Union—1854.
Days Not Published: New Year's Day, Memorial Day, Independence Day, Labor Day, Thanksgiving, Christmas
Personnel
Librarian — Mary Alice Park

208 **Indiana (Washington)**
THE WASHINGTON TIMES—HERALD
102 E Vantress St, Washington, IN 47501
812-254-0480; FAX 812-254-0480

Year established: 1867.
Newspaper Group: Donrey Media Group
Days Not Published: New Year's Day, Memorial Day, Independence Day, Labor Day, Thanksgiving, Christmas
Personnel
Director — Mary Lou Fromme

209 **Iowa (Cedar Rapids—Marion)**
THE GAZETTE
500 Third Ave SE, Cedar Rapids, IA 52406 — See Banner
319-398-8328; FAX 319-398-5846

Newspaper founded: 1883.
Hours: Mon—Fri 8am—5pm
Services to Other News Libraries: Telephone reference. Contact: Bridget Janus. Sends copies of clips. No fee.
Resources: Photo files, reference books. Microforms: roll, fiche, jackets. Clippings.
Personnel
Director — Bridget Janus, SLA
Library Asst — Marilyn Easton

210 **Iowa (Council Bluffs)**
THE DAILY NONPAREIL
117 Pearl St, Council Bluffs, IA 51501
712-328-1811

Year established: 1857.
Newspaper Group: Thomson Newspapers
Days Not Published: New Year's Day, Memorial Day, Independence Day, Labor Day, Christmas.
Personnel
Librarian — Helen Myers

211 **Iowa (Davenport)**
QUAD—CITY TIMES
PO Box 3828, Davenport, IA 52808
319-383-2293; FAX 319-383-2370

Personnel
Librarian — Ray Booker

212 **Iowa (Des Moines)**
DES MOINES REGISTER
715 Locust St, Des Moines, IA 50304
515-284-8442; FAX 515-286-2504

News Databases: Datatimes.
Online Databases: Datatimes.
Services to Other News Libraries: Answers questions from news libraries.
Access: Open to visiting reporters by appointment.
Special Collections: World War II Collection; Extensive collection of movie photos.
Personnel
Librarian — Phyllis Wolfe, (PWolfe@Desmoine.Gannet.Com)

213 **Iowa (Dubuque)**
TELEGRAPH HERALD—
Library Services
801 Bluff St, Dubuque, IA 52001
319-588-5770; FAX 319-588-5745; Email: THONLINE@WCINET.COM

Hours: Mon—Fri 8—5
Access: Open to other media by appointment.
News Databases: PhotoView; NewsView.
Personnel
Library Manager — Stephen McAuliff, SLA
Asst Librarians — Rob Rabe
Helen Ruby

214 **Iowa (Marshalltown)**
MARSHALLTOWN TIMES—REPUBLICAN
135 W Main St, Marshalltown, IA 50158
515-753-6611; FAX 515-753-7221

Year founded: 1858.
Days Not Published: New Year's Day, Memorial Day, Independence Day, Labor Day, Christmas
Personnel
Librarian — Amy Mills

215 **Iowa (Mason City)**
GLOBE-GAZETTE / SUNDAY GLOBE
300 N Washington (PO Box 271), Mason City, IA 50401
515-421-0525; FAX 515-421-0516

Newspaper Group: Lee Newspapers
Personnel
Librarian — Judy L. Delperdang, SLA

216 **Iowa (Sioux City)**
SIOUX CITY JOURNAL
515 Pavonia St, Sioux City, IA 51102
712-279-5080; FAX 712-279-5059

Year established: 1870.
Newspaper Group: Hagadone Newspapers
Days Not Published: New Year's Day, Christmas.
Access: By appointment. Open to other news libraries.
Online Databases: Internet.
Personnel
Librarian — Ranae Reed

217 **Iowa (Waterloo)**
WATERLOO—CEDAR FALLS COURIER
501 Commercial St, Waterloo, IA 50704-0540 See Banner
319-291-1477; FAX 319-291-2069

Newspaper founded: 1859; library founded: 1942.
Newspaper Group: Howard Publications
Hours: Mon—Fri 8am—3pm
Services to Other News Libraries: Telephone reference. Will send and FAX copies of clips.
Email: WCFCourier@aol.com.
Online Databases: SAVE; DIALOG.
Resources: Photo files, negatives, reference books, maps, pamphlet files. Microforms: roll. Clippings.
Fee-Based Research: Research Fee: $25/hour. Copies: $.50/article. Contact: Teresa Dahlgren (291-1477).
Special Collections: Sullivan Brothers.
Personnel
Librarian — Teresa E. Dahlgren, (477), SLA

218 **Kansas (Independence)**
INDEPENDENCE DAILY REPORTER
320 N 6th St (Box 869), Independence, KS 67301
316-331-3550; FAX 316-331-3550

Year founded: 1881.
Personnel
Librarian — JoAnn Swearingen, (66)

219 **Kansas (Topeka)**
THE TOPEKA CAPITAL—JOURNAL
616 SE Jefferson St, Topeka, KS 66607
913-295-1291; FAX 913-295-1230

Newspaper Group: Morris Communications Corp.
Hours: 8am—11am
Access: Open to visiting reporters, other librarians.
News Databases: Stauffer Gold.
Personnel
Librarian — Tricia Johnston

220 **Kansas (Wichita)**
THE WICHITA EAGLE
825 E Douglas Ave (Box 820), Wichita, KS 67201 See Banner
316-268-6554; FAX 316-268-6627; Email: 75765.1555@compuserve.com

Year established: 1872.
Newspaper Group: Knight-Ridder Newspapers Inc.
Access: Open to visiting reporters.
Services to Other News Libraries: Will do clip searches. Faxes/mails clips.
Online Databases: SAVE; DIALOG; Datatimes; NEXIS.
Archival Systems: SAVE.
Fee-Based Research: Research fee, will invoice.
Personnel
Librarian — Allan Tanner, SLA

221 **Kentucky (Covington)**
THE KENTUCKY POST
421 Madison Ave, Covington, KY 41011
606-292-2600; FAX 606-291-2525

Newspaper Group: Scripps-Howard
Days Not Published: Sunday.
News Databases: SAVE.
Personnel
Librarian — Barbara Herzog, (2675)

222 **Kentucky (Lexington)**
LEXINGTON HERALD—LEADER
100 Midland Ave, Lexington, KY 40508 See Banner
606-231-3335; FAX 606-231-3326

Newspaper founded: 1900; library founded: 1945.
Newspaper Group: Knight-Ridder Newspapers Inc.
Hours: Mon—Fri 9am—8pm; Sat 12n—6pm
Access: Other media.
Services to Other News Libraries: Telephone reference. Sends copies of clips through librarian's request only. Express mails clips—need requestor's account number. Telefacsimile clips—Group 3.
Email: HLLIB@LEX.INFI.NET.
Online Databases: NEXIS; DIALOG; SAVE; Kentucky Economic Information System; Dow Jones; Datatimes; Wilsonline; AOL.
News Databases: DIALOG.
Electronic Clipping Files: SAVE (in-house).
Resources: Photo files, negatives, reference books, pamphlet file. Microform: rolls. Clippings.
Archival Systems: SAVE.
CD ROM: Yes.
LAN: Yes.
WAN: Yes.
Personnel
Director — Lu-An Dunn Farrar, SLA
Librarians — Linda Minch, SLA
Linda Smith-Niemi, SLA

223 **Kentucky (Louisville)**
LOUISVILLE COURIER—JOURNAL AND LOUISVILLE TIMES
525 W Broadway (PO Box 740031), Louisville, KY 40201-7431 See Banner
Systems 502-582-4506 / Clippings 502-582-4184 / Photos 502-582-4603; FAX 502-582-4290

Newspaper founded: 1868; library founded: 1937.
Newspaper Group: Gannett Newspapers
Hours: Mon—Fri 8am—11pm; Sat, Sun 3pm—11pm
Online Databases: DIALOG; NEXIS; OCLC; CompuServe; Datatimes.
News Databases: Digital Collections; Info-Ky.
Archival Systems: TEXT and IMAGE ARCHIVES.
LAN: Yes.
WAN: Yes.
Fee-Based Research: Research Fee: $60/hour. Copies: $.25/article. FAX: $10/search. Microform Copies: $1.50/article. Credit Card or invoice. Contact: Sharon Bidwell (582-4184).
Services to Other News Libraries: Telephone reference. Contact: Sharon Bidwell. Will send copies of clips—fee. Express mails clips.
Access: Online access, online time charges and library time charge. Estimate at time of request. Not open to other special libraries.
Resources: Photo files, reference books, pamphlet file. Microforms: roll, fiche, jackets. Clippings. Computerized access to our files online in Datatimes System Nationally.
CD ROM: Newsbank.
Personnel
Librarian/Reference — Sharon Bidwell, (4184), SLA
Librarian/Systems — Leonard Tharp, (4506), SLA
Supervisor/Reference — Pat Chapman, (4602)
Supervisor/Systems — Patty Moulton, (4178)
Library Photo Tech — Judy Wadlington, (4603)
Systems Maintenance Tech — Mark Taflinger, (4133)

224 **Louisiana (Baton Rouge)**
THE ADVOCATE
525 Lafayette, Baton Rouge, LA 70802 See Banner
504-383-1111; FAX 504-383-0329

Newspaper founded: 1842; library founded: 1922.
Hours: Mon—Fri 9am—10pm
Days Not Published: Christmas Day
Access: Other media access. Identification and purpose of research required. Limited special library access.
Services to Other News Libraries: Limited telephone reference. Sends copies of clips to other news libraries, no fee.
Online Databases: NEXIS; Datatimes; DIALOG; Washington Alert; MEDLARS; CompuServe.
Resources: Photo files, negatives, reference books, maps, pamphlet file. Microforms: roll, jackets. Clippings, periodicals and newspapers. Online database of news stories.
Personnel
Director — Jill Arnold, (327;, SLA

225 **Louisiana (Lake Charles)**
LAKE CHARLES AMERICAN PRESS
4900 Hwy 90E (PO Box 2893), Lake Charles, LA 70602
318-433-3000; FAX 318-494-4008

Newspaper Group: Shearman Newspapers
Personnel
Librarian — Cassie Meaux, (494-4079)

226 **Louisiana (New Iberia)**
DAILY IBERIAN
926 E Main St, New Iberia, LA 70561-1270 See Banner
318-365-6773

Newspaper founded: 1873; library founded: 1975.
Hours: Mon—Fri 8am—4pm
Access: No telephone reference. Will send copies of clips.
Resources: Photo files, negatives, reference books, maps, pamphlet files. Microforms: roll. Clippings.
Personnel
Director — Ivy Derise, (32)

227 **Louisiana (New Orleans)**
THE TIMES—PICAYUNE
3800 Howard Ave, New Orleans, LA 70140 See Banner
504-826-3279; FAX 504-826-3369

Newspaper founded: 1837.
Newspaper Group: Newhouse Newspapers
Hours: Mon—Fri 7am—9pm
Services to Other News Libraries: Telephone reference. Sends copies of clips. No fee. Requirements: limited quantities; depends on information requested. Express mail clips, collect.
Access: Open to other media by appt only; subject to approval. Limited access. Not open to other special libraries.
News Databases: SAVE.
Online Databases: DIALOG; Datatimes; NEXIS.
Resources: Photo files, reference books, maps, pamphlet files. Microforms: roll. Newspaper index, clippings.
Personnel
Director — Nancy I. Burris, (3424), SLA

228 **Louisiana (Shreveport)**
THE TIMES
222 Lake St, Shreveport, LA 71130
318-459-3283; FAX 318-459-3381

Newspaper founded: 1871.
Newspaper Group: Gannett Newspapers
Resources: Microforms: roll, fiche, jacket. Newspaper index, clippings.
Access: No telephone reference. Will not send copies of clips. Open to other Gannett Group Newspapers only.

THE TIMES (cont'd)

Special Collections: Bound volumes of the Times 1871 to date and microfilm copies of area newspapers from 1843—1984.
Personnel
Director — Martha Matlock, SLA
Asst Director — Dot Landry

229 **Maine (Bangor)**
BANGOR DAILY NEWS
491 Main, Bangor, ME 04401 — See Banner
207-990-8226 / 800-432-7964; FAX 207-990-8081

Year founded: 1889.
Access: Open to other media by appointment.
Services to Other News Libraries: Telephone reference. Sends copies of clips.
Online Databases: NEXIS; Datatimes.
News Databases: BASIS.
Personnel
Librarian — Charles A. Campo, (300)

230 **Maine (Brunswick)**
BRUNSWICK TIMES RECORD
Industry Rd (PO Box 10), Brunswick, ME 04011
207-729-3311; FAX 207-729-5728

Hours: 8am—5pm
Access: Not open to public. Telephone requests for special information.
News Databases: Stauffer Gold.
Personnel
Librarian — Laura Mosqueda, (237)

231 **Maine (Portland)**
PORTLAND PRESS HERALD/MAINE SUNDAY TELEGRAM
390 Congress St (PO Box 1460), Portland, ME 04104 — See Banner
207-791-6390; FAX 207-791-6920

Newspaper founded: 1882; library founded: 1912.
Newspaper Group: Guy Gannett Communications
Hours: Mon—Fri 11am—9pm; Sat 12n—7:30pm; Sun 1:30pm—9pm
Access: Open to other media by appointment. Open to public for fee.
Services to Other News Libraries: Telephone/mail reference. Courtesy service to librarians (791-6391).
Archival Systems: SAVE.
News Databases: SAVE.
CD ROM: Yes.
Fee-Based Research: Research Fee: $25. Copies: $1—$5. FAX: $1/page. Microform Copies: $1/article. Prepay or will invoice. Call 791-6391.
Resources: Photo files, reference books, maps, pamphlet files. Microforms: roll, jackets. Clippings.
Online Databases: NEXIS; Datatimes.
Special Collections: Maine Registers to date; Portland City Directories to date.
Personnel
Librarian — Marcia MacVane, SLA
Asst Librarians — Julia McCue
Elizabeth Murphy
Linda Madsen
Susan Butler

232 **Maryland (Annapolis)**
THE CAPITAL
2000 Capital Dr (PO Box 911), Annapolis, MD 21401 — See Banner
410-268-5000; FAX 410-268-4643

Year founded: 1727; library founded: 1966.
Hours: Mon—Fri 8:30—4
Days Not Published: New Year's Day, Memorial Day, Labor Day, Christmas.
Access: Open to other newspaper librarians. Not open to other media.
Online Databases: LEXIS/NEXIS.
News Databases: SAVE.
Electronic Clipping Files: NewsView
Resources: Photo files, maps, pamphlet file. Microforms: fiche. Clippings.
Personnel
Director — Janice C. Wolod

233 **Maryland (Baltimore)**
BALTIMORE SUN
501 N Calvert St, Baltimore, MD 21278 — See Banner
410-332-6255; FAX 410-332-6918

Newspaper founded: 1837.
Newspaper Group: Times Mirror Co.
Hours: Mon—Fri 8am—9pm; Sat, Sun 12n—8pm.
Email: slevy@clark.net.
Home Page (URL): http://www.clark.net/pub/sunsrc; http://www.baltsun.com.
Archival Systems: AP Preserver.
CD ROM: Yes.
LAN: Yes.
Fee-Based Research: Research Fee: $75. Copies: $6.95/article. FAX. Credit card, invoice. Contact: SunSource (1-800-829-8000 ext 6800 or 410-332-6800).
Online Databases: NEXIS; DIALOG; Dow Jones; Datatimes; CompuServe.
News Databases: SII.
Services to Other News Libraries: Telephone reference.
Access: Assistance to new libraries outside the state of Maryland and District of Columbia. All other requests referred to SunSource fee-based reference service.
Resources: Books, periodicals, microforms, clippings, photo files and maps.
Special Collections: Baltimore City, Maryland State History; H.L. Mencken.
Personnel
Director Lib/Info Svcs — Lisa LoVullo, (6250; llovullo@clark.net), SLA
Deputy Dir — Sandra Levy, (6256; slevy@clark.net), SLA
News Researchers — Dee Lyon, (6749), SLA
Paul McCardell, (6257; pmccarde@clark.net)
Jean Packard, (6254)
Charlene Tag, (6253), SLA
Susan Waters, (6749), SLA

234 **Maryland (Silver Spring)**
THE NEWSPAPER GUILD
8211 Second Ave, Silver Spring, MD 20910
301-585-2990

Access: Open to other media by appointment.
Special Collections: Newspaper Guild Archives.
Personnel
Dir Research/Info — Larkie Gildersleeve, (71363.3211@Compuserve.Com)

235 **Maryland (Westminster)**
CARROLL COUNTY TIMES
201 Railroad Ave, Westminster, MD 21157
410-848-4400

Newspaper Group: Landmark Communications, Inc.
Access: Open to visiting reporters.
Services to Other News Libraries: Answers questions from news libraries.
Personnel
Librarian — Robin Sealover, (751-5903)

236 **Massachusetts (Boston)**
BOSTON GLOBE
135 Morrissey Blvd, Boston, MA 02107 — See Banner
617-929-2000 / Reference ext 2540; FAX 617-929-3314

Newspaper founded: 1872; library founded: 1887.

BOSTON GLOBE (cont'd)

Hours: Mon—Fri 8am—11pm. Sat, Sun 10:30am—10:30pm
Home Page (URL): http://www.boston.com.
Archival Systems: SAVE; Merlin.
CD ROM: Yes.
Fee-Based Research: Research Fee: $25. Copies: $3.10; FAX. Microform Copies: $5. Prepay or invoice. Contact: Bill Boles (929-2546).
Online Databases: DIALOG; Dow Jones; SAVE; LEXIS/NEXIS; Datatimes.
News Databases: Datatimes; SAVE.
Services to Other News Libraries: Telephone reference (929-2546). Sends copies of clips for fee. Express mail clips. Telefacsimile clips.
Access: Other media. Requirements: non-competitive, outside 40 mile radius. Other special libraries.
Resources: Photo files, reference books, maps, pamphlet files. Microforms: roll, fiche. Newspaper index, clippings.
Special Collections: Harvard College Yearbooks, Harvard University histories, directories, early Massachusetts photographs, geneologies, lithographs.
Personnel
Director — Elisabeth Tuite, (3410; tuite@globe.com), SLA

237 **Massachusetts (Boston)**
BOSTON HERALD
1 Herald Square, Boston, MA 02106-2096 See Banner
617-426-3000; FAX 617-542-1314/1315

Library founded: 1841.
Hours: Mon—Fri 10am—9pm; Sat, Sun 11am—7pm.
Home Page (URL): http://www.BOSTONHERALD.COM.
Services to Other News Libraries: Telephone reference (news related queries only). Transmit copies of clips, etc. Contact Library staff (Ext 678, 679, 680).
Access: At discretion of chief librarian.
Resources: Photo files, clip files April 1, 1993, reference collection, maps, microfilm.
Online Databases: Datatimes; NEXIS.
Fee-Based Research: Research Fee: $50 (Copies and FAXing included in search fee). Microform Copies: $1. Invoice.
Personnel
Chief Librarian — John Cronin, (Cronin@Bostonherald.com), SLA
Library Assocs — Alan Thibeault, SLA; Chris Donnelly; Elizabeth Pakule, SLA

238 **Massachusetts (Boston)**
THE CHRISTIAN SCIENCE MONITOR
1 Norway St, Boston, MA 02115 See Banner
617-450-2683; FAX 617-450-2689

Newspaper founded: 1908.
Hours: Mon—Fri 7:30am—5pm; Sun 7:30am—3:15pm.
Days Not Published: New Year's Day, Washington's Birthday, Memorial Day, Independence Day, Labor Day, Columbus Day, Veteran's Day, Thanksgiving, Christmas, Saturday, Sunday.
Access: Media access, other special library access.
Online Databases: NEXIS; DIALOG; Datatimes; Dow Jones.
Services to Other News Libraries: Telephone reference. Sends copies of clips, express mail clips. Fee as necessary.
Resources: Reference books, maps, pamphlet files. Microforms: roll, fiche, jacket. Newspaper index, clippings.
Personnel
Director — Joyce McMillin, (McMillinj@estter.csfs.com), SLA
Asst Librarian — Joan Lindsay, (2682)

239 **Massachusetts (Boston)**
HARVARD UNIVERSITY—
Business School / Baker Library
Cole Room, Soldiers Field, Boston, MA 02163
617-495-6733; Email: 71514.151@compuserve.com
Personnel
Librarian — Guy P. Seaberg

240 **Massachusetts (Brockton)**
ENTERPRISE
60 Main St, Brockton, MA 02403
508-586-7200

Access: Open by appointment only.
Personnel
Librarian — Steven Sharp

241 **Massachusetts (Fall River)**
HERALD NEWS
207 Pocasset St, Fall River, MA 02722
508-676-8211; FAX 508-673-3375

Newspaper Group: Journal Register
Hours: Mon—Fri 8am—4pm
Access: Open to other media and librarians by appointment.
Personnel
Librarian — Judy Rebello, (2529)

242 **Massachusetts (Framingham)**
MIDDLESEX NEWS
33 New York Ave (PO Box 9149), Framingham, MA 01701
508-626-3800; FAX 508-626-4400

Newspaper Group: Harte-Hanks Communications, Inc.
Personnel
Librarian — Sandy Buentello

243 **Massachusetts (Greenfield)**
RECORDER
14 Hope St, Greenfield, MA 01301
413-772-0261

Personnel
Librarian — Diane Poirier

244 **Massachusetts (Hyannis - Cape Cod)**
CAPE COD TIMES
319 Main St, Hyannis, MA 02601 See Banner
508-775-1200; FAX 508-775-7337

Newspaper founded: 1936; library founded: 1970.
Newspaper Group: Ottaway Newspapers, Inc.
Hours: Mon—Fri 10am—2pm
Services to Other News Libraries: Telephone reference—Contact Nancy Hallaren. Sends copies of clips. Fee: $1 each payable in advance.
Resources: Photo files. Reference books, maps. Microforms: roll. Clippings.
Personnel
Librarian — Nancy B. Hallaren, (862-1172) SLA

245 **Massachusetts (Lawrence)**
EAGLE—TRIBUNE
PO Box 100, Lawrence, MA 01842 See Banner
508-685-1000

Hours: Mon—Fri 6am—3pm
Days Not Published: Christmas Day.
Services to Other News Libraries: Telephone reference.
Resources: Photo files can be ordered. Reference books. Maps. Microforms: roll. Clippings.
Personnel
Library Director — Linda M. Iannalfo, (219)

246 **Massachusetts (Lowell)**
THE SUN / THE SUNDAY SUN
15 Kearney Sq, Lowell, MA 01852
508-458-7100; FAX 508-970-4700

Access: Open to visiting reporters.
Services to Other News Libraries: Answers questions from news libraries.
Personnel
Librarian — Samuel Weisberg, (970-4665)

247 **Massachusetts (Lynn)**
DAILY EVENING ITEM
38 Exchange St, Lynn, MA 01903 — See Banner
617-593-7700; FAX 617-581-3178

Newspaper founded: 1877; library founded: 1933.
Hours: Mon—Thur 6:30am—1:30pm; Fri 6:30am—11pm
Days Not Published: New Year's Day, Washington's Birthday, Memorial Day, Independence Day, Labor Day, Columbus Day, Veteran's Day, Thanksgiving, Christmas, Patriot's Day, Sunday.
Services to Other News Libraries: Telephone reference. Sends copies of clips (fee). Will not send entire files. Will FAX clips.
Resources: Photo files, maps. Microforms: roll. Newspaper Index. Clippings.
Access: Open to other media by appointment.
Personnel
Director — Judy Johnson, (223)

248 **Massachusetts (New Bedford)**
STANDARD—TIMES
25 Elm St, New Bedford, MA 02742
508-997-7411; FAX 508-997-7491

Newspaper Group: Ottaway Newspapers, Inc.
Access: Open to visiting reporters by appointment.
Services to Other News Libraries: Answers questions from news libraries.
Personnel
Librarian — Gail Couture, (4436)

249 **Massachusetts (North Adams)**
THE TRANSCRIPT
124 American Legion Dr, North Adams, MA 01247 — See Banner
413-663-3741; FAX 413-662-2792

Newspaper founded: 1843; library founded: 1950?
Newspaper Group: American Publishing
Hours: Mon—Fri 7am—4pm
Days Not Published: New Year's Day, Christmas.
Resources: Photo files, negatives, reference books, maps. Microforms: roll. Clippings. Card file prior to 1950.
Personnel
Librarian — Gail Baily

250 **Massachusetts (Northampton)**
DAILY HAMPSHIRE GAZETTE
115 Conz St (PO Box 299), Northampton, MA 01061
413-584-5000; FAX 413-585-5222

Hours: 8:30—5
Access: Open to visiting reporters.
Personnel
Librarian — Nancy Rhodes

251 **Massachusetts (Pittsfield)**
BERKSHIRE EAGLE
75 S Church St, Pittsfield, MA 01201 — See Banner
413-447-7311; FAX 413-499-3419

Newspaper Group: New England Newspapers
Access: Open to other librarians, other media and public.
Email: DScrib@aol.com.
News Databases: Folio Views.
Personnel
Librarian — Grace McMahon, (496-6256)

252 **Massachusetts (Quincy)**
THE PATRIOT LEDGER
400 Crown Colony Dr, Quincy, MA 02345-9159
617-786-7085; FAX 617-786-7393

Access: Not open to visiting reporters.
Services to Other News Libraries: Answers questions from news libraries.
Archival Systems: Stauffer Gold.
Online Databases: DIALOG; Dow Jones; Datatimes.
News Databases: Stauffer Gold.
CD ROM: Yes.
LAN: Yes.
Personnel
Librarian — Linda Chapman, (lchapman@ledger.com), SLA

253 **Massachusetts (Springfield)**
UNION—NEWS / SUNDAY REPUBLICAN
1860 Main St, Springfield, MA 01101 — See Banner
413-788-1000

Newspaper Group: Newhouse Newspapers
Hours: 7:30am—11:30pm
Access: Open to other media by appointment.
Services to Other News Libraries: Answers questions from news libraries.

254 **Massachusetts (Wakefield)**
WAKEFIELD DAILY ITEM
26 Albion St, Wakefield, MA 01880
617-245-0080; FAX 617-246-0061

Access: Open to visiting reporters.
Services to Other News Libraries: Answers questions from news libraries.
Personnel
Librarian — Marilyn Linn

255 **Massachusetts (Worcester)**
AMERICAN ANTIQUARIAN SOCIETY—Library
185 Salisbury St, Worcester, MA 01609-1634
508-755-5221; FAX 508-753-3311; Email: Lib@MWA.ORG

Hours: Mon—Fri 9—5
Access: Open to the adult public with references and two forms of identification. Telephone reference.
Special Collections: Largest collection of American newspapers through 1876 in US, American mss, with special concentration on early American diaries and printers' papers, genealogies and state and local histories, American bindings, bookplates, broadsides, children's literature.
Personnel

President	Ellen S. Dunlap
Executive Asst	Eleanor S. Adams
Director of Research	John B. Hench
Librarian	Nancy H. Burkett

256 **Massachusetts (Worcester)**
TELEGRAM & GAZETTE, SUNDAY TELEGRAM
20 Franklin St (Box 15012), Worcester, MA 01615-0012 — See Banner
508-793-9100; Reference 508-793-9240; FAX 508-793-9281

Newspapers founded: Gazette 1866; Telegram 1886; Consolidated 1989.
Hours: Mon—Fri 7am—11pm; Sat 12n—10:30pm; Sun 12n—11pm

TELEGRAM & GAZETTE, SUNDAY TELEGRAM (cont'd)

Services to Other News Libraries: Telephone reference; FAX or mail clips. Some restrictions on competing media in the same market. No fee.
Access: Open to other media and other special libraries by appointment with chief librarian.
Archival Systems: Basis.
CD ROM: Yes.
LAN: Yes.
Fee-Based Research: Research Fee ($2.50 min). Copies: $.50. Microform Copies: $2. Prepay. Contact: Barry Parsons (793-9240).
Resources: Photo files, reference books, maps, pamphlet file. Microforms: roll. Clippings. Microfilm.
Online Databases: In-house from 1/89; available on DataTimes/Dow Jones News Retrieval from 8/90.
Personnel
Chief Librarian — George H. Labonte, (9277), SLA

257 **Michigan (Alpena)**
THE ALPENA NEWS
130 Park Pl, Alpena, MI 49707
517-354-3111; FAX 517-354-2096

Access: Open to other media by appointment.
Personnel
Librarian — Paula Zaborey

258 **Michigan (Ann Arbor)**
ANN ARBOR NEWS
340 E Huron St, Ann Arbor, MI 48106-1147
313-994-6953; FAX 313-994-6879

Year founded: 1835.
Newspaper Group: Newhouse Newspapers
Personnel
Librarian — Grace L. Puravs, SLA

259 **Michigan (Battle Creek)**
BATTLE CREEK ENQUIRER
155 W Van Buren St, Battle Creek, MI 49016
616-964-7161; FAX 616-964-0299

Year founded: 1980.
Newspaper Group: Gannett Newspapers
Hours: 8—5
Personnel
Librarian — Linda Willison, (966-0683)

260 **Michigan (Bay City)**
THE BAY CITY TIMES
311 Fifth St, Bay City, MI 48703
517-895-8551; FAX 517-895-5910

Newspaper Group: Newhouse Newspapers
Hours: 7:30—3:30
Personnel
Librarian — Ann Sauve, (894-9655)

261 **Michigan (Detroit)**
AMERICAN AUTOMOBILE MANUFACTURERS ASSOCIATION
300 New Center Bldg, Detroit, MI 48202
313-872-4311

Hours: Mon—Fri 8:30am—5:15pm
Access: Open to public by appointment.
Special Collections: Automotive photographs.
Personnel
Librarians — Peggy Dusman; Diane Primack; Dan Kirchner, (367)

262 **Michigan (Detroit)**
DETROIT FREE PRESS
321 W Lafayette, Detroit, MI 48226 — See Banner
313-222-6497; FAX 313-222-8778; Email: Library@det-freepress.com

Newspaper founded: 1831; library founded: 1925.
Newspaper Group: Knight-Ridder Newspapers Inc.
Hours: Mon—Fri 8am—9pm; Sun 11am—7pm
CD ROM: Yes.
Online Databases: NEXIS; Datatimes; DIALOG; SAVE; Dow Jones; Internet.
Services to Other News Libraries: Negotiable.
Archival Systems: SAVE; Fetch; Iron Mike Photogrid
Access: Closed to the public. We have fee-based research service. Access by other media negotiable.
Fee-Based Research: Research Fee: $120/hour. Copies: $10/each. Credit card or invoice.
Resources: Photos, newspaper clips (1927—1971), books, CDROMS, maps, online databases, microfilm (1925—present), microfiche 1971—1982.
Personnel
Library Coord — Alice Pepper, SLA
Librarians — Christine Schmuckal; Lorraine Simon; Shelley Lavey; Victoria Turk

263 **Michigan (Detroit)**
DETROIT NEWS
615 W Lafayette Blvd, Detroit, MI 48226 — See Banner
313-222-2040; FAX 313-222-6417

Newspaper founded: 1873; library founded: 1873.
Newspaper Group: Gannett Newspapers
Hours: Mon—Fri 8am—9pm; Sat 9—5.
Home Page (URL): http://detnews.com.
Online Databases: NEXIS; Datatimes.
Fee-Based Research: Research Fee: $100/min. Copies: $10/page. FAX: $20. Microform copies: $10. Prepay. Contact: 222-2090.
CD ROM: Newsbank.
Services to Other News Libraries: Telephone reference. Sends copies of clips. Fee.
Access: Not open to other media. Open to other special libraries.
Resources: Photo files, reference books, maps, pamphlet files. Microforms: roll. Newspaper index, clippings.
Personnel
Library Manager — Patricia Zacharias, SLA
Reference Dept — Linda Culpepper, SLA
Librarians — Vivian Baulch, SLA; Jennifer Nolan, SLA; Anita Mack, SLA

264 **Michigan (Escanaba)**
THE DAILY PRESS
600-2 Ludington St, Escanaba, MI 49829
906-786-2021; FAX 906-786-9006

Newspaper Group: Thomson Newspapers
Personnel
Librarian — Lori Rose

265 **Michigan (Flint)**
FLINT JOURNAL
200 East First St, Flint, MI 48502 — See Banner
818-766-6192

Newspaper founded: 1876; library founded: 1935.
Newspaper Group: Newhouse Newspapers
Hours: Mon—Fri 7:30am—5pm; Sat 8am—4:30pm
Services to Other News Libraries: Telephone reference. Contact: David Larzelere. Will send copies of clips.
Access: Open to other media. Open to other special libraries.
News Databases: SAVE.
Resources: Photo files, negatives, reference books, maps, pamphlet files. Microforms: roll, fiche. Clippings.
Special Collections: Automotive history; Michigan history.
Personnel
Director — David Larzelere, (6192), SLA

266 **Michigan (Grand Rapids)**
THE GRAND RAPIDS PRESS
155 Michigan St NW, Grand Rapids, MI 49503 See Banner
616-222-5475; FAX 616-222-5409

Library founded: 1964.
Hours: Mon—Fri 8:30am—4:30pm
Access: By appointment only.
Services to Other News Libraries: Telephone reference. Will not send copies of clips.
Online Databases: Datatimes.
Personnel
Director Ruth Dryer

267 **Michigan (Jackson)**
JACKSON CITIZEN PATRIOT
214 S Jackson St, Jackson, MI 49201-2282 See Banner
517-787-2300; FAX 517-787-9711

Newspaper Group: Newhouse Newspapers
Hours: 8—4:30
Archival Systems: Ultra/Birmy.
Personnel
Librarian Susanne M. Weible, SLA

268 **Michigan (Kalamazoo)**
KALAMAZOO GAZETTE
401 S Burdick St, Kalamazoo, MI 49007
616-345-3511; FAX 616-388-8447

Newspaper Group: Newhouse Newspapers
Personnel
Librarian June Jones, (8587)

269 **Michigan (Lansing)**
LANSING STATE JOURNAL
120 E Lenawee St, Lansing, MI 48919
517-377-1008; FAX 517-377-1298

Newspaper founded: 1855; library founded: 1950.
Newspaper Group: Gannett Newspapers
Hours: Mon—Fri 11am—7:30pm
Access: Not open to other media.
Services to Other News Libraries: Telephone reference.
Resources: Photo files. Reference books. Maps. Pamphlet file. Microform: roll. Newspaper index. Clippings.
Personnel
Library Director Pamela Gawronski, SLA

270 **Michigan (Mount Clements)**
MACOMB DAILY
100 Macomb Daily Dr (PO Box 707), Mt Clemens, MI 48043
810-469-4510; FAX 810-469-2892

Access: Open to other news librarians. Not open to other media.
Personnel
Librarian Gina Joseph, (783-0252)

271 **Michigan (Mount Pleasant)**
MORNING SUN
215 N Main St (PO Box 447), Mount Pleasant, MI 48858
517-772-2971; FAX 517-773-0382

Personnel
Librarian Karen Crawford, (230)

272 **Michigan (Muskegon)**
MUSKEGON CHRONICLE
981 Third St, Muskegon, MI 49443
616-722-0320 ext 236; FAX 616-722-2552

Newspaper Group: Newhouse Newspapers
Online Databases: Datatimes.
Personnel
Librarian Linda Thompson, (725-6386), SLA

273 **Michigan (Port Huron)**
TIMES HERALD
PO Box 5009, Port Huron, MI 48061 See Banner
810-985-7171; FAX 810-989-6294

Newspaper founded: 1910; library founded: 1927.
Hours: Mon—Fri 7:30am—2pm
Access: Open to other media 10—30—4:30.
Resources: Photo files. Microforms: roll. Clippings.
Personnel
Director Allison Arnold, (6268)

274 **Michigan (Saginaw)**
SAGINAW NEWS
203 S Washington Ave, Saginaw, MI 48607-1283 See Banner
517-776-9672; FAX 517-752-3115

Newspaper founded: 1859; library founded: 1946.
Newspaper Group: Newhouse Newspapers
Hours: Mon—Fri 7am—5pm
Services to Other News Libraries: Telephone reference. Will not send copies of clips.
Resources: Photo files, negatives, reference books, maps, pamphlet files. Microforms: roll, fiche, jackets. Clippings.
CD ROM: Yes.
LAN: Yes.
Personnel
Director Lorri D. Lea, (Llea@cris.com), SLA
Asst Suzanne Grant, (171)

275 **Michigan (Traverse City)**
TRAVERSE CITY RECORD-EAGLE
120 W Front St, Traverse City, MI 49684 See Banner
616-946-2000; FAX 616-946-8632

Newspaper founded: 1858; library founded: 1980.
Newspaper Group: Ottaway Newspapers, Inc.
Hours: Mon—Fri 3pm—5pm; Sat 10am—5pm
Days Not Published: New Year's Day, Memorial Day, Independence Day, Labor Day, Thanksgiving, Christmas.
Services to Other News Libraries: Telephone reference. Sends copies of clips. Fee: 25c/page plus postage. Will not express mail clips.
Access: Not open to other media or other special libraries.
Resources: Photo files, negatives, reference books, maps, pamphlet files. Microforms: roll. Clippings.
Personnel
Head Librarian Briget Wertz, (305)

276 **Minnesota (Duluth)**
DULUTH NEWS—TRIBUNE
PO Box 169000, Duluth, MN 55816-9000
218-723-5309; FAX 218-720-4120

Year founded: 1869.
Newspaper Group: Knight-Ridder Newspapers Inc.
Services to Other News Libraries: Call public library.
Personnel
Librarian June M. Rudd, (5309), SLA

277 **Minnesota (Mankato - North Mankato)**
FREE PRESS
418 S Second St, Mankato, MN 56001
507-625-4451; FAX 507-388-4355; Email: freepress@ic.mankato.mn.us

Newspaper Group: Ottaway Newspapers, Inc.
Hours: Mon—Fri 9—5

FREE PRESS (cont'd)

Home Page (URL): http://www.ic.mankato.mn.us/news/freepress.html.
CD ROM: Yes.
Personnel
Librarian — Edie Schmierbach
Internet Mgr — Greg Abbott

278 **Minnesota (Minneapolis)**
STAR TRIBUNE NEWSPAPER OF THE TWIN CITIES
425 Portland Ave, Minneapolis, MN 55488
612-673-7398; FAX 612-673-4459

Services to Other News Libraries: Open to other special libraries. Closed to the public.
Access: Open to visiting reporters.
Online Databases: Datatimes; NEXIS; Dow Jones; DIALOG.
News Databases: Datatimes.
Archival Systems: AP Preserver.
Personnel
Head Librarian — Robert Jansen, SLA
Asst Librarians — Sandy Date
Roberta Hovde, SLA
Linda Scheiman

279 **Minnesota (Rochester)**
POST—BULLETIN
18 First Ave SE, Rochester, MN 55904
507-285-7600; FAX 507-285-7772

Newspaper founded: 1859; library founded: 1960.
Newspaper Group: Small Newspapers
Hours: Mon—Fri 7:30am—4pm
Electronic Clipping Files: Stauffer Gold
Services to Other News Libraries: Telephone reference. FAX copies of clips. Express mail clips.
Access: Open to other media, other special libraries.
Resources: Photo files, negatives, reference books, maps, pamphlet file. Microforms: roll. Clippings
Personnel
Librarians — Gretchen Meredith, (7787)
Ethel Adams

280 **Minnesota (St. Paul)**
MINNESOTA PUBLIC RADIO—Research
45 E Seventh St, St Paul, MN 55101
612-290-1479; FAX 612-290-1295

Personnel
Contact — Teresa M. Callies, (tcallies@mpr.org), SLA

281 **Minnesota (St. Paul)**
ST. PAUL PIONEER PRESS
345 Cedar Ave, St. Paul, MN 55101 — See Banner
612-222-5011; FAX 612-222-5010; Email: PPLIB@Winternet.Com

Newspaper founded: 1848; library founded: 1906.
Newspaper Group: Knight-Ridder Newspapers Inc.
Hours: Mon—Fri 7:30am—7pm; Sat, Sun 11am—7pm
News Databases: SAVE.
Services to Other News Libraries: Telephone reference (612-228-5557). Sends copies of clips.
Access: Open to other media, other special libraries.
Online Databases: DIALOG; Dow Jones; Datatimes; NEXIS.
Electronic Clipping Files: VU/TEXT
Resources: Photo files, reference books, maps, pamphlet files. Microforms: roll. Newspaper index, clippings.
Personnel
Library Researchers — Paulette Rich
Debra Nygren
Pat Thraen
Yee Chang
David Holt
Kim Korent
Kathy Rysgaard
Ruth Ehmcke
Lisa Carlson

282 **Mississippi (Biloxi - Gulfport)**
THE SUN HERALD
205 DeBuys Rd (PO Box 4567), Biloxi, MS 39535-4567 — See Banner
601-896-2100; FAX 601-896-2104

Newspaper founded: 1884; library founded: 1974.
Newspaper Group: Knight-Ridder Newspapers Inc.
Hours: Mon—Fri 8am—5pm
Services to Other News Libraries: Telephone reference. Sends copies of clips.
Access: Open to other media, special libraries, public.
Resources: Photo files, negatives in photo studio. Reference books, maps, pamphlet file. Microforms: roll. Clippings. SAVE.
Archival Systems: SAVE.
Fee-Based Research: Copies: $.75/page. FAX. Microform Copies: $2.50/page. Invoice. Contact: Rhonda Hamrick (896-2308).
Personnel
Librarian — Rhonda Hamrick, (2308), SLA
Asst Librarian — Vincent Cowan

283 **Mississippi (Hattiesburg)**
HATTIESBURG AMERICAN
825 N Main St (PO Box 111), Hattiesburg MS 39401 — See Banner
601-582-4321; FAX 601-583-8244

Newspaper founded: 1917; library founded: 1979.
Newspaper Group: Gannett Newspapers
Hours: Mon—Fri 8am—5pm
Services to Other News Libraries: Telephone reference. Sends copies of clips. Fee. Requirements: Must pay in advance. Will express mail clips.
Access: Open to other special libraries.
Resources: Photo files, reference books. Microforms: roll, fiche. Clippings.
Personnel
Librarian — Paul E. Robards

284 **Mississippi (Jackson)**
THE CLARION LEDGER
311 E Pearl St (PO Box 40), Jackson, MS 39205 — See Banner
601-961-7000; FAX 601-961-7116

Newspaper Group: Gannett Newspapers
Access: Open to other libraries, other media, non-public.
Services to Other News Libraries: Will FAX clips. Telephone reference.
Resources: Photo subject and biographical files/clips. Microfilm back-issue of paper (almost complete).
Personnel
Librarians — Susan Garcia, (7071)
Mary Gardner

285 **Mississippi (Pascagoula)**
THE MISSISSIPPI PRESS
405 Delmas Ave (PO Box 849), Pascagoula, MI
601-762-1111; FAX 601-934-1454

Newspaper Group: Newhouse Newspapers
Access: Open to visiting reporters.
Services to Other News Libraries: Answers questions from news libraries.
Personnel
Librarian — Beverly Tike, (934-1458)

286 **Mississippi (Tupelo)**
NORTHEAST MISSISSIPPI DAILY JOURNAL
1655 S Green (PO Box 909), Tupelo, MS 38801
601-842-2611; FAX 601-842-2233

Personnel
Librarian — Judy Cambell

287 **Missouri (Cape Girardeau)**
SOUTHEAST MISSOURIAN
301 Broadway (PO Box 699), Cape Girardeau, MO 63702-0699 — See Banner
573-335-6611; FAX 573-334-7288

Newspaper founded: 1904; library founded: 1964.
Hours: Mon—Fri 9:30am—5:30pm
Days Not Published: New Year's Day, Memorial Day, Independence Day, Thanksgiving, Christmas.
Services to Other News Libraries: Telephone reference.
Archival Systems: NewsView; Multi-Ad Search.
CD ROM: Yes.
LAN: Yes.
Fee-Based Research: Research Fee: $25. Copies: $10. FAX: $15. Credit Card. Contact: Sharon Saunders (ext 136).
Resources: Photo files, negatives, reference books, maps, pamphlet file. Microforms: roll. Newspaper index, clippings.
Access: Other media, other special libraries at discretion of publisher.
News Databases: VIEW.
Personnel
Director — Sharon K. Sanders

288 **Missouri (Columbia)**
COLUMBIA DAILY TRIBUNE
101 N Fourth St (PO Box 798), Columbia, MO 65205 — See Banner
314-874-6483; FAX 314-874-6483; Email: cdteditor@trib.net

Newspaper founded: 1901; library founded 1969.
Hours: Mon—Fri 8am—4pm
Days Not Published: New Year's Day, Memorial Day, Independence Day, Labor Day, Thanksgiving, Christmas.
Services to Other News Libraries: Telephone reference. Sends copies of clips. Fee: 25c/article, $2 service charge. Will express mail clips. Requirements: charge to requesting library.
Resources: Photo files, reference books, maps. Newspaper index, clippings.
Archival Systems: Stauffer Gold.
Fee-Based Research: Copies: $.25/page. FAX: $2.50. Prepay. Contact Nina Johnson.
Personnel
Librarian — Nina Johnson, (874-6410 ext 6332; njohns01@mail.coin.missouri.edu)

289 **Missouri (Columbia)**
COLUMBIA MISSOURIAN
315 Lee Hills Hall, Univ of Missouri (PO Box 917), Columbia, MO 65205 — See Banner
573-882-4876; FAX 573-882-5702

Newspaper/Library founded: 1908.
Hours: Mon—Fri 8am—5pm
Days Not Published: New Year's Day, Memorial Day, Independence Day, Labor Day, Thanksgiving, Christmas, Saturday.
Access: Open to reporters, librarians and the public.
Services to Other News Libraries: Telephone reference. FAX copies of clips. Fee: 25c/copy.
News Databases: NewsView.
Resources: Photo files, reference books, maps, pamphlet file. Newspaper index, clippings. In-house database.
Special Collections: Local government scrapbooks.
Personnel
Chief Librarian — Rhonda Glazer, (ELRHONDA@MISSOURI.EDU)

290 **Missouri (Columbia)**
INVESTIGATIVE REPORTERS AND EDITORS (IRE)—
Resource Center
138 Neff Annex, U Missouri School of Journalism, Columbia, MO 65211
573-882-2042; FAX 573-882-5431; Email: jourire@mizzoul.missouri.edu

Hours: Mon—Fri 9—6
4,200 members. Call IRE headquarters to contact members.

Access: Free use to members (copying and mailing or faxing charges apply). A $10 search fee for non-members. Extra fees may be applied for rush work. Help available by phone or FAX request.
Home Page (URL): http://www.reporter.org.
Online Databases: ASKsam.
Resources: 10,000 full-text newspaper and magazine articles and TV and radio scripts (many audio and video tapes too) representing virtually all investigative journalism done in the US since 1977. Fully indexed and abstracted on ASKsam with a paper and electronic index to holdings available upon request.
Special Collections: 20 years worth of the IRE Journal, the only publication dedicated solely to investigative reporting, fully indexed. About 4 years worth of Uplink, a newspaper for journalists working on Computer-Assisted Reporting, also indexed; 20 years worth of tapes, tip-sheets and other material from IRE annual conferences. Records and legal papers on the founding of IRE and the Arizona Project.
Personnel
Executive Director — Rosemary Armao
IRE Operations Dir — Bruce Moores

291 **Missouri (Hannibal)**
HANNIBAL COURIER-POST
200 N 3rd (PO Box A), Hannibal, MO 63401
314-221-2800; FAX 573-221-1568

Newspaper Group: Morris Enterprises
News Databases: Stauffer Gold.
Personnel
Librarian — Beverly Darr

292 **Missouri (Joplin)**
JOPLIN GLOBE
117 E Fourth St, Joplin, MO 64801 — See Banner
417-623-3480

Newspaper Group: Ottaway Newspapers, Inc.
Personnel
Librarian — Bill Caldwell

293 **Missouri (Kansas City)**
KANSAS CITY STAR
1729 Grand Ave, Kansas City, MO 64108 — See Banner
816-234-4141; FAX 816-234-4925

Newspaper founded: 1880.
Newspaper Group: Capital Cities Communications Inc.
Hours: Mon—Fri 7am—12m; Sat 9am—11pm; Sun 4:30pm—12m
News Databases: Datatimes.

KANSAS CITY STAR (cont'd)

Online Databases: DIALOG; LEXIS/NEXIS; Datatimes; CompuServe; Dow Jones; Burrelle's.
Services to Other News Libraries: Telephone reference. Sends copies of clips. Express mails clips. Photo reprints. Contact Aurora Davis.
Resources: Photo files, reference books, maps, pamphlet file. Microforms: roll, fiche, jackets. Clippings.
Access: Open to visiting reporters with appointment.
Personnel

Director	Felicia Moore, (4722), SLA
Night Supv	Derek Donovan, (4429)

294 **Missouri (St. Louis)**
ST. LOUIS POST—DISPATCH
900 N Tucker Blvd, St. Louis, MO 63101 See Banner
314-340-8000/ Reference 314-340-8270; FAX 314-340-3050

Newspaper founded: 1878; library founded: 1890.
Newspaper Group: Pulitzer Publishing Co.
Hours: Mon—Fri 9:30am—12m; Sat 9am—9pm
Access: Other media and Special Libraries by appointment (fee).
News Databases: SAVE.
CD ROM: NewsBank.
Archival Systems: SAVE.
Services to Other News Libraries: Mail requests only. Sends copies of clips. Fee: $2.00. No mass copying or research projects. Contact: Gerald Brown (7148). Will express mail clips. FAX charge—$5/ order with receivers express number.
Fee-Based Research: Research fee: $25. Copies: $2. FAX: $5 plus $2/page after 2 pages. Microform Copies: $5. Prepay. Contact: Gerald Brown (340-8274).
Online Databases: Datatimes (1992—date); DIALOG 1988—date; Mead Data Central 1989—date; NewsBank 1989—date.
Resources: Photo files, reference books, maps, pamphlet file. Microforms: roll, fiche, jackets. Newspaper index, clippings.
Special Collections: Post-Dispatch Authors' Collection.
Personnel

Director	Gerald D. Brown, (8274; gbrown@pd.stlnet.com), SLA

295 **Missouri (Sedalia)**
THE SEDALIA DEMOCRAT
7th St and Massachusetts Ave, Sedalia, MO 65301
816-826-1000; FAX 816-826-0400

Newspaper Group: Dear Newspapers
Access: Not open to other media.
News Databases: Sonar Professional.
Personnel

Librarian	Milene Mittelhauser, (33)

296 **Missouri (Springfield)**
THE NEWS—LEADER
651 Boonville, Springfield, MO 65801
417-836-1215; FAX 417-837-1138

Newspaper Group: Gannett Newspapers
Access: Open to other media by appointment.
Personnel

Librarian	Maudie Lawson, (MLawson@Springfi1.Gannett.Com), SLA

297 **Missouri (Springfield)**
SPRINGFIELD NEWS—LEADER—
News Information Center
651 Boonville, Springfield, MO 65801
417-836-1215; FAX 417-837-1381

Personnel

Librarian	Maudie A. Lawson, (mlawson@ozarks.sgcl.lib.mo.us)

298 **Montana (Missoula)**
MISSOULIAN—
Newsroom Library
500 S Higgins Ave, Missoula, MT 59801
406-523-5245

Hours: Mon—Fri 9—5
Access: Open to other media by appointment.
News Databases: Stauffer Gold.
Personnel

Librarian	Kathleen R. Kimble

299 **Nebraska (Lincoln)**
LINCOLN JOURNAL STAR
926 P St (PO Box 81709), Lincoln, NE 68508 See Banner
402-473-7295; FAX 402-473-7291; Email: library@nebweb.com

Newspaper founded: Star 1902; Journal 1881; library founded: 1952.
Newspaper Group: Lee Newspapers
Hours: Mon—Fri 9am—9pm
Home Page (URL): http://www.nebweb.com.
Access: Other media, other Special Library access. Limited public access.
Services to Other News Libraries: Telephone reference. Sends copies of clips, express mails clips. Fee: $40/hr research charge; $1 per 11X18 page photo copy. Payment in advance. Contact any staff member.
Resources: Photo files, reference books, maps, pamphlet file. Microforms: roll, fiche. Clippings.
Fee-Based Research: Research fee: $40/hour (no charge to other newspaper libaries). Copies: $1/page. FAX: $10/up to 5 pages plus $1/each additional. Microform Copies: $1/page. Prepay or invoice. Contact: Patricia Sloan (473-7298).
Special Collections: Charles Starkweather, clips on microfilm for sale.
Personnel

Library Manager	Patricia Sloan, (7298), SLA
Photo Libn	Kris Mitchell, (7297)
Library Clerk	Susan Steider

300 **Nebraska (Omaha)**
OMAHA WORLD—HERALD
World-Herald Square, Omaha, NE 68102 See Banner
402-444-1000/ FAX 402-444-1560; Email: OWHLIB@Oasis.Novia.Net

Newspaper founded: 1889.
Hours: Mon—Fri 8am—7pm; Sat 8am—5pm
Access: Open to other media.
Fee-Based Research: Research fee: $40. Copies/ Microform Copies: $7. FAX. Invoice or credit card. Contact Ann Walding-Phillips.
News Databases: Datatimes.
Resources: Photo files, reference books, pamphlet file. Microforms: roll, fiche.
Online Databases: LEXIS/NEXIS; Dow Jones; Datatimes.
Personnel

Director	Jeanne Hauser, (2560)
Library Specialists	Steve Allard
	Michelle Gullett

301 **Nevada (Las Vegas)**
LAS VEGAS SUN / LAS VEGAS REVIEW—JOURNAL
800 S Valley View, Las Vegas, NV 89107
702-385-3111; FAX 702-383-7264

Newspaper Group: Donrey Media Group
Online Databases: Datatimes.
Personnel
Librarian — Padmini Pai, (0269), SLA

302 **Nevada (Reno)**
RENO GAZETTE—JOURNAL
955 Kuenzli (Box 22000), Reno, NV 89520-2000 — See Banner
702-788-6359

Newspaper founded: 1870; library founded: 1959.
Newspaper Group: Gannett Newspapers
Access: Not open to other media.
Resources: Photo files, negatives. Reference books, maps, pamphlet file. Microforms: roll. Clippings.
Personnel
Librarian — Rosita Mateo
Photo Librarian — Merry Anne Davis

303 **New Hampshire (Concord)**
CONCORD MONITOR
PO Box 1177, 1 Monitor Dr, Concord, NH 03302-1177
603-224-5301; FAX 603-224-8120

Newspaper Group: Newspapers of New England, Inc.
Access: Open to visiting reporters.
Services to Other News Libraries: Answers questions from news libraries.
Personnel
Librarian — Judy Harris, (303)

304 **New Hampshire (Manchester)**
UNION LEADER AND NEW HAMPSHIRE SUNDAY NEWS
100 William Loeb Dr, Manchester, NH 03109 — See Banner
603-668-4321; FAX 603-668-0382

Newspaper founded: 1863.
Hours: Mon—Fri 9am—5pm
Services to Other News Libraries: Telephone reference. Sends copies of clips (Minimum charge $25.00). Contact Claudette Gammon.
Resources: Photo files, reference books, maps. Microforms: roll, fiche, jackets. Newspaper index, clippings, computer printouts.
Personnel
Director — Claudette A. Gammon, (306)
Librarian — Lisa Burch, (307)

305 **New Hampshire (Portsmouth)**
PORTSMOUTH HERALD
111 Maplewood Ave, Portsmouth, NH 03801
603-436-1800; FAX 603-427-0550; Email: PHerald@aol.com

Newspaper Group: Thomson Newspapers
Home Page (URL): http://www.nh-meseacoasp.com.
News Databases: Folio Views; NewsView.
Personnel
Librarian — Robin Silver, (137)

306 **New Jersey (Asbury Park)**
ASBURY PARK PRESS
3601 Hwy 66 (Box 1550), Neptune, NJ 07754-1551
908-922-6000; FAX 908-922-4818

News Databases: SII.
Personnel
Librarian — Mollie F. Graham, SLA

307 **New Jersey (Bridgeton)**
THE NEWS
100 E Commerce St (Box 596), Bridgeton, NJ 08302
609-451-1000; FAX 609-451-7214

Hours: 8—5

308 **New Jersey (Bridgewater)**
COURIER—NEWS
1201 Route 22, Bridgewater, NJ 08807 — See Banner
908-722-8800; FAX 908-707-3252; Email: Courier@C-N.Com

Newspaper founded: 1884; library founded 1930.
Newspaper Group: Gannett Newspapers
Hours: Mon—Fri 11am-7pm
Days Not Published: New Year's Day, Memorial Day, Independence Day, Labor Day, Christmas.
Services to Other News Libraries: Telephone reference. Sends copies of clips ($1 per copy). Requirements: No extensive research.
Resources: Photo files, reference books, maps. Microforms: roll. Clippings.
Access: Open to other media and other special libraries by appointment.
Personnel
Chief Librarian — Leslie Bachhuber, (707-3172)

309 **New Jersey (East Brunswick)**
THE HOME NEWS & TRIBUNE
35 Kennedy Blvd (PO Box 1049), East Brunswick, NJ 08816-1250 — See Banner
908-246-5500; FAX 908-937-6046

Year founded: Sunday—1786; Daily—1879; library founded: 1950.
Hours: Mon—Fri 9am—4pm
Days Not Published: Christmas.
Access: Not open to the public.
Services to Other News Libraries: Telephone reference. Contact Betty Selingo (ext 7351)
Resources: Photo files. Reference books. Maps. Pamphlet file. Microfilm. Clippings. In-house Electronic Library System.
Archival Systems: LASR.
News Databases: SII.
Personnel
Director — Betty Selingo, (7351)
Librarian — Winifred Zagariello, (7351)

310 **New Jersey (Hackensack)**
THE RECORD
150 River St, Hackensack, NJ 07602 — See Banner
Reference 201-646-4090; FAX 201-646-4737; Email: newsroom@bergen-record.com

Newspaper founded: 1895; library founded: 1930.
Hours: Mon—Thurs 6am—2am; Fri 6am—8pm; Sun 2pm—12m
Access: Other media. Other special libraries. Requirements: prior appointment. Closed to the public.
Services to Other News Libraries: Telephone reference. Sends copies of clips. Contact ext 4090.
Online Databases: DIALOG; Dow Jones; NEXIS; Datatimes.
News Databases: Datatimes; DIALOG.
Fee-Based Research: Research Fee: $80. Copies: $1/article. FAX. Microform Copies: $10/page. Prepay or invoice. Contact: Margaret Hutchinson (646-4089).
Resources: Photo files, negatives, reference books, maps, pamphlet file. Microforms: roll, fiche, jackets. Clippings.
Personnel
Mgr/Edit Info Svce — Paul Schulman, SLA
Librarians — Dorothy Fersch
Donna Blair

THE RECORD (cont'd)

Margaret Hutchinson
David Mammone
Deborah Keller
Adrian Shoobs
Paul T. Wilder

311 **New Jersey (Jersey City)**
JERSEY JOURNAL
30 Journal Square, Jersey City, NJ 07306
201-653-1000; FAX 201-653-1414

Newspaper Group: Newhouse Newspapers
Access: Not open to other media.
Services to Other News Libraries: None.
Personnel
Librarian — Olga Torres

312 **New Jersey (Morristown—Parsippany)**
DAILY RECORD
629 Parsippany Rd, Parsippany, NJ 07054
201-428-6200 ext 5550; FAX 201-428-6666; Email: 75141.3363@Compuserve. Com

Newspaper founded: 1900, library founded: 1965.
Hours: Mon—Fri 9am—5pm
Services to Other News Libraries: Telephone reference.
Resources: Photo files and negatives. Reference books, maps, pamphlet files. Microforms: roll, fiche. Newspaper index. Clippings.
Personnel
Librarian — Mary Leahy, (6625)
Library Asst — Louise Carney

313 **New Jersey (Newark)**
STAR—LEDGER
1 Star-Ledger Plaza, Newark, NJ 07101
201-877-1710

Newspaper Group: Newhouse Newspapers
Hours: Mon—Fri 10am—9pm
Access: Open to other media by appointment.
Home Page (URL): http://www.nj.com.
Online Databases: Dow Jones; Datatimes; DBT; LEXIS/NEXIS; SAVE.
News Databases: Thunderstore.
Services to Other News Libraries: Telephone reference. Sends copies of clips. Contact: Betty Davis or Selma Tull (877-4284).
Resources: Photo files. Reference books. Microform: Roll. Clippings.
Archival Systems: Fetch.
CD ROM: Yes.
LAN: Yes.
Personnel
Mgr Information Svcs — M.J. Crowley, (moose@starledger.com)
Asst Editor — Christine Baird, (1785)

314 **New Jersey (Secaucus)**
PW COMMUNICATIONS
400 Plaza Dr, Secaucus, NJ 07094

Personnel
Librarian — Elizabeth Skerritt, SLA

315 **New Jersey (Trenton)**
THE TIMES
500 Perry St, Trenton, NJ 08605
609-396-3232; FAX 609-394-2819

Newspaper founded: 1783; library founded: 1950.
Newspaper Group: Newhouse Newspapers
Hours: Mon—Fri 9am—9pm
Services to Other News Libraries: Telephone reference. Sends copies of clips.
Access: Open to visiting reporters by appointment.
Resources: Photo files, negatives, reference books, maps, pamphlet file. Microforms: roll, fiche. Clippings.
Personnel
Head Librarian — Diana Groden, (989-5719)
Senior Library Asst — Lisa Belknap

316 **New Jersey (Trenton)**
TRENTONIAN
600 Perry St, Trenton, NJ 08602
609-989-7800; FAX 609-393-6072

Newspaper Group: Journal Register
Access: Not open to public, librarians, reporters
Personnel
Librarian — Patricia Shanahan

317 **New Jersey (Willingboro)**
BURLINGTON COUNTY TIMES
2241 Route 130 N, Willingboro, NJ 08046 See Banner
609-871-8000; FAX 609-871-0490

Newspaper founded: 1958; library founded: 1965.
Newspaper Group: Calkins Newspapers
Hours: Mon—Fri 8am—3:30pm
Days Not Published: New Year's Day, Memorial Day, Independence Day, Labor Day, Christmas, Saturday.
Services to Other News Libraries: Telephone reference. Sends copies of clips.
Access: Not open to other media or other special libraries. Will answer questions over the phone that require little research.
Resources: Photo files, reference books, maps, pamphlet file. Microforms: roll. Clippings.
Special Collections: Microfilm of New Jersey Mirror: May 20,1958—Dec. 1966. Times Advertiser, Pemberton, NJ: Feb. 1935—Feb. 1978.
Personnel
Librarian — Annette Parker, (8082)

318 **New Jersey (Woodbridge - Perth Amboy)**
WOODBRIDGE NEWS TRIBUNE
1 Hoover Way, Woodbridge, NJ 07095
908-442-0400; FAX 908-324-7111

Personnel
Librarian — Sharon Williams

319 **New Jersey (Woodbury)**
GLOUCESTER COUNTY TIMES
309 S Broad St, Woodbury, NJ 08096 See Banner
609-845-3300; FAX 609-845-5480

Newspaper founded: 1897; library founded: 1969.
Newspaper Group: Media News Group
Hours: Mon—Fri 8am—5pm
Services to Other News Libraries: Telephone reference. Sends copies of clips.
Resources: Photo files, negatives, reference books, maps, pamphlet files. Clippings.
Personnel
Director — Sally Ethier, (246)

320 **New Mexico (Albuquerque)**
ALBUQUERQUE JOURNAL/TRIBUNE
7777 Jefferson NE, Albuquerque, NM 87109
505-823-3490; FAX 505-823-3499

Newspaper founded: 1880; Library founded: 1960.
Access: Other special libraries, public.
Services to Other News Libraries: Telephone reference. Will FAX clips. Research. Fees charged: research—$35/hr; photocopies—$1/page.
Personnel
Director — Judy Pence, (3493)

321 **New Mexico (Carlsbad)**
CARLSBAD CURRENT—ARGUS
620 S Main St, Carlsbad, NM 88220
1-800-650-4733; FAX 505-885-1066

Newspaper Group: World Newspapers
Hours: Mon—Fri 8am—5:30pm; Sat 8am—12n
Personnel
Librarian — Theresa Lambright

322 **New Mexico (Hobbs)**
HOBBS DAILY NEWS-SUN
201 N Thorp (PO Box 860), Hobbs, NM 88240
505-393-2123; FAX 505-393-5724

News Databases: Sonar Professional.
Personnel
Librarian — Bonnie Hicks, (245)

323 **New Mexico (Las Cruces)**
LAS CRUCES SUN—NEWS
256 W Las Cruces Ave, Las Cruces, NM 88005
505-523-4581; FAX 505-527-1249

Newspaper Group: Worrell Newspapers, Inc.
Access: Open to other news media.
Personnel
Librarian — DeeDee Arzapalo, (68)

324 **New Mexico (Los Alamos)**
LOS ALAMOS NATIONAL LABORATORY
MS P363, Los Alamos, NM 87545
505-667-5809; FAX 505-665-2948

Personnel
Librarian — Donna R. Berg, (DONNA.BERG@lanl.gov)

325 **New York (Albany)**
THE CAPITAL
Box 15000, Albany, NY 12212
518-454-5734

Personnel
Librarian — Richard Maturro, SLA

326 **New York (Albany)**
TIMES—UNION / SUNDAY TIMES UNION
645 Albany-Shaker Rd (Box 15-6000), Albany, NY 12212
518-454-5454; FAX 518-454-5628

Newspaper Group: Hearst Newspapers
Hours: Mon—Fri 6am—8pm
Access: Other media, special libraries by appointment. Not open to the public.
Email: TULibrary@aol.com.
Online Databases: SAVE; DIALOG; NEXIS; Datatimes.
News Databases: LASR.
Personnel
Librarians — Richard Matturro, (5374), SLA; Kathy Fry; Margaret Williams

327 **New York (Binghamton)**
PRESS & SUN—BULLETIN
Vestal Parkway E, Binghamton, NY 13902
607-798-1234

Newspaper Group: Gannett Newspapers
Hours: 8—6
Access: Other media—limited telephone reference. Other special libraries. Closed to the public.
Personnel
Library Coordinator — Nancy L. George, (1159)

328 **New York (Brooklyn)**
BROOKLYN PUBLIC LIBRARY—
Business Library
280 Cadman Plaza W, Brooklyn, NY 11201
718-722-3329; FAX 718-722-3337; Email: jcbusz3@transit.nyser.net

Personnel
Librarian — Rita J. Ormsby

329 **New York (Brooklyn)**
BROOKLYN PUBLIC LIBRARY—
Periodicals Room
Grand Army Plaza, Brooklyn, NY 11238
718-780-7700; FAX 718-398-3947

Special Collections: Complete file of over 80 Brooklyn daily and weekly newspapers dating back to the early 1800's to present; Papers of Raymond V. Ingersoll.
Personnel
Local History Libn — Judith Walsh, (7794)

330 **New York (Brooklyn)**
BROOKLYN PUBLIC LIBRARY—
Social Science Division
Grand Army Plaza, Brooklyn, NY 11238
718-780-7746; FAX 718-783-1770

Hours: Mon, Fri, Sat 10—6; Tues—Thur 9—8; Sun 1pm—5pm
Special Collections: Complete file of the Brooklyn Eagle from 1841—1955.
Personnel
Division Chief — Sharon Vairamides, (7747)
Documents Libn — Loren Williams
Periodicals — Lesley Seigel

331 **New York (Buffalo)**
BUFFALO NEWS
1 News Plaza, Buffalo, NY 14240
716-849-4401; FAX 716-856-5150

Founded: 1880.
Hours: 8—5
Access: Other media—limited telephone reference. Other special libraries. Not open to the public.
Online Databases: DIALOG; Datatimes; NEXIS.
News Databases: SAVE.
Personnel
Library Director — Elliot Shapiro, (4423)

332 **New York (Elmira)**
STAR—GAZETTE
201 Baldwin St (PO Box 285), Elmira, NY 14902
607-734-5151; FAX 607-733-4408; Email: SGMail@aol.com

Newspaper Group: Gannett Newspapers
Personnel
Librarian — Margaret Ridosh, (272)

333 **New York (Geneva)**
FINGER LAKES TIMES—
Library
218 Genesse St, Geneva, NY 14456
315-789-7706; FAX 315-789-4077

Personnel
Librarian — Catherine A. Barnard, SLA

334 **New York (Hauppauge)**
REUTERS
88 Parkway Dr S, Hauppauge, NY 11788
516-233-6942

Personnel
Librarian — Nancy C. Moore, SLA

335 **New York (Ithaca)**
THE ITHACA JOURNAL
123 W State St, Ithaca, NY 14850
607-274-9270; FAX 607-272-4248; Email: Journal@aol.com

Newspaper Group: Gannett Newspapers
Hours: 9—5
Personnel
Librarian — Romy Mancini, (9243)

336 **New York (Jamestown)**
POST—JOURNAL
PO Box 190, Jamestown, NY 14702
716-487-1111; FAX 716-664-3119

Newspaper Group: Ogden Newspapers
Personnel
Librarian — Sandra Terry

337 **New York (Long Island)**
NEWSDAY, INC.
235 Pinelawn Rd, Melville, NY 11747 — See Banner
516-843-2335; FAX 516-843-2342; Email: newslibrary@earthlink.com

Newspaper founded: 1940; library founded: 1940.
Newspaper Group: Times Mirror Co.
Hours: Open 24 hours a day
Days Not Published: New Year's Day, Thanksgiving, Christmas.
Access: Other media and other Special Libraries by appointment.
Services to Other News Libraries: Telephone reference. Sends copies of clips. Express mails clips.
Online Databases: DIALOG; Washington Alert; Dow Jones; WDIA; PACER; Spectrum; WESTLAW; LEXIS/NEXIS; NewsNet; Blood Stock; CDB Infotek; AOL; CompuServe; Federal Election Commission (FEC); Haver Analytics; New York State Department of Motor Vehicles (NYS DMV), Livedgar; Datatimes.
News Databases: BASIS.
Archival Systems: MediaSphere; Basis.
Fee-Based Research: Research Fee: $100; Copies: $10/article. FAX: $1/page. Microform copies. Prepay. Contact: 1-800-2Findout.
Resources: Photo files, negatives, reference books, maps, pamphlet file. Microforms: roll, fiche, jackets. Clippings.
Special Collections: Long Island History Collection.
Personnel
Mgr/Edit Technology — Mary Ann Skinner, SLA
Library Director — Theresa Kiely, (2338; kiely@earthlink.com)
Secy to Director — Pearl Granat, (2337), SLA
Librarians — Dorothy Guadagno
Iris Quigley
Eileen Effrat
Loretta Wallace
Donna Mendell
Nancy Altman
Angela Johnson
Chief Photo Libn — Kathy Sweeney, (2340)

338 **New York (Medina)**
THE JOURNAL—REGISTER
409-13 Main St, Medina, NY 14103
716-798-1400; FAX 716-798-0290

Newspaper Group: Park Communications, Inc.
Days Not Published: Saturday and Sunday
Personnel
Librarian — Lynne Harling

339 **New York (Middletown)**
MIDDLETOWN TIMES HERALD—RECORD/SUNDAY RECORD
40 Mulberry St, Middletown, NY 10940 — See Banner
914-341-1100; FAX 914-343-1699

Newspaper founded: 1960.
Newspaper Group: Ottaway Newspapers, Inc.
Hours: Mon—Thur 8—5; Fri 8:30—7:30
Days Not Published: New Year's Day, Christmas.
Access: Other media and other special libraries with permission from general manager or managing editor.
Services to Other News Libraries: Telephone reference. Sends copies of clips. Express mails clips. Requirements: must be other newspaper or special library.
Resources: Photo files, negatives, reference books, maps, pamphlet file. Clippings.
Online Databases: SAVE.
News Databases: SAVE.
Special Collections: Woodstock Festival coverage.
Personnel
Director — Patricia Racine, (1490), SLA

340 **New York (Middletown)**
TIMES HERALD—RECORD—Information Retrieval Department
40 Mulberry St, Middletown, NY 10940
914-343-2181

Personnel
Librarian — Patricia Racine, SLA

341 **New York (New York)**
ABC NEWS RESEARCH CENTER
47 W 66 St, 2nd Fl, New York, NY 10023-6290
212-456-3796; FAX 212-456-2450; Email: ncc@ccabc.com

Hours: Mon—Fri 9am—12m; Sat, Sun 10—6.
Home Page (URL): http://www.abacradio.ccabc.com/main.htm.
CD ROM: UMI Proquest; Newsbank; CD Newsbank.
LAN: Novell.
Resources: Reference books, maps, periodicals. Microform: Roll, Fiche. Newspaper clippings.
Services to Other News Libraries: Telephone reference. Telefacsimile clips. Fee: none. Limited to periodicals not online.
Online Databases: DIALOG; Dow Jones; NewsNet; Datatimes; LEXIS/NEXIS; Info Globe; Reuters; Washington Alert; LEGI-SLATE; AOL; Baseline; Burrelle's; CDB Infotek; CompuServe; DataStar; Periscope; FT Profile; Wilsonline; Broadcast News.
Special Collections: News stories from both radio and TV networks.
Personnel
Director — Madeline Cohen, (4769), SLA
Supv/Online Svcs — Carlton B. Hayden, (haydenc@ccabc.com), SLA
Information Specs — Suzanne Bernard, (bernars@ccabc.com), SLA
Tony Skaggs, SLA
Candace Stuart, (stuartc@ccabc.com), SLA
Nancy Quade
Judith Ganeles, SLA
Gerard Middleton
Ruth Tenenbaum, (tenenbr@ccabc.com)
Shulamis Lichstein

342 **New York (New York)**
AMERICAN BANKER / BOND BUYER
1 State Street Plaza, 31st Floor, New York, NY 10004
212-803-8371; FAX 212-843-9613

Hours: 9:30—5:30
CD ROM: ABI Inform; Newspapers Ondisc; NY Times; Wall Street Journal.
Access: Open to visiting reporters.
News Databases: SAVE.
CD ROM: Yes.
LAN: Yes.

AMERICAN BANKER / BOND BUYER (cont'd)

Online Databases: DIALOG; Datatimes; NEXIS.
Personnel

Chief Librarian	Mary L. Callinan, (Callinan@cclink.TEN.com), SLA
Asst Librarian	Viki Goldman, SLA

343 **New York (New York)**
AMERICAN CIVIL LIBERTIES UNION LIBRARY (ACLU)—
Press Office
132 W 43rd St, New York, NY 10036
212-944-9800; FAX 212-869-9065; Email: info@aclu.org

Hours: Mon—Fri 9—5
Home Page (URL): http://www.aclu.org.
Access: For staff, public by appointment.
Special Collections: American Civil Liberties archives; General materials on civil liberties.

344 **New York (New York)**
ASSOCIATED PRESS—
News Research Center
50 Rockefeller Plaza, New York, NY 10020 See Banner
212-621-1580; FAX 212-621-6956

Founded: 1848; library founded: circa 1898.
Hours: Mon—Fri 8am—8pm
Access: Not open to the general public or reporters.
Online Databases: DIALOG; NewsNet; LEXIS/NEXIS; Datatimes; Burrelle's; Dow Jones.
Services to Other News Libraries: Copies of clips sent to AP members' newsrooms and via FAX. No research provided.
Resources: Reference books, maps. Microforms: roll, fiche. Newspaper index. Clippings.
Personnel

Director	Donald Pine
Head Researcher	Randy R. Herschaft, (5411), SLA
Librarians	Susan James, (5412)
	Arnold Wilkinson, (5413)
	Jeffrey Tishman, (5414)
	Steve Carlson, (5415), SLA

Photo Library: Mary Ann Cataldo (212-621-1916; 212-621-7546) SLA

345 **New York (New York)**
ASSOCIATED PRESS—
Photo Archive
50 Rockefeller Pl, New York, NY 10020
212-621-1909; FAX 212-621-7546

Special Collections: Photograph Collection.
Personnel

Director	Chuck Zoeller, (1915)
Editorial Dir	Grant Lamos, (1902; glamos@ap.org)
Asst to President	Hal Buell, (1909; hbuell@ap.org)

346 **New York (New York)**
BBC RADIO (LONDON)—
New York Office
United Nations, Room 309, New York, NY 10017
212-688-6266

347 **New York (New York)**
BRITISH INFORMATION SERVICES—
Library
845 Third Ave, New York, NY 10022
212-745-0200; FAX 212-758-5395; Email: Bis@panix.com

Hours: Mon—Fri 9:15—5:30
Services to Other News Libraries: Telephone reference. Contact: staff.
Access: Open to other media, other special libraries. Appointment necessary.
Home Page (URL): http://britain.nyc.ny.us.
Resources: Reference books, British Government Documents, maps. Microform: rolls. Clippings.
CD ROM: Yes.
LAN: Yes.
Personnel

Director	Margaret Gale, SLA
Info Officer	Janet Bacon
Asst Info Officers	Peter McNally
	Paul Cornish

348 **New York (New York)**
BUSINESS WEEK
1221 Ave of the Americas, 39th Fl, New York, NY 10020
212-512-4803; FAX 212-512-4286

Hours: Mon—Fri 9—7
Personnel

Librarian	Jamie B. Russell, SLA

349 **New York (New York)**
CBS NEWS—
Reference Library
524 W 57th St, New York, NY 10019
212-975-2917; FAX 212-975-7766

Hours: Mon—Fri 9:30am—7pm
Home Page (URL): http://www.cbs.com.
CD ROM: Pioneer, Meridian. Databases: UMI ProQuest; Periodical Abstracts; Newspaper Abstracts; Wilson Business Abstracts; Bibliography Index; Reader's Guide Abstracts; UMI NY Times; Washington Post; others.
Online Databases: NEXIS; DIALOG; Dow Jones; Datatimes; EPIC.
News Databases: DataTrek Professional Series.
Access: Other media, other special libraries, authors, doctoral candidates by appointment only.
Services to Other News Libraries: ILL; transcripts of CBS News broadcasts with permission of CBS News Media Relations office.
Resources: Reference and circulating books, magazines, periodical and newspaper indexes, maps, microforms, annual reports, clippings files.
Special Collections: Transcripts of CBS News Broadcasts; CBS News up to the minute online (CBSUTTM); news, sports and information on how to order tapes and transcripts.
Personnel

Director	Laura B. Kapnick, (Laurak@cbsnews.com; lauracbs@class.org), SLA
Secy to Director	Nori Choy, (2919)
Managing Librarians	Cryder Bankes, (7727)
	Carole Parnes, (2877)
	Sara Wolozin, (2877)
Librarians	Sam Register, (2877)
	Jean Stevenson, (2877)

350 **New York (New York)**
CNN—
New York Bureau Library
5 Penn Plaza, New York, NY 10001
212-714-7831; FAX 212-714-3319

Hours: Mon—Fri 5am—8pm; Sat, Sun 10am—8pm
Personnel

Contact	Grace Lile, (grace.lile@turner.com), SLA

351 **New York (New York)**
COLUMBIA UNIVERSITY—
Journalism Library
Journalism 316 SIA Bldg, 420 W 118 St, New York, NY 10027
212-854-3916

Personnel
Librarian — Elizabeth Brennan, (eb126@columbia.edu), SLA

352 **New York (New York)**
CONDE NAST PUBLICATIONS INC.—
Library
350 Madison Ave, New York, NY 10017
212-880-8343; FAX 212-880-6763

Personnel
Librarian — Cynthia A. Cathcart, (CCATH@CONDENAST.COM)

353 **New York (New York)**
COUNCIL ON FOREIGN RELATIONS—
Library
58 E 68th St, New York, NY 10021
212-734-0400

Personnel
Librarian — Marcia L. Sprules, (MSprules@email.cfr.org), SLA

354 **New York (New York)**
DAILY CHALLENGE
1360 Fulton St, Brooklyn, NY 11216
718-643-1162

Days Not Published: Sunday
Special Collections: African-American—Newspapers.

355 **New York (New York)**
DAILY EXPRESS / SUNDAY EXPRESS (LONDON)—
New York Office
220 E 42 St, Room 3108, New York, NY 10017
212-682-4111

Personnel
Librarian — Philip Finn

356 **New York (New York)**
DAILY MAIL (LONDON)—
New York Office
500 Fifth Ave, Room 312, New York, NY 10110
212-869-2570; FAX 212-302-3902

Personnel
Librarian — George Gordon

357 **New York (New York)**
ECONOMIST (LONDON)—
New York Bureau
111 W 57th St, New York, NY 10019
212-541-5730; FAX 212-541-9378

Hours: Mon—Fri 9am—5pm
Access: Not open to the public. Open to other special libraries.
Resources: Reference books. Clippings.
Services to Other News Libraries: Telephone reference.
Online Databases: DIALOG; Dow Jones; NEXIS.
Electronic Clipping Files: DIALOG NEXIS

358 **New York (New York)**
FORBES INC.
60 Fifth Ave, New York, NY 10011
212-620-2200; FAX 212-620-1811

Year founded: 1917; library founded: 1963.
Hours: Mon—Fri 9—5
CD ROM: Yes.
LAN: Yes.
WAN: Yes.
Online Databases: DIALOG; Dow Jones; RLIN; Datatimes; LEXIS/NEXIS; Info Globe; Baseline; CDA Spectrum; CompuServe; DataStar; AOL; WESTLAW.
Services to Other News Libraries: Telephone reference: contact Information Specialist.
Resources: Reference books, pamphlets. Microforms: roll, fiche. Newspaper index, clippings, extensive journal holdings.

Personnel
Director — Anne P. Mintz, (amintz@forbes.com), SLA
Sr Info Specialist — Naomi S. Prall, SLA
Info Specialists — Cynthia Crystal, SLA; Clarita Jones, SLA; Velma Van Voris, SLA; Linda Stinson, SLA

359 **New York (New York)**
FORD FOUNDATION—
Library
320 E 43rd St, New York, NY 10017
212-573-5157; FAX 212-986-9037

Personnel
Librarian — Victoria A. Dawson, (v.dawson@fordfound.org), SLA

360 **New York (New York)**
FOREIGN PRESS CENTER
110 E 59th St, New York, NY 10022
212-826-4722; FAX 212-826-4657

361 **New York (New York)**
FREEDOM FORUM—
Media Studies Center
2950 Broadway, New York, NY 10027
212-678-6600; FAX 212-678-6663

362 **New York (New York)**
INTERNATIONAL HERALD TRIBUNE—
New York Contact
212-752-3890

Personnel
Contact — Lawrence Malkin

363 **New York (New York)**
ITAR—TASS NEWS AGENCY—
New York Bureau
50 Rockefeller Plaza #501, New York, NY 10020
212-245-4250; FAX 212-245-4258

Year founded: 1894.
Hours: Mon—Fri 9am—5pm
News Databases: NEXIS.
Electronic Clipping Files: Info Globe
Online Databases: NEXIS.

364 **New York (New York)**
JOHN FAIRFAX U.S. LIMITED
1500 Broadway, Room 1002, New York, NY 10036
212-398-9494; FAX 212-819-1745

(Sydney Morning Herald, Financial Review, Australian Business Review, Electronics Australia, Electronics Australia, 2GB Radio Sydney)

Personnel
Contact: Australian Financial Review — Brian Hale
Contact: Sydney Morning Herald — Brett Thomas
Contact: Sun—Herald/The Age — Allan Atwood

365 **New York (New York)**
JOURNAL OF COMMERCE
2 World Trade Center, 27th Fl, New York, NY 10048-0298 — See Banner
212-837-7116; FAX 212-837-7079

Newspaper founded: 1827; library founded: 1977.
Newspaper Group: Economist Group
Hours: Mon—Fri 9am—5pm
Days Not Published: New Year's Day, Washington's Birthday, Memorial Day, Independence Day, Labor Day, Columbus Day, Veteran's Day, Thanksgiving, Christmas, Saturday, Sunday.
Home Page (URL): http://www.usess.interport.net/chrystia.
Archival Systems: SAVE.
CD ROM: Yes.
News Databases: SAVE; DIALOG.
Services to Other News Libraries: Limited telephone reference (contact: Librarian). Limited document delivery.
Access: Open to news organizations and other special libraries.
Resources: Reference books, pamphlet file. Clippings, DIALOG, VU/TEXT, 90 periodical titles.
Personnel
Manager — Christine Karpevych, (chrystia@interport.net), SLA

366 **New York (New York)**
LOUIS HARRIS AND ASSOCIATES, INC.—
Information Services
111 Fifth Ave, 8th Fl, New York, NY 10003
212-539-9600; FAX 212-539-9669

Hours: Mon—Fri 9:30—5:30
Access: No visitors allowed. Outside requests on surveys conducted by Louis Harris accepted by telephone or mail only.
Special Collections: The Harris Poll 1963—present.
Personnel
Mgr/Info Svcs — Alice Church

367 **New York (New York)**
THE MCGRAW HILL COMPANIES—
Standard & Poor's TM/Central Inquiry
25 Broadway, New York, NY 10004
212-208-8519; FAX 212-514-7016

Hours: Mon—Fri 9am—4:30pm
Services to Other News Libraries: For S&P Index figures (hourly taped message provided by Index Products Department) call 208-8706,7,8. Otherwise call Central Inquiry. Financial data and quotes can be provided for a fee.
Personnel
Library Manager — Carol Fitzgerald, (8520)

368 **New York (New York)**
NATIONAL BROADCASTING CO.—
Reference Library
30 Rockefeller Plaza, Room 1426, New York, NY 10112 — See Banner
212-664-5307; FAX 212-247-8063

Hours: Mon—Fri 9am—7pm; Sat, Sun: on-call.
Access: Limited access to other special libraries by appointment only.
Services to Other News Libraries: Sends copies of clips, telefacsimile clips on limited basis as time and resources permit.
Resources: Reference books, maps. Microforms: roll. Newspaper index, clippings.
CD ROM: UMI Proquest; UMI Newspapers; NewsBank.
LAN: Novell.
Online Databases: Ovid; DIALOG; Dow Jones; Burrelle's; Datatimes; LEXIS/NEXIS; Info Globe; Information America; Periscope; CQ Washington Alert; Wilsonline; CDB Infotek; IRSC; Baseline.
Personnel
VP Information Services — Vera Mayer, (5309)
Mgr/Library Info Sys — Debra Levinson, (7184; levinson@nbc.com)

VIDEO ARCHIVES: Room 902 (212-664-6423/3797)
Archives Director Nancy Cole (3044)
Mgr/News Archives Oper Stan Singer (2442)
News Focus Reports (http://www.nbc.com)

369 **New York (New York)**
NEW YORK DAILY NEWS
450 W 33rd St, New York, NY 10001 — See Banner
212-210-1509; FAX 212-244-4033

Newspaper founded: 1919; library founded: 1920.
Hours: Mon—Fri, Sun 8am—11:30pm; Sat 10am—6:30pm
Online Databases: DIALOG; NEXIS.
Services to Other News Libraries: Telephone reference. Sends copies of clips/fee. Contact Faigi Rosenthal.
Access: Open to other media/other special libraries.
Resources: Photo files, negative, reference books, pamphlet file. Microforms: roll, fiche. Clippings.
Personnel
Librarian — Faigi Rosenthal, (6395), SLA

370 **New York (New York)**
NEW YORK MAGAZINE—
Information Services
755 Second Ave, New York, NY 10017
212-880-0755; FAX 212-867-8530

Hours: Mon—Fri 11—4
Personnel
Librarian — Susy Taylor, SLA

371 **New York (New York)**
NEW YORK POST
210 South St, New York, NY 10002
212-930-8000; FAX 212-930-8548

Newspaper founded: 1801; Library founded: 1923
Hours: 24 hrs
Days Not Published: Sunday
Services to Other News Libraries: Telephone reference. Sends copies of clips. Fee: 45c/page. Handled by Reorder Service. Requirements: prepayment or COD. Express mails clips.
Resources: Photo files, reference books, maps, pamphlet file. Microforms: roll. Clippings.
Access: Other media, other special libraries. Requirement: need permission.
Personnel
Librarian — Laura Harris, (8733), SLA

372 **New York (New York)**
NEW YORK PUBLIC LIBRARY—
Newspaper Library
11 W 40 St, New York, NY 10018
212-714-8520; FAX 212-643-0832

Hours: Mon—Sat 9—5
Access: By appointment only.
Special Collections: International newspaper collection.

373 New York (New York)
NEW YORK PUBLIC LIBRARY—
Telephone Reference
455 5th St, New York, NY 10016
212-340-0926

Personnel
Librarian Ilona G. Harris

374 New York (New York)
NEW YORK TIMES
229 W 43rd St, New York, NY 10036
212-556-7428; FAX 212-556-3542

Newspaper founded: 1851; library founded: 1867. Morgue founded: 1869.
Newspaper Group: New York Times Co.
Hours: Mon—Fri 9:30am—7pm
Access: Other media. Requirements: limited, with permission of library director or Executive Editor. Other special libraries. Requirements: limited.
Services to Other News Libraries: Telephone reference—212-556-1003. No fee. Limited.
Permission to use morgue: granted by Charles Robinson, Director of Information Services (ext 4119), Linda Amster, News Research Manager (ext 1963), or Anthony Zirilli, Assistant to Director (ext 1980).

Email: CHROBI@NYTIMES.COM; ANZIRI@NYTIMES.COM.
Home Page (URL): http://www.nytimes.com.
CD ROM: Prophone; Census; NY Times (UMI).
LAN: Ethernet.
Online Databases: NEXIS; LEXIS; DIALOG; Dow Jones; Datatimes; Information America; Federal Election Commission (FEC); Periscope; Burrelle's.
Resources: Photo files, reference books, maps, pamphlet file. Microforms: roll fiche. Newspaper index, clippings, CD Rom.
Archival Systems: Merlin.
Personnel

Manager	Linda Amster, (1963; AMSTER@NYTIMES.COM) SLA
Researchers	Donna Anderson
	Judy Greenfeld
	Lora Korbut
	Linda Lake
Librarians	Marilyn Annan, SLA
	John Motyka

375 New York (New York)
NEWSWEEK MAGAZINE
251 W 57th St, New York, NY 10019
212-445-4680 (Reference); FAX 212-445-4131

Hours: Mon 9am—6pm; Tues, Wed 9am—7pm; Thur 9am—11pm; Fri 9am—1am; Sat 9am—12m
Access: Not open to other media, other special libraries.
Services to Other News Libraries: Telephone reference—contact Aidan Mooney (445-5221). Sends copies of clips—Newsweek stories only.
Resources: Reference books, maps, pamphlet file. Microforms: roll, fiche. Newspaper index, clippings.
CD ROM: UMI Proquest GPO.
LAN: Yes.
WAN: Yes.
Online Databases: DIALOG; Dow Jones; Datatimes; NEXIS.
Electronic Clipping Files: NEXIS
Personnel

Director	Madeline Cohen, (4284; cohenm@nwnet.newsweek.com), SLA
Secretary	Lynn Seiffer, (4681)
Acquisitions	Judith Hausler, (4686)
Chief Indexer	Aidan Mooney, (4673)

376 New York (New York)
PARADE PUBLICATIONS, INC.
711 Third Ave, 6th Floor, New York, NY 10017-4014 See Banner
212-450-7000; FAX 212-450-7283; Email: PARADERS6@aol.com

Founded: 1941; library founded: 1975.
Hours: Mon—Fri 9am—5pm
Archival Systems: Linotronic.
LAN: Ethernet/Local Talk.
News Databases: NEXIS.
Services to Other News Libraries: Telephone reference. Sends copies of clips. Express mails clips. Contact Caryn Friedman.
Access: Other media, other special libraries.
Resources: Reference books, clippings. Parade Magazine Index 1941—.
Personnel

Director	Roberta J. Gardner, (7189), SLA
Librarians	Anita Goss, (7193)
	Sharon Cappelson, (7192), SLA
	Louis Leventhal, (7198), SLA
	Edgar Santiago, (7188), SLA
	John Paksons, (7149), SLA

377 New York (New York)
PEOPLE MAGAZINE—
Research Operations
Time & Life Bldg, Rm 31-34B, New York, NY 10020
212-522-8111

Personnel

Librarians	Robert P. Britton, (rbritton@people.timeinc.com), SLA
	Sarah Brennan-Green, (sarah_brennan@people.timeinc.com), SLA

378 New York (New York)
SCHOLASTIC INC.
555 Broadway, New York, NY 10012
212-343-6176; FAX 212-343-6185

Hours: Mon—Fri 9am—7pm
Access: Open to other media by appointment.
Online Databases: LEXIS/NEXIS; Dow Jones; DIALOG.
Personnel
Director Bert Schachter, SLA

379 New York (New York)
IL SOLE—24 ORE / EMC—
New York Contact
10 E 53rd St, 28th Fl, New York, NY 10022
212-755-7766; FAX 212-755-8825

Personnel
Correspondent Mario Calvo-Platero

380 New York (New York)
SPORTS ILLUSTRATED
1271 Ave of the Americas, Sports Libr Room 1837B, New York, NY 10020
212-522-3397; FAX 212-522-1719

Hours: Mon—Fri 10—6
Personnel
Librarian Linda Ronan, (LRONAN@SI.TIMEINC.COM), SLA

381 New York (New York)
STATEN ISLAND ADVANCE
950 Fingerboard Rd, Staten Island, NY 10305
718-981-1234; FAX 718-981-5679

Newspaper Group: Newhouse Newspapers
Hours: 9—5

STATEN ISLAND ADVANCE (cont'd)

Access: Open to the public/other media/other special libraries by appointment.
Personnel
Librarian — Melinda Gottlieb

382 **New York (New York)**
THIRTEEN/WNET
356 W 58th St, New York, NY 10019
212-560-3065; FAX 212-560-3199

Hours: Mon—Fri 9:30am—5:30pm (closed 12:30pm—1:30pm)
Access: Open to other libraries.
LAN: Yes.
CD ROM: UMI.
Online Databases: DIALOG; NEXIS; SAVE; Datatimes; Wilsonline.
Special Collections: Thirteen Program Guides.
Personnel
Librarians — Jane Bealer, (3063; Bealer@wnet.org), SLA
Margery Frohlinger, (3063; Frohlinger@wnet.org), SLA
Harriet Obus, (3064; Obus@wnet.org)

383 **New York (New York)**
TIME WARNER—
Research Library
Time and Life Building, 1271 Ave of Americas, New York, NY 10020
212-522-7033; FAX 212-522-3027

CD ROM: NY Times; Washington Post; LA Times; Grangers World of Poetry; Books in Print; Facts on File; Corporate Affiliations; Exegy; Phone Discs; Wall Street Journal; Newsbank.
LAN: Ethernet.
Online Databases: Reuters; DIALOG; Dow Jones; CQ Washington Alert; Warner Computer Systems; Wilsonline; Datatimes; Baseline; Sovset; NewsNet; LEXIS/NEXIS; Economic Bulletin Board; Investext; Periscope; Bloomberg.
Services to Other News Libraries: Telephone assistance with Time Inc. Publications that pre-date online access.
Resources: Reference books, maps, microforms, clippings, databases of Time, Inc. Magazines, CD Rom Network; Proquest CD Rom stations; Internet; automated catalog/Ameritech Horizon
Fee-Based Research: Research Fee: $100; Invoice or prepay.
Personnel
Director — Lany W. McDonald, (9233), SLA
Assistant Director — Lynn Dombek, (4535), SLA
Admin Asst — Andi Ramos, (4266)
Catalog/Circ Svcs Mgr — Glenn Loflin, (3528)
Database Svcs Mgr — Justin Scroggs, (2779), SLA
Central Res Svcs Mgr — Patricia Clark, (6415), SLA
Business Info Svcs Mgr — Mary Danehy, (6364), SLA
Resource Training Coord — Pamela Brooks, (2469), SLA
Time Magazine Research Coord — Angela Thornton, (3388), SLA
Research Librarians — Brenda Cherry, SLA
Evelyn Cunningham, SLA
Francis Gretes, SLA
Sandra Jamison, SLA
Susan Kramer, SLA
Charles Lampach, SLA
Joan Levinstein, SLA
Karen McCree, SLA
Patricia Neering, SLA
Robert Paton, SLA
Mary Pradt, SLA
Carol Weil, SLA
Helen Whatford, SLA
Pamela Wilson, SLA
Research Assistants — Angela Azzolino
Jonathan Bolch
AnnMarie Bonardi
Dianne Cyrus
Nan DuBois
Chris Horymski
Margaret Mendelson
Elias Rodriguez
Annette Rusin
Amy Ryan
Carol Zack
Cataloger — Ed Power

384 **New York (New York)**
THE VILLAGE VOICE—
Editorial Library
36 Cooper Square, New York, NY 10003
212-475-3300; FAX 212-475-8944; Email: vlib@inch.com

Access: Not open to the public.
Online Databases: LEXIS/NEXIS; Dow Jones; Datatimes.
Personnel
Librarian — Kan Kin, SLA

385 **New York (New York)**
WALL STREET JOURNAL
200 Liberty St, New York, NY 10281 — See Banner
212-416-2000; FAX 212-416-2806

Newspaper founded: 1889; library founded: 1903.
Newspaper Group: Dow Jones & Co., Inc.
Hours: Mon—Fri 9am—5pm
Days Not Published: New Year's Day, Washington's Birthday, Memorial Day, Independence Day, Labor Day, Thanksgiving, Christmas, Saturday, Sunday.
Home Page (URL): http://www.wsj.com.
Online Databases: DIALOG; Dow Jones; Datatimes; NEXIS; Information America.
News Databases: Dow Jones.
Services to Other News Libraries: Telephone reference. Will send copies of clips to other newspaper libraries if research is not involved.
Access: Not open to the public.
Resources: Reference books, pamphlet files. Microforms: roll, fiche. Newspaper index, clippings.
Personnel
Director — Lottie Lindberg, (2676), SLA
Asst Librarian — Elizabeth Yeh

386 **New York (Niagara Falls)**
NIAGARA GAZETTE
310 Niagara St, Niagara Falls, NY 14303 — See Banner
716-282-2311; FAX: Newsroom 716-286-3895

Newspaper founded: 1854; library founded: 1940.
Newspaper Group: Gannett Newspapers
Hours: Mon—Fri 9am—5pm
Email: 102010.453@compuserve.com.
Online Databases: G.N.A.S.
Services to Other News Libraries: No telephone reference. Sends copies of clips as time allows. Fee: negotiable. Contact: Davis Sokolowski.
Access: Open to other media on-site; open to historical, genealogical libraries.
Resources: Photo files, reference books, maps. Microforms: roll. Newspaper index, clippings.
Personnel
Librarian — David Sokolowski

387 **New York (Nyack)**
THE ROCKLAND JOURNAL—NEWS
200 N Rte 303, W Nyack, NY 10994
914-694-5086

Newspaper Group: Gannett Newspapers

388 New York (Olean)
OLEAN TIMES—HERALD
639 Norton Dr, Olean, NY 14760
716-372-3121

Personnel
Librarian (vacant)

389 New York (Oneonta)
THE DAILY STAR
102 Chestnut St, Oneonta, NY 13820
607-432-1000; FAX 607-432-5847

Newspaper Group: Ottaway Newspapers, Inc.
Personnel

Librarian	Melody Morgan, (219)

390 New York (Pleasantville)
READER'S DIGEST ASSOCIATION INC.—
Editorial and Research Libraries
Pleasantville, NY 10570
914-244-5289; FAX 914-238-0534; Email: readers@delphi.com

Hours: Mon—Fri 7:30—5
Access: SLA members, other librarians only.
Services to Other News Libraries: Telephone reference. Will send copies of clips.
Special Collections: Reader's Digest Publications.
Personnel

Head Librarian	Cynthia C. Rubino, SLA
Research Librarians	Susan Doremus, (5289), SLA
	Rosanne M. Fleury, (5290), SLA
	Edward Goralske
Stack Librarian	Lynne Dolan
Index Supv	Laura Giangrande, (5194)
Index Librarians	Karen Spano
	Nancy Villen

391 New York (Poughkeepsie)
POUGHKEEPSIE JOURNAL
85 Civic Center Pl, Poughkeepsie, NY 12602
914-454-2000 ext 362

Newspaper Group: Gannett Newspapers

392 New York (Rochester)
DEMOCRAT AND CHRONICLE / TIMES—UNION
55 Exchange Blvd, Rochester, NY 14614
716-232-7100; FAX 716-258-2265; Email: Library@Rochester.Democ.com

Newspaper Group: Gannett Newspapers
Hours: Mon—Fri 7:30am—12m; weekends 4pm—12m
Access: Open to visiting reporters.
Online Databases: NEXIS; DIALOG; Datatimes.
CD ROM: Yes.
LAN: Yes.
WAN: Yes.
Access: Open to other media/other special libraries. Not open to the public.
Special Collections: Complete collection of Life Magazines; Biographical information on George Eastman. A source of information for Xerox and Kodak; 50 years of Motion Picture Almanacs and Theatre World annuals.
Personnel

Librarian	Virginia Wheeler, (258-2506), SLA

393 New York (Rochester)
FREEDOM FORUM—
Rochester Office
1600 Chase Sq, Rochester, NY 14604
716-262-3315; FAX 716-262-3760

394 New York (Saratoga Springs)
THE SARATOGIAN
20 Lake Ave, Saratoga Springs, NY 12866 — See Banner
518-584-4242; FAX 518-587-7750

Year founded: 1854.
Newspaper Group: Gannett Newspapers
Hours: 9—5
Access: Open to visiting reporters.
Fee-Based Research: Research Fee: $5. FAX/Microform Copies: $.25. Contact: Ellie Brower (ext 210).
Personnel

Librarian	Eleanor M. Brower, SLA

395 New York (Syracuse)
SYRACUSE HERALD JOURNAL / POST—STANDARD / HERALD AMERICAN POST STANDARD
Clinton Square (Box 4915), Syracuse, NY 13221 — See Banner
315-470-2231; FAX 315-470-2005

Newspaper founded: 1829; library founded: 1920.
Newspaper Group: Newhouse Newspapers
Hours: Mon—Fri 6:30am—9pm; Sat, Sun 12n—9pm
Online Databases: DIALOG; LEXIS/NEXIS; Datatimes.
News Databases: SAVE.
Services to Other News Libraries: Telephone reference. Contact: Bonnie Ross. Sends copies of clips. Express mail clips. FAX clips.
Access: Open to other media.
Resources: Photo files, negatives, reference books, maps. Microforms: roll, clippings.
Archival Systems: SAVE.
Personnel

Library Director	Bonnie L. Ross, (2242), SLA

396 New York (Syracuse)
SYRACUSE UNIVERSITY—
Newhouse School of Public Communications
Syracuse, NY 13214
315-425-6969

Personnel

Librarian	Timothy K. Barger, (tkbarger@mailbox.syr.edu), SLA

397 New York (Troy)
THE RECORD—
Editorial Library
501 Broadway, Troy, NY 12181 — See Banner
518-270-1200; FAX 518-270-1202

Newspaper founded: 1896; library founded: 1974.
Hours: Mon—Fri 8am—4pm
Services to Other News Libraries: Brief telephone reference. Dates and short answers only. Sends copies of clips.
Access: Open to other media with permission of editor, executive editor or managing editor. Open to other special libraries. Not open to the public (some exceptions are made).
Resources: Photo files (published photos only), maps. Microforms: roll. Clippings.
Special Collections: Local History.
Personnel

Director	Susan Chasney, (1280)
Librarian	Jill M. Parsons, (JP8838@nsvax.albany.edu), SLA

398 **New York (Utica)**
OBSERVER—DISPATCH—
News Department
221 Oriskany Plaza, Utica, NY 13501
315-792-5182

Personnel

Librarian	Deborah L. Dufresne, SLA

399 **New York (Watertown)**
WATERTOWN DAILY TIMES
260 Washington St, Watertown, NY 13601 — See Banner
315-782-1000; FAX 315-782-2337

Newspaper founded: 1861; library founded: 1920.
Hours: Tues—Fri 1pm—3pm
Days Not Published: New Year's Day, Memorial Day, Independence Day, Labor Day, ThanksgivingDay, Christmas.
Access: Open with approval of chief librarian.
Services to Other News Libraries: Telephone reference. Sends copies of clips. Fee: 25c/page photocopy/ $1 library fee plus postage.
Resources: Photo files, reference books, maps, pamphlet files. Microforms: roll. Clippings.
Online Databases: DIALOG.
News Databases: SAVE.
Special Collections: Old Northern New York Newspapers.
Personnel

Chief Librarian	Lisa Carr-Bourcy, (345)
Library Clerks	Esther Daniels, (347)
	Patricia Delaney, (346)
	Elizabeth Hatch, (272)

400 **New York (White Plains)**
GANNETT SUBURBAN NEWSPAPERS
1 Gannett Drive, White Plains, NY 10604 — See Banner
914-694-5000; FAX 914-694-5150

Newspaper founded: 1917; library founded: 1950.
Newspaper Group: Gannett Newspapers
Hours: Mon—Fri 9am—6pm
Access: Other news librarians only.
Services to Other News Libraries: Telephone reference—914-694-5086.
Online Databases: LEXIS/NEXIS; Prodigy; DMV Database; DIALOG; Datatimes.
News Databases: Datatimes.
Resources: Photo files, negatives, reference books, maps. Microforms: roll.
Personnel

Director	Frances Henry Riley, (5225), SLA
Librarian	Zana Varner

401 **North Carolina (Asheville)**
ASHEVILLE CITIZEN—TIMES
14 O'Henry Ave (PO Box 2090), Asheville, NC 28802
704-252-5610; FAX 704-251-0585

Founded: 1870.
Newspaper Group: Multimedia Newspapers
Hours: 9—5
Services to Other News Libraries: Will send clips to other news libraries.
Archival Systems: PhotoView; NewsView.
Fee-Based Research: Research Fee: $50. Copies: $5. FAX only to other newspaper libraries. Prepay. Contact: ext 408.
Online Databases: NEXIS.
Personnel

Librarians	Holly MacKenzie, (408)
	Jill Wolfe

402 **North Carolina (Burlington)**
TIMES—NEWS
707 S Main, Burlington, NC 27215
919-227-0131

Newspaper Group: Freedom Newspapers
Personnel

Librarian	Pat Cathey

403 **North Carolina (Chapel Hill)**
UNIVERSITY OF NORTH CAROLINA—
School of Journalism
Howell Hall CB#3365, Chapel Hill, NC 27599
919-962-1204; FAX 919-962-0620

Personnel

Librarian	Barbara P. Semonche, (semonch@gibbs.oit.unc.edu) SLA

404 **North Carolina (Charlotte)**
CHARLOTTE OBSERVER
600 S Tryon St (PO Box 32188), Charlotte NC 28232 — See Banner
704-358-5217; FAX 704-358-5203

Newspaper founded: 1886; library founded: 1956.
Hours: Mon—Thur 8am—8pm; Fri—Sun 9am—4pm
Access: Open to other media; access authorized by librarian, editor or managing editor. Open to other special libraries.
Services to Other News Libraries: Telephone reference. Contact: Sara Gesler Klemmer. Sends copies of clips; express mails clips. FAX.
Home Page (URL): http://www.charlotte.com.
News Databases: SAVE.
Online Databases: SAVE; DIALOG; NEXIS; Datatimes; AOL; CompuServe.
Resources: Photo files, reference books, maps, pamphlet files. Microforms: roll, fiche, jacket. Clippings.
Archival Systems: Digital Link Gateway; SAVE.
CD ROM: Yes.
LAN: Yes.
Fee-Based Research: Research fee: $10 first half hour, $7.50 each half after. Copies: $3. FAXing. Microform Copies: $3. Invoice or prepay. Contact: Deborah Dunn.
Personnel

Director	Sara Gesler Klemmer, (klemmer@observer.infi.net) SLA
Asst Librarian	Marion Paynter, (5219; paynter@observer.info.net), SLA
Photo Librarian	Ann Bryant, (5213), SLA

405 **North Carolina (Durham)**
HERALD—SUN
2828 Picket Rd, Durham, NC 27705 — See Banner
919-419-6500; FAX 919-419-6889

Year founded: Herald—1894.
Hours: Mon, Wed, Fri 8am—10pm; Tues, Thur 8—5:30; Sat, Sun 9—3
Access: Other media. Other news libraries.
Services to Other News Libraries: Telephone reference.
Home Page (URL): http://www.herald-sun.com.
Online Databases: DIALOG; Datatimes; LEXIS/NEXIS.
News Databases: NewsView.
Archival Systems: NewsView.
LAN: Yes.
Fee-Based Research: Research Fee: $100. Copies: $10. Microform Copies: $10. Prepay. Contact: Janet Sammons (419-6520).

HERALD—SUN (cont'd)

Resources: Photo files, reference books, map, pamphlet file. Microforms: roll fiche, jackets. Newspaper index, clippings. Photo index.
Personnel

Director	Janet Sammons, (6520; JAG@HERALD.SUN_COM), SLA
Assistant Librarians	Michelle Rosen, (MC2@HERALD.SUN_COM)
	Mary Clements, (MER@HERALD.SUN_COM)

406 **North Carolina (Fayetteville)**
FAYETTEVILLE OBSERVER—TIMES
458 Whitfield Rd, Fayetteville, NC 28306
910-323-4848; FAX 910-486-3545

Year founded: Observer—1816; Library founded: 1991.
Hours: 8am—9pm
News Databases: SII.
Archival Systems: Autologic.
Access: Open to other media by appointment.
Personnel
Librarian — Daisy D. Maxwell, SLA

407 **North Carolina (Forest City)**
THE DAILY COURIER
1111 Oak St (PO Box 1149), Forest City, NC 28043
704-245-6431

Personnel
Librarian — Virginia Rucker

408 **North Carolina (Gastonia)**
THE GASTONIA GAZETTE
2500 E Franklin Blvd, Gastonia, NC 28053
704-864-3293

Newspaper Group: Freedom Newspapers
Personnel
Librarian — Dot Wallace

409 **North Carolina (Greensboro)**
GREENSBORO NEWS & RECORD
200 E. Market St (PO Box 20848), Greensboro, NC 27420 — See Banner
910-373-7044; FAX 910-373-7382; Email: newsrecord@delphi.com

Newspaper founded: 1890; library founded: 1969.
Newspaper Group: Landmark Communications, Inc.
Hours: Mon—Fri 7:30am—8pm
Online Databases: Datatimes; NEXIS.
News Databases: SAVE.
Resources: Photo files, reference books, maps. Microforms: roll, fiche, jacket. Clippings.
Archival Systems: SAVE; Fetch.
CD ROM: Yes.
LAN: Yes.
Personnel

Director	Robert L. Beall, SLA
Staff	Gail Scullion
	Jim Thompson

410 **North Carolina (High Point)**
HIGH POINT ENTERPRISE
210 Church Ave, High Point, NC 27261
919-341-5700

Personnel
Librarian — Howard Hayes

411 **North Carolina (New Bern)**
THE SUN—JOURNAL
226 Pollock St (Box 1149), New Bern, NC 28560
919-638-8101

Newspaper Group: Freedom Newspapers
Personnel
Librarian — Ivy Louise Garris

412 **North Carolina (Raleigh)**
THE NEWS & OBSERVER
215 S McDowell St, Raleigh, NC 27602 — See Banner
919-829-4580; FAX 919-829-4529

Newspaper founded: 1865.
Hours: Mon—Fri 7:30am—8:30pm; Sat, Sun 2:30—6:30pm
Services to Other News Libraries: Sends copies of clips, request must come through requestor's library. Online with Datatimes, CD ROM marketed through NewsBank. Fee-based public research through PiSYS IQ (ext 8918)
Online Databases: Datatimes.
CD ROM: Phonedisc; Prophone; Current biography.
Resources: Photo files, reference books, maps, vertical files, newspaper clippings, CD-ROM, magnetic tape databases.
Personnel

Director	Teresa G. Leonard, (4866; TLEONARD@NANDO.COM), SLA
News Research Mgr	Christopher Hardesty, (8925; CHARDEST@NANDO.COM), SLA
Archive Manager	Colline Roberts, (4868; CROBERTS@NANDO.COM)
Asst Archive Manager	Ron Jack
Resource Manager	Sperry Krueger, (4886; SKRUEGER@NANDO.COM), SLA
Archive Enhancers	Renee Bollten
	Tonya Loggains
	Jonathan Prescott
	Hilary Shu
Data Collection Assts	James Carpenter
	Todd Lothery
	Tiffany McLeod
	Norman Reu
	Joyce Sykes
Database Researchers	Charles DeBase
	David Raynor
	Becky Dillner
News Research Clerk	Jean Hunt
Database Editor	Donna Sese
Photo Researcher	Peggy Simmons

413 **North Carolina (Raleigh)**
STATE LIBRARY OF NORTH CAROLINA—Information Services Section
109 E Jones St, Raleigh, NC 27601
919-733-3683

414 **North Carolina (Salisbury - Spencer - East Spencer)**
THE SALISBURY POST
131 W Innes St, Salisbury, NC 28144
704-633-8950

Personnel
Librarian — Nancy Fisher

415 **North Carolina (Wilmington)**
WILMINGTON MORNING STAR/SUNDAY STAR—NEWS
PO Box 840, Wilmington, NC 28401
910-343-2309; FAX 910-343-2227

Founded: Star—1867; Star—News: 1928. Library established: 1988.
Newspaper Group: New York Times Co.
Hours: Mon—Fri 8am—6pm
Access: Not open to public.
Email: Bookbabe@Wilmington.Net.
Archival Systems: PhotoView.
Electronic Clipping Files: Newsview

WILMINGTON MORNING STAR/SUNDAY STAR—NEWS (cont'd)

Online Databases: DIALOG; Datatimes; LEXIS; NEXIS.
Personnel

Librarian	Mary MacCallum, SLA
Asst Librarian	Kim; PKimPhord$wilmington.net) Hord

416 **North Carolina (Winston—Salem)**
WINSTON—SALEM JOURNAL
PO Box 3159, Winston-Salem, NC 27102-3159 See Banner
910-727-7275; FAX 910-727-4071

Newspaper founded: 1897; library founded: 1947.
Newspaper Group: Media General, Inc.
Hours: Mon—Fri 9am—12m; Sat, Sun, Holidays 2:30pm—11pm
Access: Open to non-competing news media by appointment.
Services to Other News Libraries: Telephone reference; FAX, mail to SLA members.
Resources: Photo, negative, transparency files; reference books; maps, clippings. Microforms: roll, fiche. CD-ROM Reader; AP LeafDesk; digital image storage.
Personnel

News Library Manager	Virginia D. Hauswald, (7274), SLA
Research	Marcus L. Green
Text Archive	Melinda Currie Pennington
Photo Archive	Diane A. Lamb
Text Archive	Bonnie Toenniessen Sugden

417 **North Dakota (Bismarck)**
THE BISMARCK TRIBUNE
707 E Front St, Bismarck, ND 58501 See Banner
701-223-2500 / reference ext 241; FAX 701-224-1412

Newspaper founded: 1873; library founded: 1873.
Newspaper Group: Lee Newspapers
Hours: Mon—Fri 8am—5pm
Services to Other News Libraries: Telephone reference.
Access: Open to other media, other special libraries.
Resources: Photo files, negatives, reference books, maps, pamphlet files. Microforms: roll. Newspaper index, clippings.
News Databases: ISYS.
Personnel

Librarian	Barbara Herzberg-Bender, (241)

418 **North Dakota (Fargo)**
THE FORUM
101 North 5th St, Fargo, ND 58102
701-235-7311; FAX 701-241-5487

Year founded: 1879; library founded: 1922.
Access: Closed to the public.
Services to Other News Libraries: Telephone reference. Sends copies of clips. Contact Andrea Halgrimson.
Resources: Photo files, reference books, pamphlet file. Microforms: roll. Clippings.
Personnel

Librarian	Andrea H. Halgrimson, (241-5517), SLA

419 **North Dakota (Grand Forks)**
GRAND FORKS HERALD
303 2nd Ave N, Grand Forks, ND 58203
701-780-1133; FAX 701-780-1123

Year founded: 1879.
Newspaper Group: Knight-Ridder Newspapers Inc.
Access: Open to visiting reporters.
Services to Other News Libraries: Answers questions from news libraries.
News Databases: SAVE.
Personnel

Librarians	Jenelle Stadstas
	Ann Headrick, (1100)

420 **Ohio (Akron)**
AKRON BEACON JOURNAL
44 E Exchange St, Akron, OH 44328 See Banner
216-996-3000; FAX 216-376-9235

Newspaper founded: 1839; library founded: 1939.
Newspaper Group: Knight-Ridder Newspapers Inc.
Hours: Mon—Fri 8am—10pm; Sat 1pm—10pm; Sun 1pm—10pm
Online Databases: SAVE; DIALOG; Datatimes; Dow Jones; AOL.
Services to Other News Libraries: Telephone reference. Sends copies of clips. Fee: $3/page. Will be handled only if time/personnel permits. Contact Catherine Tierney or Norma Hill. No express mail clips.
Access: Open to other media and other special libraries by appointment.
News Databases: SAVE.
CD ROM: Yes.
Resources: Photo files, reference books, maps, pamphlet files. Microforms: roll, fiche. Newspaper index (only 1930's), clippings.
Special Collections: Kent State University riot, May 4, 1970; Airships; Rubber Industry.
Personnel

Librarian	Catherine M. Tierney, (3898; ctierney@bright.net), SLA
Asst Librarian	Norma Hill, (3899)

421 **Ohio (Canton)**
REPOSITORY
500 Market Ave S, Canton, OH 44702
216-454-5611; FAX 216-454-5745

Newspaper Group: Thomson Newspapers
Hours: 8—5
Personnel

Librarian	Annie Jones, (307)

422 **Ohio (Cincinnati)**
THE CINCINNATI ENQUIRER
312 Elm St, Cincinnati, OH 45201 See Banner
513-721-2700; FAX 513-768-8011

Newspaper Group: Gannett Newspapers
News Databases: SII.
Online Databases: Datatimes; LEXIS/NEXIS.
Access: Closed to the public; open to other libraries and reporters.
Personnel

Librarian	Ray Zwick, (768-8464), SLA

423 **Ohio (Cincinnati)**
THE CINCINNATI POST
125 E Court St, Cincinnati, OH 45202
513-352-2000; FAX 513-621-3962

Newspaper Group: Scripps-Howard
Access: Open to public. Open to other libraries and reporters - call first.
Online Databases: DIALOG; Datatimes.
Personnel

Librarian	Robert C. Hahn, (2785)

424 **Ohio (Cleveland)**
THE PLAIN DEALER
1801 Superior Ave, Cleveland, OH 44114 See Banner
216-999-4195; FAX 216-999-6363

Newspaper founded: 1842; library founded: 1908.
Newspaper Group: Newhouse Newspapers

THE PLAIN DEALER (cont'd)

Hours: Mon—Fri 8am—2am; Sat 9am—1am; Sun 11am—1am
Services to Other News Libraries: Telephone reference. Contact: Patti Graziano. Sends copies of clips.
Access: Open to other media with permission of Managing Editor. Open to other special libraries.
CD ROM: Yes.
Fee-Based Research: Copies: $1. Microform Copies: $1.50. Invoice. Contact Patti Graziano (999-4195).
Online Databases: DIALOG; Datatimes; NEXIS.
Special Collections: Ohio and Cleveland history.
Personnel

Library Director	Patti A. Graziano, SLA
Asst Librarian	Mary Ann Cofta, SLA

425 **Ohio (Columbus)**
THE COLUMBUS DISPATCH
34 South Third, Columbus, OH 43216 — See Banner
614-461-5039; FAX 614-461-5107

Year founded: 1871; library founded: 1950.
Hours: Mon—Fri 8am—8:30pm; Sat, Sun 9am—8:30pm
Access: Not open to the public. Open to other libraries.
Services to Other News Libraries: Telephone reference. Sends copies of clips.
Home Page (URL): http://www.dispatch.com.
Online Databases: DIALOG; Dow Jones; NEXIS; SAVE; Datatimes; WESTLAW.
News Databases: SAVE.
Resources: Photo files, reference books. Microforms: roll, jackets. Newspaper index. Clippings. CD Rom, Image Archive.
Archival Systems: AP Preserver.
CD ROM: Yes.
LAN: Yes.
Personnel

Librarians	James J. Hunter, (Jhunter@Dispatch.com), SLA
	Dave Stephenson
	Linda Neitch
	Susan Kelley
	Matt Leach
	Beth Clark
	Diana Hughes

426 **Ohio (Dayton)**
DAYTON DAILY NEWS
4th and Ludlow Sts, Dayton, OH 45402 — See Banner
513-225-2201; FAX 513-225-2277

Newspaper founded: 1898; library founded: 1900.
Newspaper Group: Cox Enterprises
Hours: Mon—Sun 8:30am—12m
Access: Open to other media; prior appointment necessary. Open to other special libraries.
Services to Other News Libraries: Telephone reference. Sends copies of clips. FAX.
Home Page (URL): http://www.Access—Dayton.Com.
Fee-Based Research: Research Fee: $60. Copies; Microform Copies. Prepay. Contact: Michael Jesse (225-2201).
Online Databases: DIALOG; Datatimes; LEXIS/NEXIS; Dow Jones.
Resources: Photo files, reference books, maps, pamphlet files. Microforms: roll, fiche, jackets. Clippings.
LAN: Yes.
Special Collections: Dayton History.
Personnel

Director	Michael Jesse, (2201; Michael_Jesse@DNI.COM), SLA
Staff	Robert Allaire, (2202)
	Nina Butler, (2206)
	Charlotte Jones, (2449; Charlotte_Jone@DNI.COM)
	David Ross, (2202)
	Yevetta Keenan, (2449)
	Sasha Stanley, (2127)
	Dean Koolbeck, (2127)

427 **Ohio (Elyria)**
ELYRIA CHRONICLE—TELEGRAM
225 East Ave, Elyria, OH 44035 — See Banner
216-329-7000; FAX 216-329-7282

Newspaper founded: 1829; Library founded: 1954.
Hours: Mon—Fri 6am—reporters are done
Days Not Published: Christmas Day.
Services to Other News Libraries: Telephone reference.
Access: Open to other media and other special libraries.
LAN: Yes.
Resources: Photo files, negatives, reference books, maps, pamphlet files. Microforms: roll, fiche. Clippings.
Special Collections: Extensive history files of Elyria and Lorain County (Clips and Photos).
Personnel

Director	Marie M. Banks, (7114), SLA

428 **Ohio (Lake County-Geauga County)**
THE NEWS—HERALD
38879 Mentor Ave (PO Box 351), Willoughby, OH 44094
216-951-0000; FAX 216-975-2293

Newspaper Group: Ingersoll Publications Co.
Access: Telephone reference only.
Personnel

Librarian	Jane Strachan

429 **Ohio (Mansfield)**
MANSFIELD NEWS JOURNAL
70 W Fourth St (PO Box 25), Mansfield, OH 44901 — See Banner
419-522-3311; FAX 419-522-2672

Year founded: 1930.
Newspaper Group: Thomson Newspapers
Hours: Mon, Wed, Fri 7:30am—11:30pm; Tues, Thur 12n—6pm
Personnel

Librarian	Ellen C. Smith

430 **Ohio (Napoleon)**
NORTHWEST—SIGNAL
595 E Riverview Ave (PO Box 567), Napoleon, OH 43545
419-592-5055; FAX 419-592-9778

Newspaper founded: 1966; library founded: 1966.
Days Not Published: New Year's Day, Memorial Day, Independence Day, Labor Day, Thanksgiving, Christmas.
Personnel

Librarian	Irma Follett

431 **Ohio (Sandusky)**
SANDUSKY REGISTER
Market and Jackson Sts, Sandusky, OH 44870
419-625-5500; FAX 419-625-3007

Newspaper Group: Sandusky-Norwalk Newspapers
Personnel

Librarian	Deborah VonThron

432 **Ohio (Sidney)**
AMOS PRESS, INC.—
Corporate Library
911 Vandemark Rd, Sidney, OH 45365
513-498-2111; FAX 513-498-0888; Email: apilibrary@aol.com

Access: Open to other media by appointment.
Personnel
Librarian — Bill Menker, SLA

433 **Ohio (Springfield)**
SPRINGFIELD NEWS—SUN
202 N Limestone, Springfield, OH 45501
513-328-0300; FAX 513-328-0328

Newspaper Group: Cox Enterprises
Personnel
Librarian — Anita Beaver, (0348), SLA

434 **Ohio (Toledo)**
THE BLADE
541 Superior St, Toledo, OH 43660
419-245-6185; FAX 419-245-6185

Newspaper founded: 1835.
Newspaper Group: Block Newspapers
Hours: Mon—Fri 9am—10:30pm; Sat 2pm—10:30pm
Access: Not open to the public.
Services: Telephone reference (limited basis).
Resources: Photo files, reference books, maps. Microforms: roll, fiche. Clippings.
Personnel
Director — Mary F. Mackzum, SLA

435 **Ohio (Upper Sandusky)**
THE DAILY CHIEF—UNION
111 W Wyandot Ave (PO Box 180), Upper Sandusky, OH 43351
419-294-2332; FAX 419-294-5608

Newspaper Group: Ray Barnes Newspapers, Inc.
Personnel
Librarian — Dolores Moore

436 **Ohio (Warren)**
TRIBUNE CHRONICLE
240 Franklin SE, Warren, OH 44482 — See Banner
216-841-1600; FAX 216-841-1717; Email: OHWAR01@PLINKGEIS.COM

Newspaper founded: 1812; library founded: 1982.
Hours: Mon—Fri 6am—2:30pm
Services to Other News Libraries: Telephone reference. Contact: Kathi A. Kovacic. Sends copies of clips. Fee. Requirements: Payment in advance—$2.15/copy. Express mail clips.
Access: Open to other media and other special libraries.
Home Page (URL): http://www.halli.com/tribune.
Archival Systems: Stauffer Gold.
Fee-Based Research: Copies: $2.15/page. FAX add $1. Microform Copies: $2.15/page.
Resources: Photo files, reference books, maps. Microforms: roll. Newspaper index (indexed to microfilm), clippings.
Personnel
Chief Librarian — Kathi A. Kovacic, (1734; KDKovacic@aol.com), SLA

437 **Oklahoma (Lawton)**
LAWTON CONSTITUTION/THE SUNDAY CONSTITUTION
PO Box 648, Lawton, OK 73502
405-353-0620; FAX 405-353-0620

Personnel
Librarian — Fran Mello

438 **Oklahoma (Muskogee)**
MUSKOGEE DAILY PHOENIX AND TIMES—DEMOCRAT
214 Wall St, Muskogee, OK 74401
918-684-2900; FAX 918-684-2878

Year founded: 1904.
Newspaper Group: Gannett Newspapers
Personnel
Librarian — Pauline Foster

439 **Oklahoma (Oklahoma City)**
DAILY OKLAHOMAN / OKLAHOMA CITY TIMES
9000 N Broadway (PO Box 25125), Oklahoma City, OK 73116 — See Banner
405-475-3311/ Reference 405-475-3388; FAX 405-475-3971; Email: OKLIB@IONET.NET

founded: 1889; library founded: Unknown.
Hours: Mon—Fri 7am—11pm
Access: Open to other media on a limited basis; open to other special libraries.
Services to Other News Libraries: Anything within reason.
CD ROM: Newsbank; Southwest Micro-Publishing.
Resources: Electronic Archive since 11/81. Photo files, reference books, maps, pamphlet files, Microforms: roll. Clippings.
Online Databases: Datatimes; DIALOG.
News Databases: BASIS.
Special Collections: Oklahoma City bombing text and photos.
Personnel
Manager — Carol A. Campbell, (3676), SLA
Asst Manager — Melissa Hayer, (3679), SLA

440 **Oklahoma (Tulsa)**
TULSA WORLD
315 S Boulder, Tulsa, OK 74102
918-581-8583

The Tulsa Tribune ceased publication 10/92 but clippings are electronically stored.
Hours: Mon—Sat 6am—12m; Sun 3pm—12m
News Databases: Datatimes.
Online Databases: Datatimes.
Access: Open to other libraries by appointment.
Personnel
Chief Librarian — Austin G. Farley, SLA

441 **Oregon (Albany)**
ALBANY DEMOCRAT—HERALD
138 W 6th Ave, Albany, OR 97321
541-926-2211; FAX 541-926-4799

Newspaper Group: Disney Company
Hours: 8am—2pm
Access: Open to other media, libraries.
News Databases: Stauffer Gold.
Personnel
Librarian — Glenda Suklis, (100)

442 **Oregon (Bend)**
BEND BULLETIN
1526 NW Hill St, Bend, OR 97701 — See Banner
541-382-1811; FAX 541-383-5802; Email: bulletin@bendnet.com

Newspaper founded: 1903.
Archival Systems: MacArchive; LASR.
News Databases: SII.
LAN: Yes.
Online Databases: NEXIS.

443 **Oregon (Eugene)**
THE REGISTER—GUARD
975 High St (PO Box 10188), Eugene, OR 97440
503-485-1234; FAX 503-683-7631

Access: Open to the public and other libraries.
Personnel
Librarian — Suzanne Boyd, (340), SLA

444 **Oregon (Grants Pass)**
GRANTS PASS DAILY COURIER
409 SE Seventh (PO Box 1468), Grants Pass, OR 97526
503-474-3700; FAX 503-474-3824

Hours: 8—11; 1—3
Personnel
Librarian — Mary Bradford, (3722)

445 **Oregon (Medford)**
MAIL TRIBUNE
PO Box 1108, Medford, OR 97501 — See Banner
541-776-4411; FAX 541-776-4376; Email: Mailtrib@Mind.Net

Newspaper founded: 1906; library founded: 1976.
Newspaper Group: Ottaway Newspapers, Inc.
Services to Other News Libraries: Telephone reference. Copies of clips, no fee; FAX clips, shipping.
Access: By appointment only.
News Databases: Datatimes.
Resources: Photo files, maps. Microforms: roll. Newspaper index (1952-77), clippings (1978-8/30/92 using Datatimes Software).
Personnel
Librarian — Pamela S. Sieg, (3325)

446 **Oregon (Portland)**
THE OREGONIAN
1320 SW Broadway, Portland, OR 97201
503-221-8132; FAX 503-294-4021

Newspaper Group: Newhouse Newspapers
Hours: Mon—Fri 7:30am—8:30pm; Sat, Sun, Holidays 9—6
Access: Open to other media by appointment.
CD ROM: NewsBank; telephone directories; maps; property taxes.
Online Databases: SAVE; Datatimes; DIALOG; CompuServe; Oregon State Library.
News Databases: SAVE.
Fee-Based Research: Research fee; Copies; $3.50/article. FAX: $2. Microform Copies: $12.50/article. Credit card. Contact: Circulation/Back Issues (221-8131).
Archival Systems: SAVE; Fetch.
LAN: Yes.
Special Collections: Family Life; Oregon History.
Personnel
Librarian — Sandra L. Macomber, (SLMacomber@aol.com)

447 **Oregon (Roseburg)**
ROSEBURG NEWS—REVIEW
345 NE Winchester St, Roseburg, OR 97470
541-672-3321; FAX 541-673-5994

Newspaper Group: Swift-Pioneer Newspapers
Personnel
Librarian — Capra Moore

448 **Oregon (Salem)**
SALEM STATESMAN—JOURNAL
280 Church St NE (PO Box 13009), Salem, OR 97309
503-399-6611; FAX 503-399-6706

Newspaper Group: Gannett Newspapers
Personnel
Librarian — David House, (6729)

449 **Pennsylvania (Allentown)**
THE MORNING CALL
101 N 6th St (PO Box 1260), Allentown, PA 18105 — See Banner
610-820-6523; FAX 610-820-6672

Newspaper founded: 1895; library founded: 1932.
Newspaper Group: Times Mirror Co.
Hours: Mon—Fri 8am—10pm; Sat 8—6; Sun 12n—8pm.
Access: Other media, other special libraries. Subject to fee; no subjects of a voluminous nature.
Services to Other News Libraries: Telephone reference. Sends copies of clips. Telefacsimile clips.
Online Databases: DIALOG; NEXIS; Datatimes; Dow Jones.
CD ROM: Pioneer. Databases: Philadelphia Inquirer.
Electronic Clipping Files: SAVE
Resources: Photo files, reference books, maps, pamphlet file. Microforms: roll, fiche, jackets. Newspaper index, clippings.
Archival Systems: SAVE.
Fee-Based Research: Information Service—820-6115 (Public Lines). Copies: $3/page. Microform Copies: $3/page. Invoice (Services free to other newspapers).
Personnel
Dir/Library Services — Lois A. Doncevic, (doncevic@mcall.com), SLA
Librarians — Patrice Swartz, (6165)
Dianne Knauss, (6618)
Eugene Tauber, (6521)
Ruth Burns, (770-3715)

450 **Pennsylvania (Altoona)**
ALTOONA MIRROR
301 Cayuga Ave (PO Box 2008), Altoona, PA 16602
814-946-7411; FAX 814-946-7411

Personnel
Librarian — Tim Doyle

451 **Pennsylvania (Beaver)**
BEAVER COUNTY TIMES
400 Fair Ave, Beaver, PA 15009 — See Banner
412-775-3200; FAX 412-775-7212

Newspaper founded: 1874; library founded: 1957.
Newspaper Group: Calkins Newspapers
Days Not Published: New Year's Day, Memorial Day, Independence Day, Labor Day, Christmas, Saturday.
Services to Other News Libraries: Telephone reference. Contact: Linda B. DiSante. Sends copies of clips for fee.
Access: Open to other media and other special libraries. Closed to the public.
Resources: Photo files, reference books, maps, pamphlet files. Microforms: roll. Clippings.
Personnel
Librarian — Linda B. DiSante, (153), SLA
Asst Librarians — Marlene McNaughton, (230)
Gladys Wallace

452 **Pennsylvania (Doylestown)**
DOYLESTOWN INTELLIGENCER/RECORD
333 N Broad St, Doylestown, PA 18901
215-345-3000; FAX 215-345-3150

Newspaper Group: Calkins Newspapers
Personnel
Librarian — Joan Fitting, (3072)

453 **Pennsylvania (Easton—Bethlehem—Phillipsburg NJ)**
EXPRESS TIMES
30 N Fourth (PO Box 391), Easton, PA 18044-0391
610-258-7171

EXPRESS TIMES (cont'd)

Newspaper Group: Thompson Newspapers
Personnel
Librarian Carol King

454 **Pennsylvania (Erie)**
ERIE DAILY TIMES/MORNING NEWS AND WEEKENDER/TIMES NEWS
Times Square - 205 W 12th St, Erie, PA 16534
814-456-8531

Email: CMEAD@TIMESNEWS.COM.
Home Page (URL): http://www.timesnews.com.
Fee-Based Research: Copies: $30. Invoice or credit card. Contact: Lisa Ellenberger (870-1857).
Personnel
Librarian Penny Joint

455 **Pennsylvania (Greensburg/Pittsburgh)**
TRIBUNE—REVIEW
Cabin Hill Dr, Greensburg, PA 15601
412-834-1151; FAX 412-838-5170; Email: Letters@tribune.review.com

Access: Open to other media by appointment.
News Databases: Stauffer Gold.
Personnel
Librarian Ann Saul, (837-4378)

456 **Pennsylvania (Harrisburg)**
HARRISBURG PATRIOT AND EVENING NEWS / SUNDAY PATRIOT
812 King Blvd (PO Box 2265), Harrisburg, PA 17105
717-255-8100; FAX 717-255-8456; Email: PNStaff@Microserve.Com

Newspaper Group: Newhouse Newspapers
Online Databases: Datatimes.
News Databases: Datatimes.
Personnel
Librarian Deanna S. Mills, (8402), SLA

457 **Pennsylvania (Johnstown)**
JOHNSTOWN TRIBUNE—DEMOCRAT
425 Locust St (PO Box 340), Johnstown, PA 15907
814-532-5199; FAX 814-539-1409

Personnel
Librarian Ruth Rice

458 **Pennsylvania (Lancaster)**
LANCASTER NEW ERA / INTELLIGENCER JOURNAL / SUNDAY NEWS
8 W King St (PO Box 1328), Lancaster, PA 17608 See Banner
717-291-8811

Hours: 7:30am—11pm
Access: Open to other media.
News Databases: Datatimes.
Online Databases: Datatimes.
Personnel
Librarian Edward G. Wilson

459 **Pennsylvania (Lock Haven - Jersey Shore)**
EXPRESS
9-11 W Main St (PO Box 208), Lock Haven, PA 17745
717-748-6791; FAX 717-748-1544

Newspaper Group: Thomson Newspapers
Personnel
Librarian Wendy Stiver

460 **Pennsylvania (Lower Bucks County)**
BUCKS COUNTY COURIER TIMES
8400 Route 13, Levittown, PA 19057
215-949-4168; FAX 215-949-4177

Newspaper Group: Calkins Newspapers
Hours: 8:30—5:30
Access: Not open to other media.
Personnel
Head Librarian Susan Y. Ditterline, SLA

461 **Pennsylvania (New Castle)**
NEW CASTLE NEWS
27-35 N Mercer St (Box 60), New Castle, PA 16103
412-654-6651; FAX 412-654-9593

Hours: 7:30—4
Access: Not open to other media; open to others by appointment.
Personnel
Librarian Jill McConnell, (161)

462 **Pennsylvania (New Hope)**
FREEDONIA GAZETTE
335 Fieldstone Dr, New Hope, PA 18938
215-862-9734

Newspaper founded: 1978; library founded: 1978.
Hours: Mon—Fri 7pm—10pm
Services to Other News Libraries: Telephone reference. Contact: Paul Wesolowski. Will FAX clips. Fee: 10c/page, plus postage.
Access: Open to other media by appointment; open to other special libraries or any qualified researcher/writer by arrangement.
Resources: Photo files, reference books. Newspaper index, clippings.
Special Collections: 45,000 clippings (1905—present) relating to the Marx Brothers; 2400 photos of the Marx Brothers.
Personnel
Director Paul G. Wesolowski

463 **Pennsylvania (Philadelphia)**
PHILADELPHIA NEWSPAPERS
400 N Broad St, Philadelphia, PA 19101
215-854-4660; FAX 215-854-4669

Inquirer / Daily News / Philadelphia Online / Knight Ridder Video (KR Video). Newspaper founded: 1829; library founded: 1926.
Newspaper Group: Knight-Ridder Newspapers Inc.
Hours: Mon—Fri 6am—1am; Sat 8am—7pm; Sun 3pm—12m
Access: Other media, other special libraries by appointment.
Services to Other News Libraries: Telephone reference. Sends copies of clips. FAX clips.
Email: pnresearch@philly.infi.net.
Home Page (URL): http://www.phillynews.com.
Online Databases: DIALOG; Dow Jones; SAVE; Datatimes; LEXIS/NEXIS.
News Databases: SAVE.
Electronic Clipping Files: VU/TEXT
Resources: Photo files, reference books, maps, pamphlet file. Microforms: roll. Newspaper index, clippings.
Archival Systems: SAVE; Presslink Explorer Archive
CD ROM: Yes.
LAN: Yes.
Personnel
Editor News Rec/Info Svcs Constance Pickett, (4669; CPickett@PhillyNews.Com)
Researchers Denise Boal, (dboal@philly.infi.net)
Alletta Bowers, (abowers@philly.infi.net)
Joe Daley
Frank Donahue
Jenny Elliott
Jennie Graham
Gene Loielo
Michael Panzer

PHILADELPHIA NEWSPAPERS (cont'd)

	Michael Porter
	Sandy Simmons
Libr Classifiers—Photo	Steve Elliott, (selliot@philly.infi.net)
	Ed Voves

464 Pennsylvania (Pittsburgh)
PITTSBURGH POST—GAZETTE
50 Blvd of the Allies, Pittsburgh, PA 15222
412-263-1397; FAX 412-471-1981

Newspaper Group: Block Newspapers
Access: Call for appointment.
Online Databases: Datatimes; NEXIS.
Personnel
Librarian — Angelika R. Kane, SLA

465 Pennsylvania (Pottsville)
POTTSVILLE REPUBLICAN
111-113 Mahantongo St, Pottsville, PA 17901
717-622-3456; FAX 717-628-6092

Hours: Mon—Fri 8—4
Access: Open to other media.
Personnel
Librarian — Joanne Gretsky

466 Pennsylvania (Primos, Upper Darby Township)
DELAWARE COUNTY DAILY TIMES
500 Mildred Ave, Primos, PA 19018 — See Banner
610-622-8849; FAX 610-622-8887

Newspaper founded: 1876; library founded: 1952.
Hours: Mon—Fri 8—4
Days Not Published: Saturday.
Access: Open to public and other special libraries by appointment.
Services to Other News Libraries: Telephone reference.
Archival Systems: Stauffer Gold.
Resources: Photo files, negatives, clippings since 1952, bound volumes since 1957, microfilm since 1876.
Personnel
Librarian — Barbara Budgick, SLA

467 Pennsylvania (Reading)
READING TIMES / EAGLE
345 Penn St (PO Box 582), Reading, PA 19603
610-371-5000; FAX 610-371-5194

Access: Open to other media.
News Databases: Datatimes.
Online Databases: Datatimes.
Personnel
Librarian — Margaret Gannon, (5077)

468 Pennsylvania (Scranton)
SCRANTON TIMES
149 Penn Ave, Scranton, PA 18505 — See Banner
717-348-9100; FAX 717-348-9135

Personnel
Librarians — Frank Fox
William Hines, SLA

469 Pennsylvania (State College)
CENTRE DAILY TIMES
3400 E College Ave, State College, PA 16804
814-231-6462

Personnel
Librarian — Victoria P. Mazur, SLA

470 Pennsylvania (Stroudsburg - East Stroudsburg)
POCONO RECORD
511 Lenox St, Stroudsburg, PA 18360
717-421-3000; FAX 717-421-6284

Newspaper Group: Ottaway Newspapers, Inc.
Access: Open to other media.
Personnel
Librarian — Janice Dalman, (47)

471 Pennsylvania (Tarentum)
VALLEY NEWS DISPATCH
210 Fourth Ave, Tarentum, PA 15084 — See Banner
412-224-4321; 412-226-7787

Newspaper founded: 1904; library founded: 1978.
Newspaper Group: Gannett Newspapers
Hours: Mon—Fri 8am—1pm
Access: Open to other media.
Services to Other News Libraries: Telephone reference. Contact: Audrey Lang. Sends copies of clips for fee.
Resources: Photo files, negatives. Microforms: roll. Clippings.
Personnel
Director — Louise McCleary, (249)

472 Pennsylvania (Wilkes-Barre)
THE TIMES LEADER
15 N Main St, Wilkes-Barre, PA 18711
717-829-7220; FAX 717-829-5537

Newspaper founded: 1879; library founded: 1883.
Newspaper Group: ABC/Capital Cities Inc.
Hours: Wed—Fri 10—12
Access: Open to other media through AP; open to the public.
Services to Other News Libraries: Telephone reference.
Archival Systems: Fetch; Stauffer Gold.
Resources: Photo files, reference books, maps, pamphlet files. Microforms: roll. Clippings. Government Documents.
LAN: Yes.
Personnel
Director — Kathe Kier, (Kathyk@ccabc.com), SLA

473 Pennsylvania (Wilkes-Barre)
WILKES-BARRE CITIZENS' VOICE
75 N Washington St, Wilkes-Barre, PA 18711 — See Banner
717-821-2091; FAX 717-821-2249

Personnel
Librarian — Ann Latinski-Cadden, (2065)

474 Pennsylvania (York)
YORK DAILY RECORD
S George St (PO Box 12015), York, PA 17401
717-840-4000; FAX 717-840-2009

Founded: 1984.
Hours: Mon—Fri 12n—8pm
Access: Open to other media by appointment.
News Databases: Datatimes.
Online Databases: Datatimes.
Personnel
Librarian — Joan M. McInnis, SLA

475 Pennsylvania (York)
THE YORK DISPATCH & YORK SUNDAY NEWS
205 N George St, York, PA 17401
717-854-1575; FAX 717-843-2958

Personnel
Librarian — Cathy Diehl, (462)

476 **Rhode Island (Providence)**
PROVIDENCE JOURNAL—BULLETIN / SUNDAY JOURNAL
75 Fountain St, Providence, RI 02902 See Banner
401-277-7390; FAX 401-277-7665

Hours: Mon—Fri 6:30am—10pm
Access: Open to the public and other libraries by appointment only. Copies available via Journal clips (277-8111).
Services to Other News Libraries: Free research access and article copies.
LAN: Ethernet MAC.
Online Databases: DIALOG; Dow Jones; LEXIS/NEXIS; Prodigy; Datatimes.
News Databases: VU/TEXT using QL Systems software.
Special Collections: Journal-Bulletin Rhode Island Almanacs 1887—present; Rhode Island—History.
Personnel

Library Director	Linda Henderson, (LHENDERS@PROJO.COM), SLA
Library Assts	Patricia Pothier
	Bill Angell
	Betty Cordin
	Albert Wyss

477 **Rhode Island (Woonsocket)**
THE CALL
75 Main St (PO Box A), Woonsocket, RI 02895 See Banner
401-762-3000; FAX 401-765-0303

Newspaper founded: 1892; library founded: 1940.
Hours: Mon—Fri 4:30am—11pm by special arrangement.
Days Not Published: Christmas.
Services to Other News Libraries: No telephone reference.
Access: Open to other media. Not open to other special libraries.
Resources: Photo files, negatives, reference books, maps. Microforms: roll. Clippings.
Personnel

Director	Marie Cote, (158)

478 **South Carolina (Anderson)**
ANDERSON INDEPENDENT—MAIL
1000 Williamston Rd, Anderson, SC 29622
803-224-4321; FAX 803-260-1276

Newspaper Group: Harte-Hanks Communications, Inc.
Access: Not open to other media.
Personnel

Librarian	Willie McIntosh, (260-1274)

479 **South Carolina (Charleston)**
POST AND COURIER
134 Columbus St, Charleston, SC 29402 See Banner
803-937-5698; FAX 803-937-5696

Newspaper founded: 1803; library founded: 1965.
Hours: Mon—Fri 8am—6pm
Access: Open to other media and other special libraries.
Services to Other News Libraries: Telephone reference. Contact: M. Manning. Sends copies of clips. Fee: $1/copy; Database: $5/copy.
Home Page (URL): http://www.charleston.net.
Resources: Photo files, reference books, maps, pamphlet file. Microforms: roll, fiche, jacket. Clippings.
Archival Systems: AP Preserver; LASR; Fetch.
Online Databases: NEXIS.
Fee-Based Research: Research Fee: $50. Copies: $1. FAX: $5. Microform Copies: $5. Contact M. Manning (937-5698).
Special Collections: Charleston Historic House file; Spoleto Festival.
Personnel

Director	Mary S. Manning, (291), SLA
Photo Librarian	Lathornia Perry
Librarian	Pam Liles

480 **South Carolina (Columbia)**
THE STATE
1401 Shop Rd (PO Box 1333), Columbia, SC 29201
803-771-8534; FAX 803-771-8430

Newspaper founded: 1891; library founded: 1966.
Newspaper Group: Knight-Ridder Newspapers Inc.
Hours: Mon—Fri 8am—7pm; Sat 11:30am—7pm
Access: Open to other media and other special libraries.
Services to Other News Libraries: Telephone reference. Contact: Dargan Richards. Sends copies of clips.
Home Page (URL): http://www.infi.net/thestate.
Online Databases: SAVE; DIALOG; Datatimes.
News Databases: SAVE.
Archival Systems: Presslink Explorer Archive.
Resources: Photo files, reference books, maps, pamphlet files. Microforms: roll, fiche. Clippings.
Personnel

Director	Dargan A. Richards, (darganr@aol.com), SLA
Reference Librarian	Lee Hemphill, (8340; lhemphill@scsn.net), SLA

481 **South Carolina (Florence)**
FLORENCE MORNING NEWS
141 S Irby, Florence, SC 29501
803-669-1771; FAX 803-661-6558

Newspaper Group: Thomson Newspapers
Personnel

Librarian	Amy Dickerson

482 **South Carolina (Greenville)**
GREENVILLE NEWS
305 S Main St (PO Box 1688), Greenville, SC 29602 See Banner
864-298-4100; FAX 864-298-4846

Newspaper Group: Piedmont Newspaper Group of Gannett Co., Inc.
Hours: Mon—Fri 8—5
Access: Open to other media.
News Databases: SAVE.
Fee-Based Research: Research Fee: $125/hour. Copies: $1/page. FAX: $1/page. Microform Copies: $1/page. Prepay. Contact: Amy Dickerson (298-4158).
Personnel

Librarian	Amy Dickerson, (4158), SLA
Asst Librarian	Barbara Harlow

483 **South Carolina (Myrtle Beach)**
THE SUN NEWS
Hwy 17 By-Pass and 10th Ave N, Myrtle Beach, SC 29578
803-626-8555 / 1-800-568-1800; FAX 803-626-0356

Newspaper founded: 1961; library founded: 1975.
Newspaper Group: Knight-Ridder Newspapers Inc.
Services to Other News Libraries: Telephone reference. Sends copies of clips—fee: $1 minimum. Express mails clips. Contact Barbara Horner.
Access: Other media, other special libraries. Fee charged for clips. Open to public by appointment.
Resources: Photo files, reference books, maps, pamphlet file. Microforms: roll, fiche. Clippings.
Online Databases: DIALOG; SAVE.

THE SUN NEWS (cont'd)

Archival Systems: SAVE.
Fee-Based Research: Research Fee: $1. Copies: $1. Microform Copies: $2.
Personnel
Director — Barbara Horner, (0372), SLA

484 **South Carolina (Spartanburg)**
SPARTANBURG HERALD—JOURNAL
PO Box 1657 (189 W Main St), Spartanburg, SC 29304
864-582-4511; FAX 864-594-6350

Personnel
Librarian — Carolyn Edds, (7246), SLA

485 **South Dakota (Rapid City)**
RAPID CITY JOURNAL
507 Main St, Rapid City, SD 57701
605-394-8300

Newspaper Group: Lee Newspapers
Hours: Mon—Fri 8—5
Services to Other News Libraries: Telephone reference. Sends copies of clips. Express mails or FAX clips.
Access: Open to other media by appointment.
Personnel
Librarian — Sheri Sponder, (8409)

486 **Tennessee (Athens)**
ATHENS DAILY POST—ATHENIAN
320 S Jackson St (PO Box 340), Athens, TN 37303
423-745-5664; FAX 423-745-8295

Personnel
Librarian — Allene Sykes

487 **Tennessee (Chattanooga)**
CHATTANOOGA FREE PRESS
400 E 11th St, Chattanooga, TN 37401
423-756-6900; FAX 423-757-6337

Home Page (URL): http://www.chatpub.com; www.chatfreepress.com; www.chattimes.com.
Archival Systems: PhotoView.
CD ROM: Yes.
LAN: Yes.
WAN: Yes.
Personnel
Librarian — Jackie Punneo, (jpunneo@chatpub.mindspring.com)
Systems — Jim Hazard, (jhazard@chatpub.mindspring.com)

488 **Tennessee (Chattanooga)**
CHATTANOOGA TIMES
100 E 10th St (PO Box 951), Chattanooga, TN 37401 — See Banner
423-756-1234; FAX 423-752-3364

Year established: 1963.
Hours: Mon—Fri 9:30am—6:30pm
Services to Other News Libraries: Telephone reference. Sends copies of clips. Fee: postage plus 10c/copy. Requirements: date of articles.
Access: Not open to other media or other special libraries unless special arrangements are made in advance.
Home Page (URL): http://www.chattimes.com.
Resources: Photo files, negatives, reference books, maps, pamphlet files.
Archival Systems: PhotoView; NewsView.
CD ROM: Yes.
Fee-Based Research: Copies: $1. FAX: $1. Invoice. Contact: Mary Cook (752-3320) Microforms: roll. Newspaper index, clippings.
Personnel
Director — Mary Cook, (320; mcook@chattimes.mindspring.com), SLA

489 **Tennessee (Clarksville)**
CLARKSVILLE LEAF—CHRONICLE
200 Commerce St (PO Box 829), Clarksville, TN 37040
615-552-1808; FAX 615-648-8001

Newspaper Group: Multimedia Newspapers
Hours: Mon—Fri 8—5
Access: Open to other media by appointment.
Personnel
Librarian — Julie Bartosch, (274), SLA

490 **Tennessee (Cleveland)**
CLEVELAND DAILY BANNER
1505 25th St NW, Cleveland, TN 37311
423-472-5041; FAX 423-476-1046

Newspaper Group: Walls Newspapers
Personnel
Librarian — Mary Matthews

491 **Tennessee (Jackson)**
THE JACKSON SUN
245 W Lafayette, Jackson, TN 38301
901-427-3333; FAX 901-425-9639

Personnel
Librarian — Barbara Borner

492 **Tennessee (Johnson City)**
JOHNSON CITY PRESS
204 W Main St (PO Box 1717), Johnson City, TN 37605-1717 — See Banner
615-929-3111; FAX 615-929-7484

Newspaper founded: 1935; library founded: 1950.
Newspaper Group: Carl A. Jones Enterprises
Hours: Mon—Fri 8am—5pm
Days Not Published: Christmas.
Services to Other News Libraries: Telephone reference. Sends copies of clips. Research Fee: $25/hr. Express mails clips. Contact Phyllis Brown.
Access: Open to other media, other special libraries. Not open for academic research.
Resources: Photo files, negatives, reference books, maps, pamphlet file. Microforms: roll, fiche. Newspaper index, clippings.
Personnel
Librarian — Phyllis J. Brown, (395), SLA
Secretary — Lynn Jennings, (385)

493 **Tennessee (Kingsport)**
KINGSPORT TIMES—NEWS
701 Lynn Garden Dr (PO Box 479), Kingsport, TN 37662
423-246-8121; FAX 423-392-1385

Newspaper Group: Sandusky-Norwalk Newspapers
Personnel
Librarian — Kim Absher

494 **Tennessee (Knoxville)**
KNOXVILLE NEWS—SENTINEL
204 W Church Ave, Knoxville, TN 37950-9038
615-523-3131; FAX 615-521-8186

Newspaper Group: Scripps-Howard
Access: Call librarian.
Online Databases: Datatimes.
Personnel
Librarians — Shirley Carter, SLA; Anna L. Elkins
Asst Librarian — Julia Shaver

495 **Tennessee (Memphis)**
THE COMMERCIAL APPEAL
495 Union Ave, Memphis, TN 38103
901-529-2781; FAX 901-529-6460

Library founded: 1986.
Newspaper Group: Scripps-Howard

THE COMMERCIAL APPEAL (cont'd)

Hours: Mon—Thur 9—9; Fri, Sat 9am—6pm
Access: Open to other media (ad hoc) with approval from Library Director and Managing Editor only.
Archival Systems: Fetch; MacArchive.
CD ROM: Census; Magazine Article Summaries; PhoneDisc Reverse; Contemporary Authors.
Services to Other News Libraries: Telephone reference. Sends copies of clips. Express mail charged to requesting library.
Resources: Reference books, photos, maps, pamphlets, government documents, microfilm (rolls), clips, CD-ROMS; Macintosh index of stories 1986—1990.
News Databases: SAVE.
LAN: Macintosh Network.
Online Databases: DIALOG; Dow Jones; LEXIS/NEXIS; Datatimes; CompuServe; CDB Infotek.
Personnel

Director	Rosemary W. Nelms, (rnelms@delphi.com), SLA
Asst Director	Gregory J. Paraham, SLA
Reference Librarians	Janet D. Smith, SLA
	Shirley Sykes
Library Assts	Carolyn Kent
	Teri Hayslett

496 **Tennessee (Morristown)**
MORRISTOWN CITIZEN TRIBUNE
1609 W 1st North St (PO Box 625), Morristown, TN 37814
423-581-5630; FAX 423-581-3061

Hours: Mon—Fri 8—5
Access: Not open to other media.
Personnel

Librarian	Lillie Moore, (376)

497 **Tennessee (Nashville)**
COUNTRY MUSIC FOUNDATION—
Library and Media Center
4 Music Square E, Nashville, TN 37203
615-256-1639; FAX 615-255-2245

Personnel

Librarian	Linda P. Gross, (Lindapearl@delphi.com), SLA

498 **Tennessee (Nashville)**
FREEDOM FORUM—
First Amendment Center
1207 18th Avenue S, Nashville, TN 37212
615-321-9588; FAX 615-321-9599

499 **Tennessee (Nashville)**
NASHVILLE BANNER
1100 Broadway, Nashville, TN 37203 — See Banner
615-259-8800; FAX 615-259-8890

Newspaper founded: 1876; library founded: 1940.
Hours: Mon—Fri 6am—5pm
Services to Other News Libraries: Telephone reference. FAX copies of clips.
Archival Systems: LASR; PaperDesk.
Online Databases: LEXIS/NEXIS; Datatimes.
Personnel

Librarian	Sally Moran
Editor of Information	Tammy Binford, (75VW36A@prodigy.com)

500 **Tennessee (Nashville)**
THE TENNESSEAN
1100 Broadway, Nashville, TN 37202
615-742-7504; FAX 615-259-8093

Newspaper Group: Gannett Newspapers
Hours: Mon—Fri 8am—5pm
Access: Not open to the public.
Services to Other News Libraries: Telephone reference to other newspapers. $50 research fee (no fee for other media or special libraries).
News Databases: SII.
Online Databases: Datatimes; LEXIS/NEXIS.
Personnel

Head Librarian	Annette Morrison, SLA
Asst Librarians	Nancy St. Cyr, (8000)
	Glenda Washam
	Chantay Steptoe
Database Info	Lisa Green, (726-8968)

501 **Tennessee (Nashville)**
VANDERBILT UNIVERSITY—
Television News Archive
Nashville, TN 37203

Home Page (URL): gopher://tvnews.vanderbilt.edu:70/1.

502 **Texas (Abilene)**
ABILENE REPORTER—NEWS
100 Cypress (PO Box 30), Abilene, TX 79604 — See Banner
915-673-4271; FAX 915-673-1901

Newspaper Group: Harte-Hanks Communications, Inc.
Hours: Mon—Fri 8:30am—4:30pm
Services to Other News Libraries: Telephone reference. FAX copies of clips.
Access: Open to other media by appointment.
Resources: Photo files, clippings.
Personnel

Librarian	Anne Holland, (418)

503 **Texas (Amarillo)**
AMARILLO DAILY NEWS / GLOBE TIMES
900 Harrison St (PO Box 2091), Amarillo, TX 79166
806-376-4488; FAX 806-373-0810

Newspaper Group: Morris Communications Corp.
Hours: Mon—Fri 8am—5pm
Access: Open to other media by appointment.
Personnel

Librarians	Tanya Sterling, (3447)
	Kim Hudson, (3331)
	Kristi Langood, (3330)

504 **Texas (Austin)**
AUSTIN AMERICAN—STATESMAN
PO Box 670 (305 S Congress Ave), Austin, TX 78767 — See Banner
512-445-3676; FAX 512-445-3679

Newspaper founded: 1871; library founded: 1975.
Newspaper Group: Cox Enterprises
Hours: Mon—Fri 7:30am—12m; Sat, Sun 10am—12m
Online Databases: Datatimes; LEXIS/NEXIS; SmartLine BBS.
Archival Systems: NewsView; MacArchive.
CD ROM: Yes.
LAN: Yes.
Services to Other News Libraries: Telephone reference. Contact Denise Bortolussi. Sends copies of clips. Fee: 25c/page with $5 minimum charge. Requirements: Deposit for large amount of clips. Express mails clips at requestor's expense.
Access: Open to other media by appointment only; material to be used in library. Open to other special libraries/qualified researchers/writers by permission from Editor, Managing Editor or Asst Managing Editor.
Resources: Photo files, reference books, maps. Microforms: film. Newspaper index, clippings.

AUSTIN AMERICAN—STATESMAN (cont'd)

Personnel

Librarians	Renay Bowles
	Jennifer Coffey
	Lois Craigie
	Cathy Fudala
	Jalyn Mask
	Scott Uhlaender

505 **Texas (Beaumont)**
BEAUMONT ENTERPRISE
380 Walnut St (PO Box 3071), Beaumont, TX 77704
409-833-3311; FAX 409-838-2857

Newspaper Group: Jefferson-Pilot Publications, Inc.
Personnel

Librarian	Jeanne Walls

506 **Texas (Big Spring)**
BIG SPRING HERALD
710 Scurry, Big Spring, TX 79720
915-263-7331; FAX 915-264-7205

Newspaper Group: American Publishing
Access: Open to other media by appointment.
Personnel

Librarian	Gina Garza, (111)

507 **Texas (Clute)**
BRAZOSPORT FACTS
720 S Main (PO Box 549), Clute, TX 77531-0549 — See Banner
409-265-7411; FAX 409-265-9052/265-2213

Newspaper founded: 1913; library founded: 1980.
Newspaper Group: Southern Newspapers, Inc.
Hours: Mon—Fri 8am—5pm
Access: Other media libraries, other Special Libraries.
Services to Other News Libraries: Telephone reference. Sends copies of clips. Will express mail clips if account number supplied. Contact Margaret Rice.
Resources: Photo files, negatives, reference books, maps. Microforms: roll. Clippings.
Archival Systems: Stauffer Gold.
Fee-Based Research: Call for information.
Personnel

Director	Margaret R. Rice, (ext 263), SLA

508 **Texas (Corpus Christi)**
CORPUS CHRISTI CALLER—TIMES
820 Lower North Broadway, Corpus Christi, TX 78401 — See Banner
512-884-2011; FAX 512-886-3732

Newspaper Group: Harte-Hanks Communications, Inc.
Hours: Mon—Fri 10am—5pm (public); Sat 9am—7pm (staff)
Access: Open to public by appointment only.
Home Page (URL): http://www.wtr.com/cchome.
Archival Systems: Stauffer Gold.
Fee-Based Research: Research fee: $25. Copies: $1. FAXing and microform copies: $5 + $1/ page. Prepay.
Personnel

News Info Ctr Manager	Margaret Jane Neu, (886-4312; mneu@intcomm.net), SLA

509 **Texas (Dallas)**
DALLAS MORNING NEWS
Communications Center, Dallas, TX 75265 — See Banner
214-977-8222; FAX 214-977-8957; Email: dmnlib@mail.airmail.net

Newspaper founded: 1885; library founded: 1917.
Hours: Mon—Fri 7:30am—12m; Sat 9am—12m; Sun 1pm—12m
Access: Open to other new media by appointment (can perform only short searches of clip files (Mon—Fri 9:30am—12m; Sat, Sun 3:30pm—12m. No FAX requests accepted. Open to other special libraries—to be cleared by appropriate editor.
Home Page (URL): http://www.pic.NET/TOMN.html.
Online Databases: DIALOG; Dow Jones; Datatimes; LEXIS/NEXIS.
News Databases: BASIS.
Electronic Clipping Files: Datatimes
Services to Other News Libraries: Telephone reference. Sends copies of clips after request is approved. Requirements: Limited number of clips. Express mails clips—requestor's expense.
Fee-Based Research: Research fee: $80. Copies, FAX, Microform Copies. Contact: Newsource (977-7777). Not part of library.
Resources: Photo files, reference books, maps, pamphlet files. Microforms: roll, fiche. Newspaper index, clippings.
Special Collections: Texana Collection (not loaned).
Personnel

Reference Editor	Judy Sall, (8953), SLA
Text Librarian	Carmela Copeland, (8952), SLA
Photo Librarian	Jerome Sims, (8955), SLA
Night Librarian	T. Alan Doss, (8950)

510 **Texas (Del Rio)**
DEL RIO NEWS—HERALD
321 S Main St (PO Box 4020), Del Rio, TX 78840 — See Banner
210-775-1551; FAX 210-774-2610

Newspaper founded: 1929; library founded: 1978.
Newspaper Group: Thomson Newspapers
Hours: Mon—Fri 8am—5pm; Sat 8am—12n
Services to Other News Libraries: Telephone reference. FAX copies of clips.
Access: Not open to other media or other special libraries.
Resources: Photo files, negatives. Microforms: roll. Newspaper index, Clippings.
Personnel

Director	Rosa Delgado, (229)

511 **Texas (Denison)**
DENISON HERALD
329 W Woodward, Denison, TX 75020
903-465-7171; FAX 903-465-7188

Newspaper Group: Donrey Media Group
Personnel

Librarian	Teena Byington

512 **Texas (Denton)**
DENTON RECORD—CHRONICLE
Box 369, Denton, TX 76202
817-381-9597; FAX 817-381-9666

Personnel

Librarian	Julie Lehman

513 **Texas (El Paso)**
EL PASO HERALD—POST
300 N Campbell, El Paso, TX 79901
915-546-6263

Newspaper Group: Scripps-Howard
Hours: Mon—Fri 7am—9pm
Access: Open to other media by appointment.
Personnel

Librarian	Leslie Trich Humble
Library Assts	Sandra DeLaCruz
	Liz Royer

514 **Texas (El Paso)**
EL PASO TIMES
300 N Campbell, El Paso, TX 79901
915-546-6179

Newspaper founded: 1881.
Newspaper Group: Gannett Newspapers
Hours: Mon—Fri 8—5
Services to Other News Libraries: Telephone reference. Express mails clips—bill recipient.
Access: Open to other media/other special libraries.
Personnel

Librarian	Leslie Trich Humble
Library Assts	Sandra DeLaCruz
	Liz Royer

515 **Texas (Fort Worth)**
FORT WORTH STAR—TELEGRAM
400 W 7th St, Fort Worth, TX 76102
817-390-7742; FAX 817-390-7255; Email: fwstlib@class.org

Newspaper Group: Capital Cities Communications Inc.
Hours: 8am—5pm
Access: Open to other media/other special libraries. Closed to the public.
Archival Systems: EyeQ Publisher; Basis.
LAN: Yes.
Online Databases: Datatimes; Dow Jones; NewsBank.
Services to Other News Libraries: Telephone reference. Sends copies of clips (less than 5). Express mails clips with requestor's account number. Contact Janice Fennell.
Resources: Photo files, negatives, reference books. Microforms: roll, fiche. Clippings.
Personnel

Head Librarian	Janice C. Fennell, (7741), SLA

516 **Texas (Galveston)**
GALVESTON DAILY NEWS
8522 Teichman Rd, Galveston, TX 77553
409-744-3611; FAX 409-740-3421

Personnel

Librarian	Calvin Whitner, (247)

517 **Texas (Houston)**
HOUSTON CHRONICLE
801 Texas Ave (PO Box 4260), Houston, TX 77210
713-220-7171; FAX 713-220-7275

Newspaper founded: 1901; library founded: 1961.
Newspaper Group: Hearst Newspapers
Hours: Mon—Fri 7:30am—10:45pm
Access: Open to other newspaper libraries; open to other special libraries and other newspapers.
Services to Other News Libraries: Telephone reference (contact: Sherry Adams). Sends copies of clips. Express mail clips. Requirements: Federal Express account number needed. FAX copies of clips.
Online Databases: Datatimes; DIALOG; NewsNet; NEXIS.
News Databases: BASIS.
Electronic Clipping Files: Datatimes; NEXIS
CD ROM: NewsBank; Houston Chronicle; New York Times; Dallas Morning News; Austin American—Statesman.
Resources: Photo files, negatives, reference books, pamphlet files. Microforms: roll, fiche. Clippings.
Personnel

Librarian	Sherry Adams, (7312; sherry.adams@chron.com), SLA
Asst Librarian	Melissa Mantel, (7313; melissa.mante@chron.com), SLA
Photo Sales	Jo Gutierrez, (7314)

518 **Texas (Houston)**
TAFT BROADCASTING—
US National Aeronautical Space Administration
16441 Space Center Blvd Bldg A, Houston, TX 77058
713-483-6923

Personnel

Librarian	Kathryn I. Claus

519 **Texas (Jacksonville)**
JACKSONVILLE DAILY PROGRESS
201 Austin St, Jacksonville, TX 75766
903-586-2236; FAX 903-586-0987

Newspaper Group: Donrey Media Group
Personnel

Librarian	Pat Jackson

520 **Texas (Lubbock)**
LUBBOCK AVALANCHE JOURNAL
8th St and Ave J (PO Box 491), Lubbock, TX 79408
806-762-8844; FAX 806-744-9603

Newspaper Group: Morris Communications Corp.
Access: Open to other media by appointment.
Personnel

Librarians	Bobbie Morelle
	Ruth Alexander

521 **Texas (Port Arthur)**
PORT ARTHUR NEWS
549 4th St, Port Arthur, TX 77640
409-985-5541; FAX 409-985-6128

Newspaper Group: American Publishing
Access: Not open to other media.
Personnel

Librarian	Voletta Collins, (122)

522 **Texas (San Angelo)**
SAN ANGELO STANDARD—TIMES
PO Box 5111, San Angelo, TX 76902
915-653-1221 ext 210

Newspaper Group: Harte-Hanks Communications, Inc.
Hours: Mon—Fri 8am—5pm
Services to Other News Libraries: Limited research service on a time-available basis. $2/search fee. 75c/photocopies. $1/microfilm copies.
Access: Open to the public and other libraries (see above).
Personnel

Chief Librarian	Suzanne M. Perry, SLA
Librarian	Edna A. Sedeno

523 **Texas (San Antonio)**
SAN ANTONIO EXPRESS—NEWS
Ave E and 3rd St, San Antonio, TX 78205
210-225-7411; FAX 210-225-8351

Newspaper Group: Hearst Newspapers
Access: Open to other media by appointment.
Online Databases: LEXIS/NEXIS; Datatimes.
Personnel

Librarians	Judith Zipp
	Kathy Foley

524 **Texas (Temple)**
TEMPLE DAILY TELEGRAM
10 S Third St (PO Box 6114), Temple, TX 76501 See Banner
817-778-4444

Newspaper founded: 1907; library founded: 1907.
Hours: Mon—Fri 8am—3:30pm
Access: Open to public by appointment only.

TEMPLE DAILY TELEGRAM (cont'd)

Services to Other News Libraries: Telephone reference. Contact: Steve Walters. Sends copies of clips. Fee: $1.50.

Personnel

Managing Editor	Steve Walters
Library Clerk	Mary Lopez

525 **Texas (Texarkana)**
TEXARKANA GAZETTE
313-17 Pine St, Texarkana, TX 75501
903-794-3311; FAX 903-794-3310

Access: Open to other media by appointment.

Personnel

Librarian	Ruth Evans, (7257)

526 **Texas (Waco)**
WACO TRIBUNE—HERALD
900 Franklin (PO Box 2588), Waco, TX 76702
817-757-5757; FAX 817-756-6906; Email: LET@Wacotrib.jetbbs.com

Newspaper founded: 1892; library founded: 1980.
Newspaper Group: Cox Enterprises
Hours: Mon—Fri 8:30am—5:30pm
Services to Other News Libraries: Telephone reference. FAX copies of clips.
Access: Open to other media by appointment; each request will be determined individually.
Resources: Photo files, negatives, reference books, maps, pamphlet file. Microforms: roll, fiche, jackets. Newspaper index, clippings.

Personnel

Chief Librarian	Colleen Curran, (5725)

527 **Texas (Wichita Falls)**
WICHITA FALLS TIMES RECORD NEWS
1301 Lamar St (PO Box 120), Wichita Falls, TX 76307
817-767-8341

Newspaper Group: Harte-Hanks Communications, Inc.
Hours: Mon—Fri 8:30—5:30
Access: Open to other media by appointment.

Personnel

Librarian	Edith Bosche, (545)

528 **Utah (Ogden)**
STANDARD—EXAMINER
455-23rd St, Ogden, UT 84401
801-394-7711; FAX 801-625-4299

Newspaper Group: Sandusky Newspapers
Access: Not open to other media.

Personnel

Librarian	Kim Perrin, (625-4236)

529 **Utah (Salt Lake City)**
DESERET NEWS
30 E 100 South (PO Box 1257), Salt Lake City, UT 84110
801-237-2155; FAX 801-237-2121

Hours: Mon—Fri 8—5
Home Page (URL): http://www.desnews.com.
Online Databases: SAVE.
News Databases: SAVE.
Archival Systems: SAVE; Fetch.
Fee-Based Research: Research Fee: $50. Copies: $.50. FAX: $2. Microform Copies: $2. Contact colleen Randall (237-2155).

Personnel

Library Manager	Colleen Randall, SLA
Systems Manager	Dave Croft, (2134)
Dir/Online Svcs	Stewart Shelline, (2139; stewart@desnews.com)

530 **Utah (Salt Lake City)**
SALT LAKE TRIBUNE
143 South Main St (PO Box 867), Salt Lake City, UT 84110 — See Banner
801-237-2001; FAX 801-521-9418

Newspaper founded: 1871.
Hours: Mon—Fri 9:30am—5:30pm
Home Page (URL): http://www.sltrib.com.
Archival Systems: PhotoView.
Services to Other News Libraries: Telephone reference. FAX copies of clips.
Access: Open to other newspapers by appointment.
Resources: Photo files, reference books, maps, pamphlet files. Microforms: roll. Newspaper index, clippings. Database to Sept. 91 (full text).
Online Databases: Datatimes; NEXIS.

Personnel

Librarians	Anna Daraban, (2002), SLA
	Becky Hodges
	Linda Hardy
	Antonio Ramirez

531 **Vermont (Burlington)**
BURLINGTON FREE PRESS
191 College St, Burlington, VT 05401
802-863-3441; FAX 802-660-1802

Newspaper Group: Gannett Newspapers
Hours: Mon—Fri 9—6
Access: Open to other media by appointment.
News Databases: NewsView.
Online Databases: Grateful Med; LEXIS/NEXIS.

Personnel

Librarian	Susan Keeler, (660-1872)

532 **Virginia (Arlington)**
FREEDOM FORUM WORLD CENTER
1101 Wilson Blvd, Arlington, VA 22209
703-528-0800; FAX 703-522-4831

Personnel

Staff	Christine Wells, (284-2860; CWELL@freedomforum.org) SLA
	Phyllis Lyons, (LYONS@ TFFWC.MHS.CompuServe. COM (Phyllis Lyons)

533 **Virginia (Arlington)**
USA TODAY
1000 Wilson Blvd, Arlington, VA 22229 — See Banner
Reference 703-276-5588; FAX 703-247-3139

Newspaper founded: 1982; library founded: 1982.
Newspaper Group: Gannett Newspapers
Hours: Mon—Thur 9am—12m; Fri 9am—6pm; Sun 10am—12m
Days Not Published: Saturday, Sunday.
Home Page (URL): http://www.usatoday.com.
CD ROM: NY Times; Thomas' Register; Prophone; Gates Quotations; LA Times; WSJ; Washington Post; Reader's Guide.
Online Databases: NEXIS; DIALOG; Datatimes; Burrelle's plus in-house Data Base; WESTLAW; Washington Alert.
News Databases: PLS.
Services to Other News Libraries: Telephone requests.
Resources: Photo files, negatives, reference books, magazines, newspapers, maps, pamphlet files. Microforms: roll, fiche. Newspaper index, clippings.
Archival Systems: AP Preserver.
LAN: Yes.

USA TODAY (cont'd)

Fee-Based Research: Research Fee: $85/hour. Copies: $10.50. FAX: $5. Microform Copies: $10.50. Prepay or invoice. Contact Ruth Fogle (276-5835).

Personnel

Director	Barbara Maxwell, (3797; bellenb@cligex.access.net), SLA
Asst Director	Jeanette Brown, (5592), SLA
Librarians	Gini Blodgett, SLA
	Teresa Campbell
	Tristan Coffelt
	Lynette Constantinides
	Ruth Fogle
	Joe Hagarty
	Raymond Hicks
	Clarencetta Jelks
	Lisa Leevy-Washington
	George Mitchell
	JoAnn Mzil
	Susan O'Brian
	Mary Priestland
	Bruce Rosenstein
	Arabella Stewart-Stern
	Jean Sudlow
	Angela Titone
	Tish Wells

534 **Virginia (Covington)**
COVINGTON VIRGINIAN
343 Monroe Ave, Covington, VA 24426
703-962-2121

Personnel

Librarian	Mary Lamb

535 **Virginia (Lynchburg)**
THE NEWS AND DAILY ADVANCE
101 Wyndale Dr, Lynchburg, VA 24501
804-237-2941

Newspaper Group: Worrell Newspapers, Inc.

Personnel

Librarian	Gloria Staples

536 **Virginia (Martinsville)**
MARTINSVILLE BULLETIN
204 Broad St, Martinsville, VA 24115
703-638-8801

Personnel

Librarian	Sue Carter

537 **Virginia (Newport News)**
NEWPORT NEWS DAILY PRESS
7505 Warwick Blvd, Newport News, VA 23607 — See Banner
804-247-4882; FAX 804-247-4881

Newspaper founded: Daily Press: 1898; Times Herald: 1901; library founded: 1961.
Hours: Mon—Fri 8am—10pm; Sat, Sun 4pm—10pm
Access: Open to other media, academic, special libraries by appointment.
Services to Other News Libraries: Telephone reference. Sends copies of clips. Fee varies.
Home Page (URL): http://www.xso.com/dailypress/taste/htm; http://www.xso.com/dailypress.dproo.htm.
CD ROM: Yes.
LAN: Yes.
Online Databases: DIALOG; SAVE.
News Databases: TEQLIB; SAVE.
Resources: Photo files, negatives, reference books, maps, pamphlet files. Microforms: roll, fiche. Newspaper index, clippings.
Fee-Based Research: Research fee: $60. Copies, FAX, Microform Copies: $1. Invoice. Contact Melissa Simpson.
Archival Systems: Digital Link Gateway; AP Preserver; Fetch.

Personnel

Library Manager	Melissa Simpson, (melissa400@aol.com), SLA
Senior Librarian	Elizabeth Joines

538 **Virginia (Norfolk)**
VIRGINIAN—PILOT AND LEDGER—STAR
150 W Brambleton Ave, Norfolk, VA 23510 — See Banner
804-446-2240; FAX 804-446-2974

Newspaper founded: 1865; library founded: 1947.
Newspaper Group: Landmark Communications, Inc.
Hours: Mon—Fri 7:30am—8pm
Days Not Published: Christmas
Services to Other News Libraries: Telephone reference. Contact: Ann Kinken Johnson. Sends copies of clips. Fee: $1/page. Fee waived on small requests.
Access: Open to other media; permission in advance. No free lancers. Open to other special libraries.
Resources: Photo files, negatives, reference books, maps, pamphlet files. Microforms: roll. Newspaper index, clippings.
Online Databases: DIALOG; Datatimes; NEXIS.

Personnel

Director	Ann Kinken Johnson, SLA
Asst Librarian	Clara P. Basnight, (2242), SLA

539 **Virginia (Reston)**
NEWSPAPER ASSOCIATION OF AMERICA (NAA)
11600 Sunrise Valley Dr, Reston, VA 22091
703-648-1090; FAX 703-648-1092; Email: NAAINFO@attmail.com

Hours: Mon—Fri 9am—5pm
Access: Open to other media/special libraries. Open to public by appointment.
Services to Other News Libraries: Telephone reference. Sends copies of clips. Will express mail clips. Requirements: Limited to 12 pages.
Home Page (URL): http://www.infi.net/naa.
Resources: Books, reports, serials. Microforms: roll, fiche. Clippings.
CD ROM: Editor & Publisher; Standard & Poor's; Newsbank; ABI Inform; F&S Index
Fee-Based Research: Research Fee: $100. Copies: $.10/page. FAX: $.25 (first 5 free). Microform Copies: $.25. Prepay. Contact: Sharon Wray (648-1091).
Special Collections: Books, pamphlets, clippings on newspaper publishing, plus selected holdings in related fields of journalism, advertising, telecommunications and broadcasting; History of Newspaper publishing in the US.

Personnel

Director	Belida LaBarbera, (NAANETWORK!NAA!BILIS@NAAATT.ATTMAIL.COM)
Manager	Sharon Wray, (NAANETWORK!NAA!WRAYS@NAAATT.ATTMAIL.COM)
Information Spec	Katherine LaVallee, (NAANETWORK!NAA!LAVAK@NAAATT.ATTMAIL.COM)
Info Center Asst	Suzanne Bilinski, (NAANETWORK!NAA!BILIS@NAAATT.ATTMAIL.COM)

540 **Virginia (Richmond)**
RICHMOND TIMES—DISPATCH
333 E Grace St, Richmond, VA 23219
804-649-6000/ Research 804-649-6224; FAX 804-649-6848

Newspaper Group: Media General, Inc.
Online Databases: SAVE; Datatimes; DIALOG; Dow Jones.
News Databases: SAVE.
Access: Open to other media/other special libraries/ public.
Personnel
Librarian — Charles Saunders, (6286), SLA

541 **Virginia (Roanoke)**
THE ROANOKE TIMES
201 W Campbell Ave (PO Box 2491), Roanoke, VA 24011 — See Banner
540-981-3279; FAX 540-981-3346

Year founded: Times—1886; World News—1889; library founded: 1956.
Newspaper Group: Landmark Communications, Inc.
Hours: Mon—Fri 8am—5pm
Services to Other News Libraries: Telephone reference. Sends copies of clips. Express mails clips with recipients billing number. FAX.
Access: Open to other media/other special libraries. 50c/page photocopies; $2/page copies from film or fiche.
Home Page (URL): http://www.infi.net/roatimes.
Online Databases: Datatimes; NEXIS; Dow Jones.
Archival Systems: SAVE.
LAN: Yes.
Resources: Photo files, reference books, maps, pamphlet file. Microforms: roll, fiche. Clippings.
News Databases: SAVE.
Fee-Based Research: Copies: $.50. Microform Copies: $2.
Personnel
Chief Librarian — Belinda J. Harris, (3280; belin39255@aol.com), SLA
Library Clerk — Steven Urquhart

542 **Virginia (Springfield)**
TIMES JOURNAL CO.
6883 Commercial Drive, Springfield, VA 22159 — See Banner
703-750-8696

News Databases: QL Systems.
Services to Other News Libraries: Telephone reference. Contact: Patricia White-Williams. Sends copies of clips. Fee: 20c/page. Requirements: Small staff limits what we can do.
Access: Open to other media and other special libraries.
Resources: Photo files, reference books. Microforms: roll, fiche, jackets. Newspaper index, clippings.
Personnel
Librarian — Patricia White-Williams, (8007), SLA

543 **Washington (Bellevue)**
JOURNAL—AMERICAN
1705 132 Ave NE, Bellevue, WA 98005
206-453-4249; FAX 206-635-0603

Newspaper Group: Horwitz Newspapers
Hours: Mon—Fri 9am—6pm
Access: Not open to public and other libraries but will give quick information over the phone and answer questions.
Archival Systems: NewsView; PhotoView; Software Folio.
Services to Other News Libraries: We sell copies of photographs taken by our staff. Fee: $15/print.
Personnel
Librarian — Renee Valois, (4249), SLA

544 **Washington (Bellingham)**
BELLINGHAM HERALD
1155 N State St (PO Box 1277), Bellingham, WA 98225 — See Banner
360-676-2620; FAX 360-647-9260; Email: herald@3.com

Newspaper founded: 1890; library founded: 1978.
Newspaper Group: A.M. Publications
Hours: Mon—Fri 8:30am—4pm
Services to Other News Libraries: Telephone reference. Contact: Carole Teshima Morris.
Access: Open to other media and libraries, limited.
Archival Systems: Gannett Archivist; Kudo Image Browser.
Fee-Based Research: Limited Copies. FAX. Microform Copies.
Special Collections: Local History.
Personnel
Director — Carole Teshima Morris, (283), SLA

545 **Washington (Bremerton)**
BREMERTON SUN
545 Fifth St (PO Box 259), Bremerton, WA 98337
360-377-3711; FAX 360-479-7681; Email: SunNews@aol.com

Newspaper Group: John P. Scripps Newspapers Group
Hours: 9—5
Access: Not open to other media.
Archival Systems: Stauffer Gold.
LAN: Yes.
Personnel
Librarian — Deb Smith

546 **Washington (Centralia - Chehalis)**
THE CHRONICLE
PO Box 580, Centralia, WA 98531
360-736-3311; FAX 360-736-4796

Access: Open to other media by appointment.
Personnel
Librarian — Linda Stewart, (254)

547 **Washington (Everett)**
THE HERALD
Grand and California, Everett, WA 98201
206-339-3000; FAX 206-339-3049

Newspaper Group: Washington Post Co.
Personnel
Librarian — Jenetta Rose Coffin, (3479)

548 **Washington (Longview)**
THE DAILY NEWS
770 11th Ave (PO Box 189), Longview, WA 98632 — See Banner
360-577-2511; FAX 360-577-2536

Newspaper founded: 1923; library founded: 1953.
Hours: Mon—Fri 8am—12n
Days Not Published: Christmas, Sunday
Services to Other News Libraries: Telephone reference. Contact: Donna Yardley. Sends copies of clips. Fee: $1/copy plus tax and postage. Requirements: fee in advance.
News Databases: Sonar Professional.
Access: Open to other media with publisher's permission. Must do own research in extensive requests. Open to other special libraries.
Resources: Photo files, reference books, maps, pamphlet files. Clippings.
Personnel
Librarian — Donna Yardley

549 **Washington (Olympia)**
THE OLYMPIAN
1268 4th Ave E (PO Box 407), Olympia, WA 98507
360-754-5400; FAX 360-357-0202; Email: olympian@halcyon.com

Hours: 8—4
CD ROM: Yes.
Personnel
Librarians — Patricia Gennotti
Lori Buker

550 **Washington (Pasco - Kennewick - Richland)**
TRI—CITY HERALD
PO Box 2608, Tri-Cities, WA 99302
509-582-1500; FAX 509-582-1510

Newspaper Group: McClatchy Newspapers
Access: Not open to other media.
News Databases: SCS 800.
Personnel
Librarian — Donna Ball, (1530)

551 **Washington (Port Angeles)**
PENINSULA DAILY NEWS
305 W First (PO Box 1330), Port Angeles, WA 98362
360-452-2345; FAX 360-417-3521

Newspaper founded: 1916.
Newspaper Group: Horwitz Newspapers
Personnel
Librarian — Geri Zanone, (417-3527)

552 **Washington (Seattle)**
SEATTLE POST—INTELLIGENCER
101 Elliott Avenue W, Seattle, WA 98119 See Banner
206-448-8359; FAX 206-448-8166

Newspaper founded: 1863; library founded: 1926.
Newspaper Group: Hearst Newspapers
Hours: Mon—Fri 9am—11pm
Online Databases: DIALOG; SAVE; Datatimes.
News Databases: SAVE.
Electronic Clipping Files: VU/TEXT
Services to Other News Libraries: Telephone reference. FAX copies of clips.
Access: Not open to other media.
Resources: Photo files, reference books, maps, pamphlet files. Microforms: roll. Newspaper index.
Personnel
Librarian — Lytton E. Smith, (Lyttonsmith@Seattle_PI.Com), SLA

553 **Washington (Seattle)**
SEATTLE TIMES
PO Box 70, Seattle, WA 98111 See Banner
206-464-2307

Newspaper founded: 1896; library founded: 1910.
Hours: Mon—Thur 5am—11pm; Fri 5am—1am; Sat 9am—10pm; Sun 12n—11pm
Online Databases: DIALOG; NEXIS; BASIS; SAVE; Datatimes.
News Databases: Datatimes.
Services to Other News Libraries: Telephone reference. FAX copies of clips, with approval from Time's Library Manager.
Access: Open to other media on approval from Time's Library Manager. Open to other special libraries.
Resources: Photo files, reference books, maps, pamphlet files. Microforms: roll, fiche. Newspaper index, clippings.
Personnel
Database Ed — Tom Boyer
Librarian — Cathy Donaldson

554 **Washington (Spokane)**
SPOKESMAN—REVIEW
PO Box 2160, Spokane, WA 99210-1615
509-459-5528; FAX 509-459-3815

Hours: Mon—Fri 7:30am—8pm
Access: Open to visiting reporters.
Services to Other News Libraries: Clip searches; will mail clips.
Archival Systems: AP Preserver; SAVE.
CD ROM: Yes.
LAN: Yes.
Fee-Based Research: Research Fee: $50/business; $30/individuals. Copies: $1/page. FAX: $1/page. Microform Copies: $2/page. Invoice.
Online Databases: Datatimes.
Personnel
Library Supervisor — Susan W. Mulvihill, SLA
Librarians — Angie Flint, (angief@spokesman.com)
Tracy Santrop, (tracyso@spokesman.com)
Sara Lindgren, (saral@spokesman.com)
Jeanette McDonald, (jeanettem@spokesman.com)

555 **Washington (Tacoma)**
THE NEWS TRIBUNE
1950 S State St (PO Box 11000), Tacoma, WA 98411 See Banner
206-597-8511; FAX 206-597-8274

Newspaper founded: 1883; library founded: 1955.
Newspaper Group: McClatchy Newspapers
Hours: Mon—Fri 9am—5pm
Online Databases: Datatimes.
Services to Other News Libraries: Telephone reference. Sends copies of clips. Contact Pilaivan Britton.
Access: Not open to other media.
Resources: Photo files, reference books, maps, pamphlet files. Microforms: roll, fiche. Newspaper index, clippings.
Personnel
Director — Pilaivan H. Britton, (8626; PHB@P.Tribnet.Com), SLA
Library Assts — Stephanie Clark, (6049)
Lisa Love, (8629), SLA

556 **Washington (Vancouver)**
VANCOUVER COLUMBIAN NEWSPAPER
701 W 8th St (PO Box 180), Vancouver, WA 98660 See Banner
360-694-3391

Hours: Mon—Fri 8am—5pm
Home Page (URL): http://www.columbian.com.
Services to Other News Libraries: Research: $50/hour.
Access: Open to other media by appointment.
News Databases: NewsView.
Online Databases: LEXIS/NEXIS; AOL; Datatimes; Internet.
Personnel
Info Specialist — Dareth Murray, (2337), SLA
Asst Librarian — Diane Gibson, (2336; Diane.Gibso@Columbia.Com), SLA

557 **Washington (Walla Walla)**
WALLA WALLA UNION-BULLETIN
First and Poplar Sts, Walla Walla, WA 99362
509-525-3300

Newspaper founded: 1869; library founded: 1869.
Hours: Mon—Fri 8am—5pm
Days Not Published: Christmas.

WALLA WALLA UNION-BULLETIN (cont'd)

Services to Other News Libraries: Telephone reference. Will send paper when available at cost. Contact Janet Collins.
Resources: Photo files, negatives, reference books, maps. Microforms: roll, jackets. Newspaper index, clippings.
Personnel
Librarian — Janet G. Collins, (281)

558 **Washington (Wenatchee)**
WENATCHEE WORLD
14 N Mission St (PO Box 1511), Wenatchee, WA 98801
509-663-5161

Newspaper founded: 1905; library founded: 1983.
Hours: Mon—Fri 6am—2pm
Days Not Published: Christmas.
Services to Other News Libraries: Telephone reference. Contact: Linda Barta. Sends copies of clips on microfiche only. Fee: $2.50/first page; $1 each additional page.
Resources: Photo files, reference books, maps. Microforms: roll. Newspaper index, clippings.
Personnel
Librarian — Linda Barta, (229)

559 **Washington (Yakima)**
YAKIMA HERALD-REPUBLIC
PO Box 9668, Yakima, WA 98909
509-248-1251

Newspaper Group: Garden State Newspapers
Personnel
Librarian — Donean Sinsel

560 **West Virginia (Charleston)**
CHARLESTON DAILY MAIL
1001 Virginia St, Charleston, WV 25301
304-348-5140; FAX 304-348-4847; Email: curst@maim.citynet.net

Newspaper Group: Thomson Newspapers
News Databases: Documaster.
Online Databases: NEXIS.

561 **West Virginia (Charleston)**
CHARLESTON GAZETTE AND SUNDAY GAZETTE-MAIL
1001 Virginia St E, Charleston, WV 25301
304-348-5140

News Databases: Documaster.
Online Databases: NEXIS.

562 **West Virginia (Huntington)**
HUNTINGTON HERALD-DISPATCH
946 5th Ave, Huntington, WV 25701 — See Banner
304-526-4000

Newspaper Group: Gannett Newspapers
Personnel
Librarian — Patty Clay

563 **West Virginia (Parkersburg)**
PARKERSBURG NEWS AND SENTINEL
519 Juliana, Parkersburg, WV 26101
304-485-1891

Newspaper Group: Ogden Newspapers

564 **West Virginia (Welch)**
WELCH DAILY NEWS
125 Wyoming St (PO Box 569), Welch, WV 24801 — See Banner
304-436-3144

Newspaper founded: 1923; library founded: 1923.
Newspaper Group: Moffitt Newspapers
Hours: Mon—Fri 8am—5pm
Days Not Published: New Year's Day, Memorial Day, Independence Day, Labor Day, Christmas, Saturday, Sunday.
Services to Other News Libraries: Will not do telephone reference or send clips.
Access: Not open to other media.
Personnel
Director — Brenda West

565 **West Virginia (Wheeling)**
WHEELING INTELLIGENCER AND NEWS REGISTER
1500 Main St, Wheeling, WV 26003
304-233-0100

Newspaper Group: Ogden Newspapers

566 **Wisconsin (Appleton - Neenah - Menasha)**
APPLETON POST-CRESCENT
306 W Washington St (PO Box 59), Appleton, WI 54912
414-733-4411

Newspaper Group: Post Corp. Newspapers

567 **Wisconsin (Eau Claire)**
LEADER TELEGRAM
701 S Farwell St, Eau Claire, WI 54701
715-833-9208

Newspaper founded: 1881; library founded: 1980.
Hours: Mon—Fri 8am—3pm
Days Not Published: New Year's Day, Memorial Day, Independence Day, Labor Day, Christmas.
Services to Other News Libraries: Telephone reference. Sends copies of clips—fee. Contact Dale Peterson.
Access: Not open to other media/other special libraries.
Resources: Photo files, negatives, reference books, maps, pamphlet file. Clippings.
Personnel
Librarian — Dale A. Peterson, (303)

568 **Wisconsin (Green Bay)**
GREEN BAY PRESS-GAZETTE
435 E Walnut (PO Box 19430), Green Bay, WI 54307
414-435-4411

Newspaper Group: Gannett Newspapers
Personnel
Librarian — Diane Laes, (362)

569 **Wisconsin (Kenosha)**
KENOSHA NEWS
715 58th St (Caller Box 190), Kenosha, WI 53141
414-657-1000; FAX 414-657-8455

Newspaper Group: United Communications Corp.
CD ROM: Stauffer Gold. Databases: Kenosha News articles only.
Archival Systems: Fetch.
Personnel
Librarian — Michelle M. Arkens, (markens@omnifest.uwm.edu)

570 **Wisconsin (La Crosse)**
LA CROSSE TRIBUNE
401 N 3rd St, La Crosse, WI 54601

Newspaper Group: Lee Newspapers
Hours: Mon—Fri 7:30am—4pm
Access: Open to the public and other libraries.
Personnel
Librarian — Marilyn R. Walden

571 Wisconsin (Madison)
WISCONSIN STATE JOURNAL
1901 Fish Hatchery Rd (PO Box 8058), Madison, WI 53708 — See Banner
608-252-6112; FAX 608-252-6119

Newspaper founded: 1852; library founded: 1920.
Newspaper Group: Lee Newspapers
Hours: Mon—Fri 7am—6pm; Sat 7am—2:30pm
Access: Closed to public.
Services to Other News Libraries: Telephone reference. Contact: Dennis McCormick. Sends copies of clips. Fee: $1/copy. Will not express mail clips.
Resources: Photo files, negatives, reference books, maps, pamphlet file. Microforms: roll. Newspaper index, clippings.
Online Databases: DIALOG; NEXIS; Datatimes.
News Databases: SAVE.
Archival Systems: SAVE; Fetch.
Personnel

Director	Ronald Larson, (6113; rlarson@binc.net), SLA
Librarians	Dennis McCormick, (6412)
	Donna Howard
	Carol Schmitt, (6114)

572 Wisconsin (Milwaukee)
MILWAUKEE JOURNAL SENTINEL
333 W State St (PO Box 661), Milwaukee, WI 53201
414-224-2376; FAX 414-224-2388

Newspaper Group: Journal Communications
Hours: Mon—Fri 8am—12m; Sat 10am—12m; Sun 2pm—12m
Access: Very limited access to the public and other libraries.
Services to Other News Libraries: Telephone reference. Sends copies of clips.
Online Databases: Datatimes; NEXIS.
Archival Systems: LASR.
Fee-Based Research: Research fee; Copies; Microform Copies.
CD ROM: Yes.
Personnel

Manager	Rosemary Jensen, (QJKZ29C@prodigy.com), SLA

573 Wisconsin (Oshkosh)
OSHKOSH NORTHWESTERN
224 State St (PO Box 2926), Oshkosh, WI 54901
414-235-7700

574 Wisconsin (Racine)
JOURNAL—TIMES
212 4th St, Racine, WI 53403
414-634-3322; FAX 414-631-1702

Newspaper Group: Lee Newspapers
LAN: Netware.
Personnel

Librarian	Peggy A. Anderson

575 Wisconsin (Sheboygan)
SHEBOYGAN PRESS
632 Center Ave, Sheboygan, WI 53081 — See Banner
414-457-7711 / reference ext 147

Newspaper founded: 1907; library founded: 1924.
Hours: Mon—Fri 8am—5pm
Days Not Published: New Year's Day, Memorial Day, Independence Day, Labor Day, Thanksgiving, Christmas.
Services to Other News Libraries: Telephone reference. Sends copies of clips. Will express mail clips.
Resources: Photo files, negatives, reference books, maps, pamphlet file. Microforms: roll. Newspaper index, clippings.
Personnel

Director	Janice Hildebrand, (147)

576 Wisconsin (Superior)
SUPERIOR EVENING TELEGRAM
1226 Ogden Ave, Superior, WI 54880
715-394-4411

Newspaper Group: Morgan Murphy Newspapers
Personnel

Librarian	Michel Peyton

577 Wisconsin (Waukesha)
WAUKESHA FREEMAN
200 Park Pl (PO Box 7), Waukesha, WI 53187
414-542-2501

Newspaper Group: Thomson Newspapers
Personnel

Librarian	Kathleen A. Scholzen

578 Wisconsin (Wausau)
WAUSAU DAILY HERALD
800 Scott St (PO Box 1286), Wausau, WI 54401
715-842-2101 / Library 715-845-0602; FAX 715-848-9361

Newspaper Group: Gannett Newspapers
Personnel

Librarian	Debra Siburt

579 Wisconsin (Wisconsin Rapids)
WISCONSIN RAPIDS DAILY TRIBUNE
220 1st Ave So, Wisconsin Rapids, WI 54494
715-423-7200

Personnel

Librarian	Roseann Arndt, (6723)

580 Wyoming (Casper)
CASPER STAR-TRIBUNE
Box 80, Casper, WY 82602
307-266-0500

NEWS LIBRARIES CANADA

581 **Canada (Alberta - Calgary)**
CALGARY HERALD
215 16th St SE, Calgary, AB, Canada, T2P 0W8 — See Banner
403-235-7100; FAX 403-235-7379

Newspaper founded: 1883; library founded: 1950.
Newspaper Group: Southam
Hours: Mon—Fri 7am—7pm; Sat, Sun 8am—4pm
Days Not Published: New Year's Day, Labor Day, Thanksgiving, Christmas, Good Friday, Canada Day, Victoria Day.
Access: Not open to other media; open to other special library for telephone reference.
Services to Other News Libraries: Telephone reference. Will FAX copies of clips. Requirements: will send one or two clips on an issue.
Online Databases: Info Globe; QL Systems; SAVE; NEXIS; Infomart.
News Databases: Infomart.
Resources: Photo files, reference books, maps. Microforms: roll, fiche. Clippings
Personnel

Library Team Mgr	Karen Crosby, (7287), SLA
Library Team	Norma Marr
	Pauletta McMillan
	Jacci Firkys

582 **Canada (Alberta - Calgary)**
CALGARY SUN
2615 12 St NE, Calgary, AB, Canada, T2E 7W9
403-250-4135; FAX 403-250-4180

Newspaper founded: 1980; Library founded: 1980.
Hours: Mon—Sun 9am—10pm
Resources: Clipping files, Biography files, photos/slides, Reference books. Microforms: rolls. Movie/TV kits.
Personnel

Chief Librarian	Kathryn M. Dilts, SLA

583 **Canada (Alberta - Edmonton)**
THE EDMONTON JOURNAL
101st St & 100th Ave (Box 2421), Edmonton, AB, Canada, T5J 2S6
403-429-5200; FAX 403-429-5221

Newspaper Group: Southam
Access: Open to other media by appointment.
Personnel

Librarian	Elaine Mantua, (5263; EMANTUA@THEJOURNAL.SOUTHAM.CA), SLA

584 **Canada (Alberta - Edmonton)**
EDMONTON SUN
#250, 4990 92 Ave, Edmonton, AB, Canada, T6B 3A1 — See Banner
403-468-0261; FAX 403-468-0350 or 403-468-0148; Email edmonton.sun@ccinet.ab.ca

Newspaper Founded: 1978; library founded: 1978.
Newspaper Group: Toronto Sun Corp.
Hours: Mon—Fri 7:30am—12m; Sat 8am—11pm; Sun 12n—11pm
Days Not Published: Christmas.
Online Databases: Canadian Press; AP.
CD ROM: Yes.
Fee-Based Research: Research Fee: $50. Copies: $3. FAX: $3. Invoice.
Services to Other News Libraries: Telephone reference. Will FAX copies of clips. Fee: $3/each. Requirements: Prepayment; No service to competing newspapers.
Access: Open to other, non-competitive media; open to other special libraries by appointment.
Resources: Photo files, reference books, maps. Microforms: roll, fiche. Clippings.
Archival Systems: Fetch.
Special Collections: Wayne Gretzky; Edmonton Oilers; Edmonton Eskimos; Commonwealth Games, 1978; Universiade 1983.
Personnel

Chief Librarian	John M. Sinclair, SLA
Asst Chief Librarian	Bruce Grant
Library Clerk	Kathy Levesque

585 **Canada (Alberta - Medicine Hat)**
NEWS
3257 Dunmore Rd SE (Box 10), Medicine Hat, AB, Canada, T1A 7E6
403-527-1101; FAX 403-527-6029

Newspaper Group: Southam
Hours: Mon—Fri 8—4
Access: Open to other media by appointment.
Personnel

Librarian	Peter Mehrer

586 **Canada (Alberta - Red Deer)**
RED DEER ADVOCATE
2950 Bremner Ave, Red Deer, AB, Canada, T4N 5G3 — See Banner
403-343-2400; FAX 403-341-6560

Newspaper founded: 1903; library founded: 1974.
Hours: Mon—Fri 8am—3:30pm
Days Not Published: New Year's Day, Labor Day, Thanksgiving, Christmas, Good Friday, Family Day.
Services to Other News Libraries: Telephone reference. Will FAX copies of clips. Fee: 25c/page.
Access: Open to other media by appointment.
Resources: Photo files, reference books, maps, pamphlet files. Microforms: roll. Newspaper index, clippings.
Special Collections: Statutes of Alberta; Alberta Hansard; Current Year's Canadian Hansard.
Personnel

Director	Patricia Goulet, (253)

587 **Canada (British Columbia - Vancouver)**
CANADIAN BROADCASTING CORP.—
TV News Library
700 Hamilton St, Vancouver, BC, Canada, V6B 2R5
604-662-6855; FAX 604-622-6878

Home Page (URL): http://www.cbc.ca/index.html.
Special Collections: News stories in French and English; sports; ordering information.
Personnel

Director	Colin Preston

588 Canada (British Columbia - Vancouver)
THE PROVINCE / VANCOUVER SUN
2250 Granville St, Vancouver, BC, Canada, V6H 3G2 See Banner
604-732-2933; FAX 604-732-2353; Infoline 604-732-2607

Newspaper founded: Province—1898; Vancouver Sun—1912. Library founded: c. 1950.
Newspaper Group: Southam
Hours: 24 hours a day.
Days Not Published: New Year's Day, Good Friday, Victoria Day, Canada Day, BC Day, Labour Day, Thanksgiving, Remembrance Day, Christmas, Boxing Day.
Access: Open to other news media and journalists. Contact D. Millward.
Services to Other News Libraries: Telephone quick reference. Contact D. Millward. Clips mailed, FAXed for a fee. Contact Infoline.
Online Databases: Infomart; LEXIS/NEXIS; Datatimes; Dow Jones; QuickLaw; Globe Information Services; BC Online; Netscape.
Electronic Clipping Files: Infomart/Dialog
Archival Systems: Merlin.
CD ROM: Yes.
Fee-Based Research: Research Fee: $60. Copies: $10 + $1/pp. FAX: $15 + $1/pp. Invoice or prepay. Contact: Infoline (732-2607).
Resources: Photo archive, negatives, electronic image archive, reference books, maps, statistics collection, directories, government documents - mun, prov, fed. Microforms: rollfilm, fiche of indexed clippings.
Special Collections: Journalism books; Photo/negative archive.
Personnel

Mgr/Editorial Svcs/ Chief Libn	Debra Millward, (2933; debbiem@wimsey.com), SLA
Graphics Libn	Kathryn Abbott, (2699; katea@wimsey.com), SLA
Systems Libn	Deborah Schachter, (2584; debbies@wimsey.com), SLA
Librarian	Deanna Norris, (deanna@wimsey.com)

589 Canada (British Columbia - Vernon)
DAILY NEWS
4301 27th St, Vernon, BC, Canada, V1T 4Y5
604-545-0671; FAX 604-545-7193

Newspaper Group: Thomson Newspapers
Services to Other News Libraries: Will answer questions from news libraries.

590 Canada (Manitoba - Brandon)
THE BRANDON SUN
501 Rosser Ave, Brandon, MB, Canada, R7A 0K4
204-727-2451; FAX 204-727-0385

Newspaper Group: Sun Publishing Co. Ltd.
Access: Open to other media by appointment.
Personnel

Librarian	Betty Cochrane, (237)

591 Canada (Manitoba - Winnipeg)
WINNIPEG FREE PRESS
1355 Mountain Ave, Winnipeg, MB, Canada, R2X 3B6 See Banner
204-697-7289; FAX 204-697-7412; Email: library@freepress.mb.ca

Newspaper founded: 1872; library founded: about 1926.
Newspaper Group: Thomson Newspapers
Hours: Mon—Fri 8am—4:30pm
Days Not Published: New Year's Day, Labor Day, Thanksgiving, Christmas, Good Friday, Victoria Day, Canada Day, August Civic Holiday, Boxing Day, Remembrance Day.
Services to Other News Libraries: Telephone reference. Will FAX copies of clips.
Access: Not open to other media; open to other special libraries.
Home Page (URL): http://www.freepress.mb.ca/Freepress.
Resources: Photo files, negatives, reference books, pamphlet files. Microforms: roll, fiche, jackets. Clippings. Electronic Library.
News Databases: Stauffer Gold.
Online Databases: C-Text.
Archival Systems: Stauffer Gold.
LAN: Yes.
Personnel

Director	Joan Williamson, (7290)
Photo Librarian	Marjorie Jamieson, (7291)

592 Canada (Manitoba - Winnipeg)
THE WINNIPEG SUN
1700 Church Ave, Winnipeg, MB, Canada, R2X 3A2
204-694-2022; FAX 204-694-2347

Newspaper Group: Groupe Quebecor Inc.
Hours: Mon—Fri 8:30—4
Access: Open to other media by appointment.
Personnel

Librarian	Denette Ruff

593 Canada (New Brunswick - Fredericton)
THE DAILY GLEANER
12 Prospect St (Box 3370), Fredericton, NB, Canada, E3B 5A2
506-452-6671; FAX 506-452-7405

Newspaper Group: Summit Publishing Ltd.
Personnel

Librarian	Eliza Aitken

594 Canada (New Brunswick - Moncton)
MONCTON TIMES—TRANSCRIPT
939 Main St, Moncton, NB, Canada, E1C 8P3 See Banner
506-859-4900; FAX 506-859-4904

Newspaper founded: 1877; library founded: 1968.
Days Not Published: New Year's Day, Labor Day, Christmas, Sunday.
Access: Open to other media/other special libraries.
News Databases: ATEX.
Resources: Photo files, reference books, clippings.
Fee-Based Research: Research Fee: $80. Copies. FAX. Microform Copies. Prepay or invoice. Contact: Frederick Leidemer.
Personnel

Librarian	Frederick Leidemer
Library Asst	Bob Poirier

595 Canada (New Brunswick - Saint John)
EVENING TIMES—GLOBE—TELEGRAPH—JOURNAL
210 Crown St (Box 2350), Saint John, NB, Canada, E2L 3V9
506-632-8888; FAX 506-648-2654

Newspaper Group: NB Publishing Co. Ltd.
Hours: Mon—Fri 8:30—5:30
Access: Open to other media by appointment.
Personnel

Librarian	Claire Hickman

596 Canada (Newfoundland - St. John's)
EVENING TELEGRAM
Columbus Dr (Box 5970), St. John's, NF, Canada, A1C 5X7
709-364-2323; FAX 709-364-9333

Newspaper Group: Canadian Newspapers Co. Ltd.

597 **Canada (Nova Scotia - Halifax)**
THE CHRONICLE—HERALD / MAIL STAR
1650 Argyle St (PO Box 610), Halifax, NS, Canada, B3J 2T2
902-426-3080; FAX 902-426-1164

598 **Canada (Nova Scotia - Halifax)**
THE DAILY NEWS
11 Thornhill Dr (Box 8330), Halifax, NS, Canada, B3K 5M1
902-468-1222; FAX 902-468-3609

Newspaper Group: Robinson-Blackmore Printing & Publishing Ltd.
Personnel
Librarian — Katrina Sidney

599 **Canada (Ontario - Agincourt)**
ETV TELEVISION NETWORK—
News Research Library
9 Channel Nine Ct, Agincourt, ON, Canada, M1S 4B5
416-609-7399

Personnel
Librarian — Patricia A. Treble

600 **Canada (Ontario - Hamilton)**
THE SPECTATOR
44 Frid St, Hamilton, ON, Canada, L8N 3G3 — See Banner
905-526-3333; FAX 905-526-3399

Year founded: 1846; library founded: 1937.
Newspaper Group: Southam
Hours: Mon—Fri 9am—4:30pm
Days Not Published: New Year's Day, Labor Day, Victoria Day, Thanksgiving, Christmas, Canada Day, Good Friday, Sunday.
Access: by appointment.
Services to Other News Libraries: Sends copies of clips—25c/page. Faxes clips. Contact reference 526-3315.
Resources: Photo files, negatives, reference books, pamphlet file. Microforms: roll, fiche. Clippings.
Online Databases: Infomart; Info Globe.
Personnel
Senior Info Technician — Tammie Danciu

601 **Canada (Ontario - Kitchener)**
KITCHENER—WATERLOO RECORD
225 Fairway Rd, Kitchener, ON, Canada, N2G 4E5
519-894-2231; FAX 519-894-3829; Email newsroom@therecord.com

Founded: 1879; library founded: 1972.
Hours: Mon—Fri 9am—5pm
Access: Other media, special libraries and public by appointment.
Services to Other News Libraries: Telephone reference. Sends copies of clips.
Online Databases: Infomart.
Archival Systems: Merlin.
Fee-Based Research: Research Fee: $15. Copies: $5/article. FAX: $2.50/article. Invoice. Contact: Michael Fox (ext 697).
Resources: Photo files, negatives, reference books, maps, pamphlet file. Microforms: roll. Clippings (all available through Infomart Online)
Personnel
Director — Michael Fox, (697), SLA
Asst Librarian — Christine Masterman, (695)

602 **Canada (Ontario - London)**
LONDON FREE PRESS
369 York St (PO Box 2280), London, ON, Canada, N6A 4G1 — See Banner
519-679-1111; FAX 519-667-4528

Newspaper founded: 1849; library founded: 1950.
Hours: Mon—Fri 8:30am—5:30pm
Days Not Published: All national holidays.
Home Page (URL): http://www.lfpress.com.
News Databases: Folio Views.
CD ROM: Yes.
Fee-Based Research: Resesarch Fee: $35. Copies: $5. FAX: $1. Microform Copies: $1. Invoice. Contact: Anita McCallum (ext 2097).
Online Databases: DIALOG.
Personnel
Librarian — Anita McCallum, (2097; amccallu@lfpress.com)

603 **Canada (Ontario - Niagara Falls)**
NIAGARA FALLS REVIEW
4801 Valley Way (PO Box 270), Niagara Falls, ON, Canada, L2E 6T6
905-358-5711; FAX 905-356-0785

Year founded: 1879; library founded: 1967.
Newspaper Group: Thomson Newspapers
Hours: Mon—Fri 6:30am—11am.
Days Not Published: New Year's Day, Good Friday, Victoria Day, Thanksgiving, Christmas.
Services to Other News Libraries: Telephone reference. Sends copies/Faxes clips.
Resources: Photo files, negatives, reference books, maps. Microforms: rolls.
For information contact City Editor

604 **Canada (Ontario - North Bay)**
THE NORTH BAY NUGGET
259 Worthington St W (Box 570), North Bay, ON, Canada, P1B 8J6
705-472-3200; FAX 705-472-5128

Newspaper Group: Southam
Hours: Mon—Fri 8—5
Access: Open to other media by appointment.
Personnel
Librarian — Allison Barrett, (303)

605 **Canada (Ontario - Ottawa)**
OTTAWA CITIZEN
1101 Baxter Rd, Ottawa, ON, Canada, K2C 3M4 — See Banner
613-596-3744; FAX 613-726-1198; Email: 01715@Freenet.Carleton.Ca

Newspaper founded: 1846: library founded: 1960.
Newspaper Group: Southam
Hours: Mon—Fri 8am—3pm
Days Not Published: New Year's Day, Thanksgiving, Christmas.
Access: Open to other media and other special libraries.
Services to Other News Libraries: Telephone reference. Contact: Ron Tysick. Sends copies of clips. Express mails clips.
Online Databases: DIALOG; SAVE; Datatimes; Info Globe; NEXIS; Canadian Press; Infomart.
News Databases: Info Globe; QL Systems; SAVE; Infomart.
Electronic Clipping Files: Infomart Online
Fee-Based Research: Research Fee: $60. Copies: $1. FAX: $2/search. Invoice or prepay.
CD ROM: Yes.
Resources: Photo files, negatives, reference books, maps. Microforms: roll, fiche. Newspaper index, clippings.

OTTAWA CITIZEN (cont'd)

Personnel
Head Librarian — Ronald P. Tysick, (3744), SLA
Asst Librarian — Jim Scheer, (3691), SLA
Librarians — Charlene Ruberry, (3745)
Liisa Tuominen, (3744; LTUOMINEN@THECITIZEN.SOUTHAM.CA)
Lois Kirkup, (3745)

606 **Canada (Ontario - Ottawa)**
OTTAWA SUN
380 Hunt Club Rd (PO Box 9729, Station T), Ottawa, ON, Canada, K1G 5H7
613-739-7000; FAX 613-739-0930; Email: OTTLIB@OTTAWA.NET

Newspaper founded: 1988; Library founded: 1988.
Newspaper Group: Toronto Sun Corp.
Hours: Mon—Thur 9am—9pm; Sat, Sun 2pm—10pm
Days Not Published: New Year's Day, Easter Friday, Christmas, Saturday.
Access: Open to other media by appointment.
Services to Other News Libraries: Telephone reference—739-5115. Telefacsimile clips. Contact Librarian.
Resources: Photo files, reference books, maps, pamphlet file. Microforms: roll. Clippings.
Online Databases: Infomart; Info Globe; Toronto Sun Database.
News Databases: Smarterm; Symphony.
Personnel
Director — Catherine Flegg, (5115), SLA
Asst Libn — Dale Overall, (5115)

607 **Canada (Ontario - Ottawa)**
LA PRESSE—
Ottawa Bureau
#715, 150 Wellington, Ottawa, ON, Canada, K1P 5A4
613-238-8051

Personnel
Documentalist/Researcher — Sylvie Dallaire

608 **Canada (Ontario - Ottawa)**
SOUTHAM NEWS—
Library
151 Sparks St, Ste 512, Ottawa, ON, Canada, K1P 5E3
613-236-0491; FAX 613-236-1788

Personnel
Librarian — Kirsten J. Smith, SLA

609 **Canada (Ontario - Sault Ste. Marie)**
SAULT STAR
145 Old Garden River Rd (Box 460), Saut Ste. Marie, ON, Canada, P6A 5M5
705-759-3030; FAX 705-759-0102

Newspaper Group: Southam
Access: Open to other media by appointment.
Personnel
Librarian — Joan Dorse, (285)

610 **Canada (Ontario - Toronto)**
CANADIAN BROADCASTING CORP.
250 Front St W (PO Box 500, Station A), Toronto, ON, Canada, M5V 3G5
416-205-3244; FAX 416-205-4707

Library founded: 1948.
Hours: Mon—Fri 7:30am—9pm
Access: Open to other media. Access determined on request-by-request basis.
Services to Other News Libraries: Telephone reference. Faxes clips.
Resources: Reference books. Microforms: fiche. Clippings.
Online Databases: DIALOG; Dow Jones; SAVE; Datatimes; Info Globe; NEXIS; Canadian Press; QL Systems; Infomart.
Personnel
Director — Leone Earls, (3243)
Reference Librarians — Anne Mercer
Gail Strachan
Louise Goldberg

611 **Canada (Ontario - Toronto)**
CANADIAN BROADCASTING CORP.—
News Library
PO Box 500, Station A, Toronto, ON, Canada, M5W 1E6
416-205-2737; FAX 416-975-6257

Personnel
Director — Jeannette Kopak, (2737)

612 **Canada (Ontario - Toronto)**
CANADIAN BROADCASTING CORP.—
Radio Archives
Box 500, Station A, Toronto, ON, Canada, M5W 1E6
416-205-5868

Access: Open to other media by appointment.
Personnel
Director — Laura Struthers

613 **Canada (Ontario - Toronto)**
CANADIAN BROADCASTING CORP.—
Reference Library
PO Box 500, Station A, Toronto, ON, Canada, M5W 1E6
416-205-3243; FAX 416-205-3555

Personnel
Librarian — Leone Earls, (Learls@delphi.com), SLA

614 **Canada (Ontario - Toronto)**
THE CANADIAN PRESS
36 King St E, Toronto, ON, Canada, M5C 2L9
416-364-0321; FAX 416-364-6634

Established: 1917.
Hours: Mon—Fri 9am—7pm
Wire Service

Online Databases: NEWSTEX.
Services to Other News Libraries: Telephone reference.
Access: Other librarians by telephone or written request.
Special Collections: Microfiche collection on: War Diary; Canada at War (WW II); Canadians in Korea; Korean War; CP News Diary.
Personnel
Librarian — Asma S. Khan, (293), SLA
Asst Librarian — Perry Tom, (399)

615 **Canada (Ontario - Toronto)**
CORRIERE CANADESE
890 Caledonia Rd, Toronto, ON, Canada, M5B 3Y1
416-785-4303; FAX 416-785-4329

Newspaper Group: October Press Ltd.
Personnel
Contacts — Tina Losiggio
Ron Kitchener

616 **Canada (Ontario - Toronto)**
CTV TELEVISION NETWORK—
Research Library
42 Charles St E, Toronto, ON, Canada, M4Y 1T5
416-595-4100; FAX 416-928-0907

Personnel
Contact — Carol Ashurst

617 **Canada (Ontario - Toronto)**
THE FINANCIAL POST
333 King St E, Toronto, ON, Canada, M5A 4N2
416-350-6300; FAX 416-350-6301

Newspaper Group: Toronto Sun Corp.
Access: Open to other media by appointment.
Personnel
Librarian — Theresa M. Butcher, (6693), SLA

618 **Canada (Ontario - Toronto)**
MACLEAN'S MAGAZINE
777 Bay St (7th floor), Toronto, ON, Canada, M5W 1A7 — See Banner
416-596-5340; FAX 416-596-7730; Email: 76702.2247@compuserve.com; letters@macleans.ca

Founded: 1905; library founded: 1978.
Newspaper Group: Maclean-Hunter Telecommunications
Hours: Mon—Fri 9am—6pm
Access: Other news librarians; other special librarians.
Services to Other News Libraries: Telephone reference. Contact Basil Guinane.
Online Databases: DIALOG; Info Globe; QL Systems; Dow Jones; Profile; Datatimes; LEXIS/NEXIS; Infomart.
WAN: Yes.
LAN: Yes.
CD ROM: Macleans, Globe & Mail, EBSCO full text elite, ProQuest.
Resources: Reference books, maps, pamphlet file. Clipping files. Magazine index.
Personnel
Librarian — Basil Guinane, SLA
Library Technicians — Maryjane Culbert; George Serhijczuk
Library Clerk — Robin Selz

619 **Canada (Ontario - Toronto)**
ONTARIO LEGISLATIVE LIBRARY—Information and Reference Servcies
45 Carlton St, #1201, Toronto, ON, Canada, M5B 2H9
416-325-3945; FAX 416-325-3925

Personnel
Librarian — Donna M. Burton, SLA

620 **Canada (Ontario - Toronto)**
TORONTO GLOBE AND MAIL
444 Front St W, Toronto, ON, Canada, M5V 2S9 — See Banner
416-585-5075; FAX 416-585-5085

Newspaper founded: Mail: 1936; Globe: 1944; library founded: 1936.
Newspaper Group: Thomson Newspapers
Hours: Mon—Fri 9am—9:30pm; Sun 11am—9:30pm
Days Not Published: Christmas.
Access: Open to other reporters by appointment, Contact 585-5076. Available on Infoglobe.
Online Databases: Dow Jones; Info Globe; LEXIS/NEXIS; Infomart; Profile; Textline.
Resources: Photo files, negatives, reference books, maps, pamphlet files. Microforms: roll, fiche. Newspaper index, clippings.
Personnel
Director — Amanda Valpy, (5075), SLA
Assoc Librarian — Celia Donnelly, (5076), SLA
Picture Librarian — Sonja Lindegger, SLA

621 **Canada (Ontario - Toronto)**
TORONTO STAR
One Yonge St, Toronto, ON, Canada, M5E 1E6 — See Banner
416-367-2000; FAX 416-865-3994

Founded: Newspaper—1892; Library—1923
Hours: Mon—Sun 9am—10pm
Days Not Published: Christmas, Good Friday.
Online Databases: DIALOG; QL Law; Info Globe; LEXIS/NEXIS; Infomart.
News Databases: QL Systems.
Electronic Clipping Files: Infomart Online
Services to Other News Libraries: Telephone reference (869-4491). Will FAX copies of clips.
Access: Open to out-of-town journalists by appointment; not open to other special libraries.
Resources: Photo files, negatives, reference books, maps, pamphlet files. Microforms: roll, fiche, jackets. Clippings.
Special Collections: Ernest Hemingway: Biographical and bibliography of articles published in his Toronto years in the Toronto Star and the Star Weekly.
Personnel
Director — Sonja Noble, (4490; SNoble@thestar.ca), SLA

622 **Canada (Ontario - Toronto)**
TORONTO SUN
333 King St E, Toronto, ON, Canada, M5A 3X5 — See Banner
416-947-2257

Newspaper founded: 1971.
Newspaper Group: Toronto Sun Corp.
Hours: 9am—11pm
Days Not Published: New Year's Day, Canada Day, Civic Holiday, Christmas, Good Friday.
Online Databases: DIALOG; Info Globe; Infomart; NEXIS; SAVE.
News Databases: SAVE (in-house); Infomart (clients).
Services to Other News Libraries: Telephone reference. Contact: Julie Kirsh. Will FAX copies of clips.
Fee-Based Research: Research Fee: $53.50; $3.50 per copy of article. Requests by mail only.
Resources: Photo files, reference books, maps, pamphlet files. Microforms: roll, fiche. Clippings.
Special Collections: Holdings for the Toronto Telegram editions on microfilm.
Personnel
Mgr/News Research — Julie Kirsh, (2257), SLA
Asst Mgr/News Research — Katherine Webb Nelson, (2258)
News Researchers — Glenna Tapscott, (2258); Joyce Wagler, (2258); Julie Hornby, (2258); Bob Johnston; Susan Dugas, (2238); Barbara White, (2238); Jillian Goddard, (2258)

623 **Canada (Ontario - Windsor)**
WINDSOR STAR
167 Ferry St, Windsor, ON, Canada, N9A 4M5 — See Banner
519-255-5711; FAX 519-255-5515

Newspaper founded: 1918; library founded: 1948.
Newspaper Group: Southam
Days Not Published: New Year's Day, Canada Day, Labor Day, Victoria Day, Thanksgiving, Christmas, Good Friday, Sunday.
Access: Open to other media, special libraries.
Services to Other News Libraries: Telephone reference (ext 601). Sends copies of clips. Fee: free to most news libraries.
CD ROM: Yes.
LAN: Yes.
WAN: Yes.
Online Databases: Southam News Service; Info Globe Infomart; Canadian Press.
Archival Systems: Merlin.
News Databases: Infomart Online.

WINDSOR STAR (cont'd)

Electronic Clipping Files: Datatimes, Infomart Online.
Resources: Photo files, reference books, maps, pamphlet file. Microforms: roll, fiche, jackets. Clippings. Journals. Electronic Bulletin Boards.
Personnel

Director	Deborah J. Jessop, (672), SLA
Library Assts	Denise Chuk, (746)
	Ute Hertel, (601)
	Maureen Williams, (601)
	Susan Patterson, (640)
	Mike Ricketts, (640)

624 Canada (Quebec - Hull)
CIDA—
Center for International Training
200 Promenade Du Portage, #863, Hull, PQ, Canada, K1A 0G4
819-994-0761

Personnel

Librarian	Patrick J. Hunt, (patrick.hunt@devcan.ca), SLA

625 Canada (Quebec - Montreal)
LE DEVOIR
2050 de Bleury, 9th Fl, Montreal, PQ, Canada, H3A 3M9 See Banner
514-985-3333; FAX 514-985-3360

Newspaper founded: 1910; library founded: 1972.
Hours: Mon—Fri 9am—7pm
Days Not Published: New Year's Day, Labor Day, Christmas, Sunday.
Services to Other News Libraries: No telephone reference. Sends copies of clips. Will not express mail clips.
Access: Accept other libraries' requests only. Open to other special libraries
Resources: Photo files, reference boks. Microforms: roll, fiche, jackets. Newspaper index, clippings.
Personnel

Director	Gilles Pare, SLA

626 Canada (Quebec - Montreal)
HYDRO—QUEBEC—
Autochtones Et Collectivites
75 Blvd Rene-Levesque W 21 fl, Montreal, PQ, Canada H2Z 1A4
514-289-4759; FAX 514-289-3251

Personnel

Librarian	Christiane Gouin

627 Canada (Quebec - Montreal)
MONTREAL GAZETTE
250 St. Antoine W, Montreal, PQ, Canada H2Y 3R7 See Banner
514-987-2583; FAX 514-587-2433

Newspaper founded: 1778; library founded: 1950.
Newspaper Group: Southam
Hours: Mon—Fri 9am-12m; Sun 12n-12m
Days Not Published: New Year's Day, Labor Day, Thanksgiving, Christmas, St. Jean Baptiste, Victoria Day, Canada Day, Good Friday.
Access: Other media, other libraries, general public.
Services to Other News Libraries: Telephone reference. Sends copies of clips. Fee: 25c/page. Express mails clips.
Online Databases: NEWSTEX; SAVE; Datatimes; Info Globe; NEXIS; Canadian Press; Infomart; Infodex.
News Databases: Infomart.
Electronic Clipping Files: Infomart Online
Resources: Photo files, reference books, maps, pamphlet files. Microforms: roll, fiche, jackets. Clippings.
Fee-Based Research: Research fee: $25. Copies: 25c. FAX: $10/search. Microform Copies: $.25/page. Invoice. Contact: Patricia Duggar (987-2621).
Archival Systems: Merlin.
Personnel

Chief Librarian	Agnes McFarlane, SLA

628 Canada (Quebec - Montreal)
LA PRESSE
7 Rue St Jacques, Montreal, PQ, Canada, H2Y 1K9 See Banner
514-285-7019; FAX 514-285-6988

Newspaper founded: 1884; library founded: 1965.
Newspaper Group: Trans-Canada
Hours: Mon—Fri 8am—12m; Sat, Sun 4am—12n
Days Not Published: New Year's Day, Labor Day, Thanksgiving, Christmas, Boxing Day.
News Databases: Bibliographic-Minisis.
Electronic Clipping Files: CEDRON
Services to Other News Libraries: Telephone reference. FAX copies of clips.
Access: Other media, other special libraries.
Resources: Photo files, negatives, reference books, maps. Microforms: roll, fiche, jackets. Newspaper index, clippings.
Special Collections: World War I and II photos.
Personnel

Chief Librarian	Gerard Monette, (7019)

629 Canada (Quebec - Montreal)
READER'S DIGEST MAGAZINES LTD.
215 Redfern Ave, Montreal, PQ, Canada, H3Z 2V9
514-934-0751; FAX 514-934-2357

Hours: Mon—Fri 9am—5pm
Online Databases: Info Globe; Infomart; Financial Post Online; LEXIS/NEXIS; QuickLaw.
Access: Not open to the public; open to other libraries by phone, FAX or letter request.
Personnel

Librarian	Pierre Charlebois

630 Canada (Quebec - Montreal)
SOCIETE RADIO-CANADA—
Library
1400 Blvd Rene-Levesque E, Montreal, PQ, Canada, H2L 2M2
514-597-6265; FAX 514-597-6236

Personnel

Librarian	Michelle Bachand, SLA

631 Canada (Quebec - Quebec)
LE SOLEIL
925 Chemin St Louis, Quebec, PQ, Canada, G1K 7J6 See Banner
418-686-3394; FAX 418-686-3374

Newspaper founded: 1896.
Newspaper Group: Uni Media, Inc.
Hours: Mon—Fri 8:30am—4:30pm
Days Not Published: New Year's Day, June 24th, Labor Day, Christmas, Sunday.
Services to Other News Libraries: Telephone reference. Contact: Claudine Gagnon. Sends copies of clips for fee.
Access: Not open to other media or the public.
Personnel

Director	Andre Forgues
Coordinator	Claudine Gagnon

632 Canada (Quebec - Trois-Rivieres)
LE NOUVELLISTE
1920, rue Bellefeuille, CP 668, Trois-Rivieres, PQ, Canada, G9A 5J6
819-376-2501; FAX 819-691-4356

LE NOUVELLISTE (cont'd)

Newspaper Group: Power Corp.
Personnel
Librarian — Robert Marchand, (216)

633 **Canada (Saskatchewan - Regina)**
THE LEADER POST
1964 Park St (PO Box 2020), Regina, SK, Canada, S4P 3G4
306-565-8234; FAX 306-565-2588

Founded: 1883.
Newspaper Group: Armadale Publishing
Hours: Mon—Fri 8:30am—4:30pm
Days Not Published: New Year's Day, Good Friday, Remembrance Day, Labor Day, Victoria Day, Thanksgiving, Christmas, Canada Day, Sunday
Services to Other News Libraries: Telephone reference. Sends copies of clips—25c/copy/$1 minimum. Service limited. Contact Eric Jenkins.
Access: Other media, other special libraries. Limited access.
Resources: Photo files, reference books. Microforms: roll, fiche. Newspaper index, clippings. Government Documents.
Personnel
Director — Eric Jenkins

634 **Canada (Saskatchewan - Saskatoon)**
SASKATOON STAR—PHOENIX
204 5th Avenue N, Saskatoon, SK, Canada, S7K 2P1 — See Banner
306-652-9200; FAX 306-664-0437

Newspaper founded: 1902; Library founded: 1960.
Newspaper Group: Armadale Publishing
Hours: Mon—Fri 9am—4:30pm
Days Not Published: Sunday, New Year's Day, Good Friday, Easter, Remembrance Day, Labor Day, Victoria Day, Thanksgiving, Christmas.
Access: Not open to other media or the public.

NEWS LIBRARIES INTERNATIONAL

635 **Australia (Adelaide)**
THE ADELAIDE ADVERTISER
121 King William St, Adelaide, South Australia, 5000
618 206 2000; FAX 618 206 3622

Personnel

Librarian	Sharon Doyle

636 **Australia (Bowen Hills)**
THE COURIER MAIL
41 Campbell St (GPO Box 130, Brisbane 4001), Bowen Hills, Queensland, 4006
617 252 6011; FAX 617 252 6696

Personnel

Librarian	Brian Breingan

637 **Australia (Melbourne)**
THE AGE/SUNDAY AGE
250 Spencer St, Melbourne, Victoria, Australia, 3000
61 3 601 2806; FAX 61 3 670 1059

Newspaper founded: 1854; Library founded: 1960.
Hours: Mon—Sat 8am—11pm; Sun 2pm—11pm
Access: Open to other media, other special libraries for negotiated fee.
Services to Other News Libraries: Telephone reference. Sends copies of clips, telefacsimile clips. Contact Manager, Editorial Library.
Home Page (URL): http://www.theage.com.au.
Resources: Photo files, negatives, reference books, maps, pamphlet file. Microforms: roll, fiche. Newspaper index, clippings.
Online Databases: BRS; DIALOG; Ausinet; Presscom; LEXIS/NEXIS; QNIS; Reuters; Datatimes.
CD ROM: Yes.
LAN: Yes.
Fee-Based Research: Age Search. Fee: $110 (negotiable). Copies. FAX. Microform Copies. Contact: Jude Whelan (9601-2874).

Personnel

Mgr/Edit Info Svcs	Frank Prain, (frank@theage.com.au), AUKML
Deputy Library Mgr	Catherine Ryan, (cryan@theage.com.au)
Age Search Manager	Jude Whelan, (jwhelan@theage.com.au)

638 **Australia (Melbourne)**
HERALD AND WEEKLY TIMES
44 Flinders St, Melbourne, Victoria, Australia, 3000
61 3 9292 2000; FAX 61 3 9602 1856

Library founded: 1922.
Newspaper Group: News Corporation
Days Not Published: Christmas.
Access: Open to other special libraries.
Services to Other News Libraries: Telephone reference, sends copies of clips. Telefacsimile clips.
Resources: Photo files, negatives, reference books, maps. Microforms: roll, fiche. Clippings.
News Databases: BASIS.

Personnel

Chief Librarian	Vickie Ritchie

639 **Australia (Perth)**
THE WEST AUSTRALIAN
219 St George's Terrace, Perth, Western Australia, 6000
61 9 482 3111; FAX 61 9 482 3747

Newspaper founded: 1833; Library founded: 1959.
Hours: Mon—Fri 7am—12m; Sat 8am—4pm; Sun 12n—12m
Days Not Published: Christmas.
News Databases: SII.
Access: Open to other special libraries.
Resources: Photo files, negatives, reference books, maps, pamphlet file. Microforms: roll, fiche, jackets. Newspaper index, clippings.

Personnel

Chief Librarian	David Andrews, (3768; DAVIDA@WANEWS.COM.AU)
Deputy Chief Librarian	Tracey Bennett, (3766)
Librarians	Peter Todd, (3769)
	David Schokman, (3769)

640 **Australia (Queensland - Brisbane)**
QUEENSLAND NEWSPAPERS
Campbell St Bowen Hills, Brisbane, Queensland Australia, 4006 — See Banner
61 7 252 6405; FAX 61 7 252 6723

Newspaper founded: 1846; Library founded: 1930.
Newspaper Group: News Limited
Hours: Mon—Fri 7:45am—1pm; Sat 9am—11pm; Sun 12n—11pm
Days Not Published: Good Friday, Christmas.
Access: Open to other media, other special libraries. Call first for permission.
Services to Other News Libraries: Telephone reference. Sends copies of clips if available (some only stored electronically). Fee. Contact: Librarian.
Resources: Photo files, negatives, reference books, maps, pamphlet file. Microform: roll, fiche. Newspaper index, clippings.
Online Databases: Biosis.
News Databases: BASIS.
Electronic Clipping Files: VU/TEXT

Personnel

Director	Brian Breingan, (6405), SLA
Deputy Librarian	Rosemary Kunst, (6216)

641 **Australia (Sydney)**
AUSTRALIAN BROADCASTING CORPORATION
GPO Box 9994, Sydney, NSW, Australia 2001,
61 2 333 2653; FAX 61 2 333 2558

Personnel

Head—Program/Info Res	John Bartholomaeus, (BARTHOLOMAEUS.JOHN@a2.abc.com.au)

642 **Australia (Sydney)**
FAIRFAX EDITORIAL LIBRARY
201 Sussex St (GPO Box 506), Sydney 2000, NSW, Australia,
61 2 282 2196; FAX 61 2 282 2301

FAIRFAX EDITORIAL LIBRARY (cont'd)

Hours: Mon—Fri 9am—11pm; Sat 9—9; Sun 11am—10pm
Access: Open to the public by appointment.
News Databases: NewsLink.
Personnel

Info Svcs Manager	Kathryn Woolley, (3325)
Deputy Libn	Cathy Houston, (1615)
Collection Supv	Helen Bayliss
Data Prod Supv	Simon Jones
Indexing Supv	Frank Bopf
Business Supv	Brigette Mills

643 **Australia (Sydney)**
JOHN FAIRFAX GROUP—Library
GPO Box 506, Sydney, NSW, Australia, 2000
61 22 82 3325; FAX 61 22 82 3001; Email: library1@magna.com.au

Services: Research, Statistical research, Readers' enquiries, Book ordering, Serials/Periodicals, Indexing, Cuttings.
Online Databases: DIALOG; FT Profile; LEXIS/NEXIS.
Personnel
Librarian — Kathy Woolley, AUKML

644 **Australia (Sydney)**
SYDNEY MORNING HERALD
235 Jones St, Broadway, NSW, Australia,
61 2 282 2002; FAX 61 2 212 2424

Personnel
Librarian — Crystal Condous, (1615)

645 **Belgium (Antwerp)**
GAZET VAN ANTWERPEN
2 Katwilgweg, 2050 Antwerp, Belgium,
32 3 210 0210; FAX 32 2 219 4165

Founded: 1891.

646 **Belgium (Antwerp)**
NIEUWE GAZET
10 Leopoldstraat, 2000 Antwerp, Belgium,
323 231 9680; FAX 323 234 1688

Founded: 1897

647 **Belgium (Berchem)**
DE FINANCIELE ECONOMISCHE TIJD
Posthoflei 3, bus 9, 2600 Berchem,
32 3 286 0383; FAX 32 3 286 0380

Newspaper founded: 1988.
Hours: by appointment.
CD ROM: Yes.
Fee-Based Research: Research Fee: $10. Copies: $1. FAX: $1. Invoice. Contact Franky Van Hamme.
Home Page (URL): http://www.tyd.be.
Personnel
Contacts — Franky Van Hamme, (franky.van.hamm@tijd.be); Hans Stevens, (Hans.Stevens@tijd.be); Luc Gijsbrechts, (Luc.gijsbrechts@tijd.be); Marc Schauvaerts, (Marc.Schauvaerts@tijd.be)

648 **Belgium (Brussels)**
LA DERNIERE HEURE / LES SPORTS
Emile Jacqmainlaan 127, 1000 Brussels, Belgium,
32 2 211 2888; FAX 32 2 211 2870

Founded: 1906.

649 **Belgium (Brussels)**
EUROPEAN COMMISSION
200, rue de la Loi (JECL 1/58), 1049 Brussels, Belgium
32 2 295 59 38; FAX 32 2 296 11 49

Personnel
Librarian — Linda Jones, (linda.jones@dg10.cec.be)

650 **Belgium (Brussels)**
HET LAATSTE NIEUWS
Brusslsesteenweg 347, 1730 Asse-Koblegen, Belgium,
32 2 454 2211; FAX 32 2 454 2822

Founded: 1888

651 **Belgium (Brussels)**
DE MORGEN
Brogniezstraat 54, 1070 Brussels, Belgium,
32 2 556 6811; FAX 32 2 520 3516

Personnel
Contacts — Jan Jonckheere; Armand Plottier

652 **Belgium (Brussels)**
NEWSPAPER DE MORGEN—Documentation
Brogniezstraat 54, Brussels, Belgium,
32 2 527 0030; FAX 32 2 520 4192

Personnel
Librarian — Jan Jonckheere

653 **Belgium (Brussels)**
DE NIEUWE GIDA
105 Koningastraat, 1000 Brussels, Belgium,
32 2 216 5605; FAX 32 2 218 5906

Founded: 1944.

654 **Belgium (Brussels)**
LE SOIR
21 place de Louvain, 1000 Brussels, Belgium,
32 2 225 5555; FAX 32 2 225 5909

655 **Belgium (Brussels)**
TVV/HUMO/TELEMOUSTIQUE/L'INSTANT/GAEL
De Jonckerstraat 46, 1060 Brussels, Belgium,
32 2 537 0800; FAX 32 2 537 45 63, 537 79 75

Personnel
Contacts — Lut Delanoy; Genevieve Corbisier; Iris Heiremans; Nadine Laurent; Anna Van Beneden

656 **Belgium (Brussels)**
WALL STREET JOURNAL EUROPE
Blvd Brand Whitlock 87, 1200 Brussels, Belgium,
32 2 741 12 81; FAX 32 2 741 16 01

Personnel

Chief Librarian	Mary McGlynn
Asst Librarian	Noel Farrell

657 **Belgium (Charleroi)**
RTBF CHARLEROI
Passage de la Bourse, 6000 Charleroi, Belgium,
32 71 20 92 11; FAX 32 71 20 94 05

Personnel
Contacts — Anne De Bock; Christian Vandelois

658 **Belgium (Ghent)**
HET VOLK
Forelstraat 22, 9000 Ghent, Belgium,
32 91 225 5701; FAX 32 91 225 3527

Personnel
Contact — Ann Vantournhout

659 **Belgium (Groot Bijgaarden)**
DE STANDAARD
Gossetlaan 28, 1702 Groot Bijgaarden, Belgium,
32 2 267 22 37; FAX 32 2 463 17 97; Email: docum@vum.be

Personnel
Librarian — Paul Gybels

660 **Belgium (Hasselt)**
HET BELANG VAN LIMBURG
Herckienrodesingel 10, 3500 Hasselt, Belgium,
3211 87 81 11; FAX 3211 87 84 97

Personnel
Contact — Jan Bex

661 **Bermuda (Hamilton)**
ACE LTD.—
Information Services
30 Woodbourne Ave, Hamilton, Bermuda HM DX,
809-295-5200; FAX 809-295-5221

Personnel
Librarian — Frances K. Marshall, SLA

662 **Bermuda (Hamilton)**
ROYAL GAZETTE—
Library
PO Box 1025, Hamilton, Bermuda HM DX,
809-295-5881

Personnel
Librarian — Deborah A. Charles, SLA

663 **Brazil (Sao Paulo)**
EDITORA ABRIL SA
Dedoc/Ave Otaviano Alves, De Lima 4400, Sao Paulo, SP, Brazil, 02909
55 11 876 0056

Personnel
Contact — Susana H. Camarso

664 **Czech Republic**
LIDOVE NOVINY, A.S.—
Documentation Department
Narodni 9, 121 21 Praha 1, Czech Republic,
42 2 248 1413; FAX 42 2 232 1369

Personnel
Manager — Alena Klimova

665 **Czech Republic**
MLADA FRONTA DNES—
Documentation Department
Na porici 30, 112 86 Praha 1, Czech Republic,
42 2 232 4141; FAX 42 2 232 0924

Personnel
Manager — Jaroslav Vozobule

666 **Denmark (Aabybro)**
TV/NORD
Soparken 4, 9440 Aabybro, Denmark,
45 9 824 4600

Personnel
Librarian — Peter Steen Nielsen

667 **Denmark (Aalborg)**
AALBORG STIFTSTIDENDE
Langagervej 1, 9290 Aalborg 0, Denmark,
45 9 935 3423; FAX 45 9 935 3375

Services: Research, Serials/Periodicals, Book Ordering, Statistical Research.
Online Databases: FT Profile; DIALOG; DataStar.
Personnel
Librarian — Ann Langballe Madsen, AUKML

668 **Denmark (Aalborg)**
AALBORG TVR
Riihimakivej 6, 9200 Aalborg, Denmark,
45 9 934 9914; FAX 45 9 818 8440

Personnel
Librarian — Lise Larsen

669 **Denmark (Arhus)**
ARHUS STIFSTIDENDE
Olof Palmes Alle 39, 8200 Arhus N, Denmark,
45 8 678 4000; FAX 45 8 678 4401

Personnel
Librarian — Grethe Waldorf

670 **Denmark (Arhus)**
DANMARKS JOURNALISTHOJSKOLE
Olof Palmes Alle 11, 8200 Arhus, Denmark,
45 8 616 1122; FAX 45 8 616 8910

Personnel
Librarians — Birgit Farbol Sorensen, (bis@djh.dk)
Niels Mork, (nim@djk.dk)
Birgitte Normand, (bn@djk.dk)
Birgit Farbol Sorensen

671 **Denmark (Arhus)**
TV-P—
Library
Olof Palmes Alle 10, 8200 Arhus N, Denmark,
45 8 739 7028; FAX 45 8 739 7104

Personnel
Librarian — Elsa Holmer

672 **Denmark (Copenhagen)**
BERLINGSKE TIDENDE
Pilestrade 34, DK-1147, Copenhagen K, Denmark,
45 3 375 2230; FAX 34 3 313 1012

Personnel
Chief/Editorial Archives — Jorgen Larsen
Librarians — Nils Ulrik Pedersen, (nup@berlingske.dk)
Mette Marie Rude

673 **Denmark (Copenhagen)**
BERLINGSKE TIDENDE—NORDFOTO
Pilestraede 34, 1147 Copenhagen K, Denmark,
45 3 375 7575; FAX 45 3 375 2035

Personnel
Librarian — Hanne Blenner

674 **Denmark (Copenhagen)**
BOERSEN
19, Moentergade, DK-1140, Copenhagen K, Denmark, See Banner
45 3 332 0102; FAX 45 3 393 6686

Founded: Borsen—1896; Library—1970.
Hours: Mon—Fri 8am—6pm

BOERSEN (cont'd)

Access: Telephone reference. Open to the public and other libraries. Will send copies of clippings by post/telefax. Fee: 100 DKK + 10 DKK/page.
Resources: Books, reference books, pamphlet files, business annual reports, government documents, periodicals, statistics. Microforms: fiche, jackets. Clippings (1970 -).
Home Page (URL): http://www.borsen.dk.
Online Databases: Alis; Retsinformation; Polinfo; Artikelbasen; Profile; DIALOG; Teleboersen; Rex; Publicom; FT Profile; DataStar; Avisdata; Kompass/Affars-Data.
Fee-Based Research: Research fee: 125 DKK; Copies: 12.50 DKK. FAX: 50 DKK. Invoice.
Special Collections: Business annual reports.
Personnel
Mgr/Editorial Archives — Margrethe Mose Mortensen, (MMOSE@borsen.dk), SLA,AUKML
Librarian — Lise Nestelso

675 **Denmark (Copenhagen)**
BORN & UNGE BUPL
Blegdamsvej 124, 2100 Copenhagen, Denmark,
45 3 543 1000

Personnel
Librarian — Jette Otterstrom

676 **Denmark (Copenhagen)**
BORSENS NYHEDSMAGASIN
Montergade 19 (PO Box 2242), 1019 Copenhagen K, Denmark,
45 3 332 4400; FAX 45 3 311 5906

Personnel
Librarian — Birgitte Gether

677 **Denmark (Copenhagen)**
DANMARKS BIBLIOTEKSSKOLE
Birketinget 6, 2300 Copenhagen S, Denmark,
45 3 158 6066; FAX 45 3 284 0201

Personnel
Librarian — Fagleder Susanne Ornager

678 **Denmark (Copenhagen)**
DET FRI AKTUELT
Radhuspladsen 45-47, 1595 Copenhagen V, Denmark,
45 3 332 4001; FAX 45 3 313 0048

Personnel
Librarian — Gertrud Brejnholm

679 **Denmark (Copenhagen)**
FAGBLADET JOURNALISTEN
Gl. Strand 46, 1202 Copenhagen, Denmark,
45 3 314 2388; FAX 45 3 332 0308; Email: Journa@inet.uni-c-dk

Personnel
Librarian — Tine Hauge Moller

680 **Denmark (Copenhagen)**
INFORMATION
Store Kongensgade 40C (PO Box 188), 1006 Copenhagen K, Denmark,
45 3 314 1426; FAX 45 3 393 8083; Email: info-dk@uni-c.dk

Hours: 9—5
Access: Open to other media by appointment.
Personnel
Editorial Archive Director — Dorrit Kampmann, (339 191 66)
Librarian — Poul Siersback

681 **Denmark (Copenhagen)**
JYLLANDS—POSTEN
Ostergade 26, 1100 Copenhagen K, Denmark,
45 3 330 3030; 45 3 330 3001

Personnel
Librarian — Susanne Jacobsen

682 **Denmark (Copenhagen)**
KRISTELIGT DAGBLAD
Fanogade 15, 2100 Copenhagen, Denmark,
45 3 927 1235; FAX 45 3 927 0800

Personnel
Librarians — Lisbeth Marcussen
Majbrit Simonsen

683 **Denmark (Copenhagen)**
MANEDSBLADET PRESS
Studiestraede 24, 1, 1455 Copenhagen K, Denmark,
FAX 45 3 311 6866

Personnel
Librarian — Mette Jensen

684 **Denmark (Copenhagen)**
POLITIKEN NEWSPAPERS—
Library
Raadhuspladsen 37, 1785 Copenhagen, Denmark,
45 3 311 8511; FAX 45 3 332 0410; Email: library@pol.dk

Hours: Mon—Fri 9am—8pm
Access: Telephone service in the library. Fee based research.
Resources: Reference books, newspapers, journals and magazines, databases, press cuttings (until 1975).
Online Databases: DIALOG; DataStar; FT Profile; Genios; Datatimes; Polinfo; LEXIS/NEXIS.
Personnel
Librarians — Johs. Chr. Johansen
Lise Moller, (LISE_MOLLER@online.pol.dk)
Aase Andreasen, (Aase_Andreasen@online.pol.dk), SLA,AUKML
Michaela Rosendal, (MICHAELA_ROSENDAL@online.pol.dk)
Gitte Ronberg, (GITTE_RONBERG@online.pol.dk)
Solveig Skovmand

685 **Denmark (Frederiksberg)**
BIBLIOTEKARFORBUNDET
Lindevangs Alle 2, 2000 Frederiksberg, Denmark,
45 3 888 2233; FAX 45 3 888 3201

Personnel
Librarians — Suzan Gemzoe
Jesper Laursen

686 **Denmark (Frederiksberg)**
DANMARKS RADIO
Rosenorns Alle 22, DK1970 Frederiksberg C Denmark,

687 **Denmark (Frederiksberg)**
DR—RADIO—
Library
Radiohuset, 1999 Frederiksberg C, Denmark,
45 3 520 5582; FAX 45 3 520 5590

Personnel
Librarian — Ingvild Alnaes

688 Denmark (Herning)
HERNING FOLKEBLAD
Ostergade 25, 7400 Herning, Denmark,
45 9 712 3700; FAX 45 9 722 3600

Personnel
Hansen, Anne-Marie

689 Denmark (Holstebro)
TV/MIDT-VEST
Sovej 2, 7500 Holstebro, Denmark,
45 9 740 3300; FAX 45 9 740 1444; Email: TVMV@mail.teledanmark.dk

Personnel
Librarian — Pia Hald

690 Denmark (Odense)
FYENS STIFTSTIDENDE—ARKIVET
Blangstedgardsvej 2-6 (PO Box 418), 5220 Odense S0, Denmark,
45 6 611 1111; FAX 45 6 593 2574

Personnel
Librarian — Hanne Schwensen

691 Denmark (Odense)
TV2—
Library
Rugaardsvej 25, 5100 Odense C, Denmark,
45 6 591 9191; FAX 45 6 591 3322

Personnel
Librarians — Helle Bjernemose, (HeBj@tv2.dk)
Lis R. Moldrup, (LIMO@tv2.dk)

692 Denmark (Soborg)
BILLEDARKIVET
TV-Byen, 2860 Soborg, Denmark,
45 3 520 3040

Personnel
Librarian — Lisette Rungsoe

693 Denmark (Soborg)
DANMARKS RADIO
Blok M, K/1, 2860 Soborg, Denmark,
45 3 520 2193

Personnel
Librarian — Mette Charis Buchmann

694 Denmark (Soborg)
TV—ARC TEKST
TV-Byen, 2860 Soborg, Denmark,
45 3 520 3820; FAX 45 3 520 3817

Personnel
Librarian — Gunhild Leth Andersen

695 Denmark (Valby)
KOMMUNERNES GENSIDIGE FORSIKRINGSSELSKAB
Krumtappen 2, 2500 Valby, Denmark,
45 3 644 1688

Personnel
Librarian — Gertrud Baun

696 Denmark (Viby)
JYLLANDS—POSTEN-ARKIVET
Grondalsvej 3, 8260 Viby J, Denmark,
45 87383838; FAX 45 87383199

Personnel
Librarian — Kirsten Mathiesen

697 Denmark (Viby)
MORGENAVISEN JYLLANDS POSTEN
DK-8260 Viby J, Denmark,
45 8 738 3838; FAX 45 8 738 3199

CD ROM: Yes.
Fee-Based Research: Research fee. Copies. FAX. Microform Copies. Invoice. Contact K. Mathiesen.
Home Page (URL): http://www.jp.dr.
Personnel
Editorial Archive — Kirsten Mathiesen
Directors — Steve Vinther Moller

698 Finland (Helsinki)
ILTA-SANOMAT
Korkeavourenkatu 34, 00130 Helsinki, Finland,
358 0 122 1000; FAX 358 0 122 3419

Newspaper Group: Sanhoma Corp.

699 Finland (Yleisradia)
FINNISH BROADCASTING CO.—
Library - Information Services
PO Box 113, Yleisradia, Finland, 00024
358 1 480 5622; FAX 358 1 480 5616

Hours: Mon—Fri 9—6
Personnel
Head/Lib Info Svcs — Ratva Valiaho
Info Specialist — Janne Ranta

700 France (Paris)
CFPJ
33, rue du Louvre, 75002 Paris, France,
33 14 482 2000; FAX 33 14 482 2002

Personnel
Librarian — Sylvie Foutrier

701 France (Paris)
LE FIGARO MAGAZINE
37 rue du Louvre, 75002 Paris, France,
33 13 4221 6200; FAX 33 13 1221 6105

Founded: 1828.

702 France (Paris)
INTERNATIONAL HERALD TRIBUNE
181, av. Charles-de-Gaulle, 92521 Neuilly Cedex, France, See Banner
33 14 143 9300; FAX 33 14 143 9338; Email: Library@IHT.COM

Newspaper founded: 1887; Library founded: 1887.
Hours: Sun—Fri 8:30am—12m
Days Not Published: New Year's Day, May Day, Christmas.
Newspaper Group: Co-owned by the New York Times and Washington Post.

Access: Open to other media by appointment.
Resources: Photo files, reference books, maps. Microforms: roll. Newspaper index, clippings.
Services to Other News Libraries: Telephone reference. Sends copies of clips—3 pages maximum; no long distance FAX. Telefacsimile clips in greater Paris area.
Online Databases: Minitel; Datatimes; LEXIS/NEXIS
Personnel
Director — Daniel Reasor, (9321), SLA
Asst Librarian — Bradford Spurgeon

703 France (Paris)
LE MONDE
15 rue Falguierre, 75501 Paris Cedex 03, France,
33 13 4065 2525; FAX 33 13 4065 2599

Founded: 1944

LE MONDE (cont'd)

Home Page (URL): http://www.lemonde.fr.
Personnel
Librarian — Daniel Conrod-Magnian

704 **Germany (Baden-Baden)**
BADISCHES TAGBLATT
Stefanienstr. 1 PF 120, 76481 Baden-Baden, Germany,
49 72 212 1500; FAX 49 72 212 1529

Personnel
Director — Eckard Lange, (21 92 3358)

705 **Germany (Berlin)**
BERLINER ZEITUNG
Kurl Liebknecht Str. 29, 10176 Berlin, Germany,
49 30 232 79; FAX 49 30 232 75 533

Founded: 1945.

706 **Germany (Bonn)**
AGENCE FRANCE—PRESS (AFP)
Adenauerallee 266, 53113 Bonn, Germany,
49 228 917 2552; FAX 49 228 917 2559

Personnel
Librarian — Sabine Sendker

707 **Germany (Darmstadt)**
THE EUROPEAN STARS AND STRIPES
Unit 29480, APO AE 09211,
49 61 55601400 / Reference 49 61 55601214; FAX 49 61 55601416

Newspaper founded: 1942.
Hours: Mon—Fri 8am—5pm
Days Not Published: New Year's Day, Independence Day, Christmas.
Services to Other News Libraries: Telephone reference, sends copies of clips. Contact: Debra Tesh.
Resources: Photo files, negatives, reference books, maps. Microforms: roll. Newspaper index (1983—present); clippings (before 1984).
Special Collections: World War II era.
Personnel
Library Supervisor — Charlene Neuwiller, (49 6155 601 400), SLA
Photo Technician — Ortwin Nossinski
Research Specialist — Debra Tesh

708 **Germany (Darmstadt)**
INCA-FIEJ RESEARCH ASSOCIATION
Washingtonplatz 1, 6428 Darmstadt, Germany,
49 61 51 7005 49; FAX 49 61 51 7005 74

Hours: Mon—Fri 8am—5pm
Access: Open to the public and other libraries. Will send clippings.
Special Collections: Sample newspaper collection of over 300 international newspapers.
Files of newspaper production equipment, newspaper files and technoloy index describing operations at 200-300 int'l newspapers, based on clippings from trade press, press releases, visit memos, etc.

Also a register of newspapers in Europe, America, Australia, using inhouse electronic library systems. A register of int'l and national news databases that are publicly accessible.

Personnel
Documentalists — Heike Schmockel
Susanne Finkler

709 **Germany (Dusseldorf)**
EUROPEAN INSTITUTE FOR THE MEDIA
KaistraDFe 13, 40221 Dusseldorf, Germany,
49 211 9010 459; FAX 49 211 9010 456; Email: 100443.1710@compuserve.com

Personnel
Librarians — Angela Mounier
Helga Schmid

710 **Germany (Dusseldorf)**
HANDELSBLATT
Kasernenstrasse 67, 40213 Dusseldorf, Germany,
49 211 88 7 0; FAX 49 211 32 67 59

Personnel
Librariain — M. Niedermeier

711 **Germany (Frankfurt)**
FRANKFURTER ALLGEMEINE ZEITUNG
Hellerhofstr 2 (Postfach 100808), 60267 Frankfurt, Germany,
49 69 75910; FAX 49 69 75911535

Personnel
Archivist — E. Ganzmann
Librarian — Franz-Josef Gasterich

712 **Germany (Hamburg)**
AXEL—SPRINGER PUBLISHING CORP.
Hamburg 20350, Germany,
49 40 347 4000

Library founded: 1946.
Hours: Mon—Fri 8am—12m
Resources: Reference books. Microforms: roll, fiche. Clippings.
Services to Other News Libraries: Telephone reference. Sends copies of clips.
News Databases: BASIS.
Personnel
Supv Director — Richard Everett
Director — Beate Pauluth-Cassel, (22146)

713 **Germany (Munich)**
SUDDEUTSCHE ZEITUNG
Sendlinger Strasse 8, 80331 Munich, Germany,
49 89 2183 1; FAX 49 89 2183 787

Personnel
Archivists — M. Hess
Hella Schmidt

714 **Hong Kong (Wanchai)**
FREEDOM FORUM—
Asian Center
1305-06, 13th Fl, Shui on Centre, Wanchai, Hong Kong,
85 2 2596 0018; FAX 85 2 2598 8818

715 **Iceland (Reykjavik)**
DAGBLADID-VISIR
Tnverholt 11 (PO Box 5380), 105 Reykjavik, Iceland, See Banner
354 1 27022; FAX 354 1 27079

Library founded: 1981.
Newspaper Group: Frjals fjolmidlun Ltd.
Days Not Published: Sunday, Christmas.

716 **Ireland (Cork)**
THE CORK EXAMINER / EVENING ECHO
95 Patrick St, Cork, Ireland,
353 21 272722

717 **Ireland (Dublin)**
IRISH INDEPENDENT / EVENING HERALD
Middle Abbey St, Dublin 2, Ireland,
353 01 731333

718 **Ireland (Dublin)**
IRISH PRESS / EVENING PRESS
Tara House, Tara St, Dublin 2, Ireland,
353 01 713333

719 **Ireland (Dublin)**
IRISH TIMES
11-15 D'Olier St, Dublin 2, Ireland,
353 01 792022

720 **Israel (Haifa)**
BAHAI WORLD CENTRE—
Library
PO Box 155, 31 001 Haifa Israel,
972 8 4 358 570; FAX 972 8 4 358 280; Email: Libper@bwc.Org.il

Personnel
Librarian — Bryn Deamer

721 **Israel (Jerusalem)**
JERUSALEM POST
PO Box 81, Jerusalem, Israel, — See Banner
972 2 315641/2; FAX 972 2 385070 / 972 2 389572

Newspaper founded: 1932.
Services to Other News Libraries: Telephone reference. Sends articles by Email; clippings by mail.
LAN: ATEX, IBM.
Archival Systems: ATEX.
Resources: Photo files, microform/fiche. Commercial newspaper database available on CD Rom from 10/88; also offered on LEXIS/NEXIS/Mead Data Central, Datastar, Datatimes, Telebase and ACC networks. Clippings Research library and CD Rom stations for public access at main offices in Jerusalem.
Special Collections: The Jerusalem Post is the only daily English language newspaper which has recorded the events in Palestine, Israel, and the Middle East over the past fifty years.
Personnel
Director — Nina Keren-David, SLA

722 **Italy (Rome)**
ANSA—
Italian News Agency Library
39 6 67741; FAX 39 6 67824

723 **Italy (Rome)**
BRITISH COUNCIL
Via Quattro Fontane 20, 00184, Rome, Italy,
39 6 478 14213; FAX 39 6 481 4206; Email: bcrome@itcaspur.caspur.it

Personnel
Librarian — Christine Cole, AUKML

724 **Italy (Rome)**
RAI RADIOTELEVISIONE ITALIANA
Viale Mazzini 14, 00195 Rome, Italy,
39 6 384004; FAX 39 6 3612012

Personnel
Librarian — Stefano Nespolesi, (39 6 3386 4249)

New York Bureau: 1350 Ave of Americas, NY 10019 (212-468-2466; FAX: 212-765-1956)
Washington DC Bureau: 1234 34th St NW #7, Washington DC 20007

725 **Italy (Rome)**
LA REPUBBLICA
Piazza Indipendenza 11/b, 00185 Rome, Italy,
39 6 49 821; FAX 39 6 49 387 7049; Email: Library.Repubblica@Agora.Stm

Hours: Sat, Sun 8am—12m
Access: Open to other media by appointment.
Archival Systems: Baseview Library System; AP Preserver; Digital Link Gateway; Photofile; Image Central; PaperDesk; TEXT and IMAGE ARCHIVES.
LAN: Ethernet.
CD ROM: Yes.
Fee-Based Research: Research Fee: $30. Copies; Microform Copies; FAX. Contact Stefano Fabbri or Patrizia Deales.
Personnel
Archivist — Vittorio Caraffa, (22777)

726 **Japan**
NIPPON TOSHOKAN KYOKAI (ASSOCIATION OF JAPANESE LIBRARIES)
81 3 3410 6411; FAX 81 3 3410 6566

Personnel
Secretary — Nori Yoshikio

727 **Japan (Kita-Kyushu)**
ASAHI SHIMBUN
1-12-1, Sunatsu, Kokura-kita-ku, Kitakyushu City, 802 Japan,
81 3 5541 8557 (Tokyo Office)

Personnel
Librarian — Keiko Nakamichi

728 **Japan (Tokyo)**
ASAHI SHIMBUN
5-3-2 Tsukiji, Chou-ku, Tokyo 104-11, Japan,
81 3 545 0131; FAX 81 3 545 8450

729 **Japan (Tokyo)**
ASSOCIATED PRESS—
Library
Asahi Shimbun Bldg 11th Fl, 3-2 Tsukjii 5-chome, Chuo-Ku, Tokyo 104-11 Japan,

Personnel
Librarian — Watanabe Chisaki

730 **Japan (Tokyo)**
NIHON KEIZAI SHIMBUN
1-9-5 Ohte-Machi, Chiyoda-ku, Tokyo 100-66 Japan,
81 3 327 00251; FAX 81 3 278 0614

Founded: 1876.

731 **Japan (Tokyo)**
NIKKET BP INC.
2-7-6 Hirakawa-cho, Chiyoda-ku, Tokyo 102, Japan,
81 3 13 5210 8349

Personnel
Librarian — Tomoko Ueno, SLA

732 **Japan (Tokyo)**
SANKEI SHIMBUN
1-7-2 Ohte-machi, Chiyoda-ku, Tokyo 100-77 Japan,
81 3 323 17111; FAX 81 3 246 1168

Founded: 1933.

733 **Japan (Tokyo)**
YOMIURI SHIMBUN
1-7-1 Ohte-Machi, Chiyoda-ku, Tokyo 10055 Japan,
81 3 324 21111; FAX 81 3 246 0890

Founded: 1874.

734 **Malaysia (Kuala Lampur)**
NEW STRAITS TIMES PRESS BERHAD—
Resource Center-RIS Department
Balai Berita 31 Jalan Riong, 59100 Kuala Lampur, Malaysia,
60 3 282 3322; FAX 60 3 282 1434

Personnel
Librarian — Cecilia Chun Huang Tan, SLA

735 **Mexico**
REFORMA / EL NORTE / INFOSEL—
Servicios de Informacion
52 8 318 8835; FAX 52 8 340 0560

Home Page (URL): http://www.infosel.com.mx/.
Personnel
Director — Rogelio Hinojosa, (rhinojos@infosel.net.mx)

736 **Mexico (Monterrey)**
SERVICIOS DE INFORMACION
Washington 629 Oriente Apdo, 64000 Monterey, N.L., Mexico,
52 8 318 8835; FAX 52 8 340 0560

Home Page (URL): http://www.infosel.com.mx/.
Personnel
Director — Rogelio Hinojosa, (rhinojos@infosel.net.mx)

737 **Netherlands**
BRABANT PERS BV
PO Box 90, 5680 AB Best, Netherlands,
31 499 36 33 98; FAX 31 499 39 71 80

Personnel
Documentation Dept Head — Wil Roestenburg

738 **Netherlands**
CHW/FJC
Campus 2-6, 8017 Cazwolle, Netherlands,
31 38 469 96 17; FAX 31 38 465 42 88

Personnel
Librarian — Thea Dengerink, (denger@chw.nl)

739 **Netherlands**
DE GELDERLANDER
Postbus 36, 6500 da Nijmegen, Netherlands,
31 24 365 05 91; FAX 31 24 365 04 59

Personnel
Librarian — Ruud Jacobs

740 **Netherlands**
NOS—JOURNAAL—
Documentation Department
Postbus 2G 150, 1202 Hc Hilversum, Netherlands,
31 35 677 37 45; FAX 31 35 21 88 70

Personnel
Librarian — Ineke de Waard, (idewaard@nos.nl)

741 **Netherlands**
TROS BROADCASTING
PO Box 28000, 1202 La Hilversum, Netherlands,
31 35 671 53 51; FAX 31 35 671 54 21

Personnel
Librarians — Margot Bacsa, (margot.bacsa@tros.nl)
Anne Werst, (anne.werst@tros.nl)

742 **Netherlands (Amsterdam)**
TELEGRAAPH DAGBLAD
31 20 585 2101

Personnel
Librarian — M. van der Linden

743 **New Zealand (Auckland)**
AUCKLAND STAR LIMITED
155 New North Rd (PO Box 1409), Auckland, New Zealand, See Banner
64 9 797 626; FAX 64 9 390 258

Library founded: 1950.
Newspaper Group: Independent Newspapers Ltd.
Hours: Mon—Fri 7am—4:30pm; Sat 12n—8pm
Days Not Published: New Year's Day, Good Friday, Anzac Day, Christmas, Saturday.
Access: Not open to other media. Opens occasionally to other special libraries.
Resources: Photo files, negatives, reference books, maps, pamphlet file. Microforms: fiche. Newspaper index, clippings, cartoons.
Special Collections: Bromhead cartoons.
Personnel
Director — Andrea J. Millar, (8806)
Deputy Librarian — Jennifer Reed, (8803)
Library Assts — Marshar Kaye, (8803)
Barbara Niccol, (8804)
Anna Harding, (8804)

744 **New Zealand (Auckland)**
FOURTH ESTATE PERIODICALS LTD.
PO Box 1734, Auckland, New Zealand,
64 9 371 629

Hours: 9am—5pm
Access: Open to the public and other special libraries. Will send clippings.
Personnel
Librarian — Catherine M. Grebenar

745 **New Zealand (Auckland)**
NEW ZEALAND HERALD
46 Albert St (PO Box 32), Auckland, New Zealand,
64 9 795 050; FAX 64 9 366 1568

Newspaper founded: 1863; library founded: 1927.
Hours: Mon—Fri 8:30am—11pm; Sun 2:30pm—11pm
Days Not Published: New Year's Day, Anzac Day, Easter Friday, Christmas, Sunday.
Services to Other News Libraries: Telephone reference, within reason. Sends copies of clips.
Access: Not open to the public or other special libraries. Although official policy is no public access, we usually handle quick telephone queries and some mail requests within reason.
Resources: Photo files, reference books, pamphlet files. Microforms: roll. Clippings.
Personnel
Head Librarian — Carol Edmonds
Deputy Librarian — Pauline Murphy

746 **New Zealand (Christchurch)**
CHRISTCHURCH STAR
293 Tuam St (PO Box 1461), Christchurch, New Zealand, See Banner
64 3 379 7100; FAX 64 3 366 0180

Newspaper founded: 1868; Library founded: 1960's.
Newspaper Group: Wilson and Horton Ltd.
Hours: Mon—Fri 7:30am—4pm
Access: Open to other media and other special libraries with the permission of the editor.
Resources: Photo files, reference books, maps, pamphlet file. Microforms: roll. Newspaper index, clippings.
Services to Other News Libraries: Telephone reference. Sends copies of clips—Fee: $20. Express mails clips. Must have permission of the editor.

747 **New Zealand (Wellington)**
THE DOMINION / DOMINION SUNDAY TIMES—
Library
40 Boulcott St (PO Box 1297), Wellington, New Zealand, See Banner
64 4 740 222; FAX 64 4 740 350

Newspaper founded: 1907; Library founded: 1960's.
Newspaper Group: Independent Newspapers Ltd.
Hours: Mon—Fri 9am—10pm

THE DOMINION / DOMINION SUNDAY TIMES (cont'd)

Days Not Published: Boxing Day, Anzac Day, Good Friday, January 2nd.
Access: Open to other media with editor's permission; open to other special libraries if time allows.
Services to Other News Libraries: Telephone reference (64 4 740 169), sends copies of clips.
Resources: Photo files, negatives, reference books, maps, pamphlet file. Microforms: fiche. Clippings.
Personnel
Chief Librarian — Mary Slatter

748 **New Zealand (Wellington)**
EVENING POST
PO Box 3740, Wellington, New Zealand,
64 4 729 009; FAX 64 4 740 237

749 **Norway (Bergen)**
BERGENS TIDENDE
Postboks 875, N-5001 Bergen, Norway,
47 5 21 45 00; FAX 47 5 31 92 31
Newspaper founded: 1868.

750 **Norway (Oslo)**
AFTENPOSTEN
51 Postboks 1178 Sentrum, N-0107 Oslo 1, Norway,
47 2 86 34 78; FAX 47 2 42 63 25
Newspaper founded: 1860.
Personnel
Librarians — Anniken Lorentzen
Hilde Flaten Arkivar

751 **Norway (Oslo)**
DAGBLADET
Postboks 1184 Sentrum, N-0107 Oslo 1, Norway,
47 2 20 20 90; FAX 47 2 42 95 48
Newspaper founded: 1869.
Personnel
Adm Director — Dagfinn Bakken

752 **Norway (Oslo)**
VERDENS GANG
Akersgt. 34, N-0107, Oslo 1, Norway, See Banner
47 2 11 40 40; FAX 47 2 33 37 78
Newspaper founded: 1945; Library founded: 1975.
Newspaper Group: Schibsted-Gruppen
Hours: 8:45am—12m
Resources: Reference books, maps. Microforms: rolls. Clippings.
Services to Other News Libraries: Telephone reference. Sends copies of clips, express mails clips.
News Databases: SII.
Personnel
Director — Bjorg Saether Foss, (375)
Librarians — Tone Eliassen, (371)
Ellen Anette Smeby
Karin Benjaminsen

753 **Saudi Arabia**
KACST—
Library
PO Box 6086, Riyadh, 11442 Saudi Arabia,
966 1 481 3215
Personnel
Librarian — Abdulrahman Alhamidi

754 **Singapore**
LIANHE WANABAO
82 Genting Lane, Singapore 1334,
65 743 8800; FAX 65 743 2427

755 **Singapore**
LIANHE ZAOBAO
82 Genting Lane, Singapore 349567,
65 743-8800; FAX 65 748-2652
Home Page (URL): http://www.asia1.com.og/zaobao.

756 **Singapore**
STRAITS TIMES AND BUSINESS TIMES
390 Kim Seng Rd, Singapore, 0923
65 737 0011; FAX 65 747 8501
Personnel
Librarian — Lee Meow Hui

757 **Slovak Republic**
NARODNA OBRODA—
Documentation Department
Trnavska cesta 112, 830 00 Bratislava, Slovakia,
42 7 299 2238; FAX 42 7 296 281
Personnel
Manager — Dr. Drahoslava Rehakova

758 **Slovak Republic**
NOVY CAS—
Documentation Department
Gorkeho 5, 812 78 Bratislava, Slovakia,
42 7 363 070; FAX 42 7 363 104

759 **Slovak Republic**
PRACA—
Documentation Department
Odborarske namestie 3, 812 71 Bratislava, Slovakia,
42 7 642 46; FAX 42 7 212 985
Personnel
Manager — Jana Ciernikova

760 **Slovak Republic**
PRAVDA—
Newsroom and Information Services
Pribinova 25, 819 08 Bratislava, Slovakia,
42 7 210 4771; FAX 42 7 210 4759
Personnel
Manager — Peter Bulak

761 **Slovak Republic (Bratislava)**
CENTER FOR INDEPENDENT JOURNALISM—
Freedom Forum Library
9 Sturova, Bratislava, Slovakia, 81102
42 7 322 707; FAX 42 7 322 706
Personnel
Librarian — Luba Horvathova

762 **South Africa (Johannesburg)**
TIMES MEDIA LTD.
PO Box 1138, Johannesburg 2000 South Africa,
27 11 497 2138; FAX 27 11 834 1686; Email: 100075.1167@compuserve.com
Services: Research, Readers' enquiries, Serials/periodicals, Cuttings.
Personnel
Librarian — Michelle Leon, (michelle@tml.com.za), AUKML

763 **Sweden (Goteborg)**
GOTEBORGS—POSTEN
405 02 Goteborg, Sweden,
46 31 62 46 89; FAX 46 31 15 06 63
Personnel
Librarians — Susanne Kilner, (sanna.kilner@gp.se)
Lars Svensson, (lars.svensson@gp.se)

764 **Sweden (Stockholm)**
SWEDISH BROADCASTING CORPORATION
10510, Stockholm, Sweden,
46 8 784 17 35

Hours: Mon—Fri 8am—7pm; Sat, Sun 12n—7pm
Access: Open to other libraries; not open to the public.
Personnel
Chief Librarian — Ronald D. Vaverka

765 **Switzerland (Zurich)**
FREEDOM FORUM— European Center
Bahnhofstrasse 16, CH-8001, Zurich, Switzerland,
41 1 212 3355; FAX 41 1 212 3365

766 **Switzerland (Zurich)**
NEUE ZURCHER ZEITUNG— Redaktionsinformatikerin
Falkenstrasse 11, 8021 Zurich Switzerland,
41 1 258 1014; FAX 41 1 258 1070; Email: nzzspi@dm.rs.ch

Personnel
Info Systems Editor — Ruth Spitzenpfeil
Archivist — Hans-Peter Jaun, (1220)

767 **United Kingdom (Aberystwyth)**
UNIVERSITY OF WALES— Department of Information & Library Studies
Llanbadarn Campus, Aberystwyth, SY23 3AS, Wales,
44 1970 623 111; FAX 44 1970 622 190

Services: Research.
Online Databases: Blaise; DataStar; DIALOG.
Personnel
Librarian — Jamie Medhurst, (2152, jsm@aber-ac.uk), AUKML

768 **United Kingdom (Belfast)**
IRISH NEWS
113-117 Donegal St, Belfast, BT1 2GE, N Ireland,
44 232 322 226; FAX 44 232 337 505

Year founded: 1855; Library founded: 1982.
Hours: Mon—Fri 9—5:30
Days Not Published: Christmas, Sunday
Services to Other News Libraries: Telephone reference. Sends copies/Faxes clips.
Resources: Photo files, reference books, maps, pamphlets. Microfiche. Clippings.
Personnel
Director — Kathleen Bell, (565), AUKML

769 **United Kingdom (Birmingham)**
BIRMINGHAM POST AND MAIL
PO Box 18, 28 Colmore Circus, Birmingham, B4 6AX, England,
44 121 234 5717; FAX 44 121 233 0271

Year founded: 1732; library founded: 1920.
Hours: Mon—Thur 8am—10pm; Fri 8—5; Sat 10—8; Sun 3pm—10:30pm.
Days Not Published: Christmas
Resources: Photo files, reference books, maps, pamphlets. Microforms: roll, fiche, jackets. Clippings.
Online Databases: FT Profile.
Personnel
Chief Librarian — Christine Cole, (5717)
Deputy Librarian — Anna Burke, AUKML
Librarians — Jackie Curley
Teresa Kinchin-Sevier
Mike Evetts
Tim Stanton
Gill Shaw
Alison Sharpe

770 **United Kingdom (Birmingham)**
CENTRAL BROADCASTING
Central House, Broad St, Birmingham, B1 2JP, England,
44 21 643 9898; FAX 44 21 634 4055

Online Databases: FT Profile.
Personnel
Librarian — Margaret Duerden, (4535), AUKML

771 **United Kingdom (Birmingham)**
MIDLAND INDEPENDENT NEWSPAPERS
28 Colmore Circus (PO Box 18), Birmingham, B4 6AX, England,
44 21 234 5717

Year founded: 1732; library founded: 1920.
Hours: Mon—Thur 8am—10pm; Fri 8—5:30; Sat 10—8; Sun 3pm—10pm.
Days Not Published: Christmas.
Resources: Photo files, reference books, maps, pamphlets. Microforms: roll, fiche, jackets. Clippings.
Personnel
Chief Librarian — Christine Cole
Deputy Librarian — Anna Burke, (236-3366)
Librarians — Jackie Curley, (5414)
Teresa Kinchin-Sevier, (5681)
Mike Evetts
Tim Stanton
Gill Shaw
Alison Sharpe

772 **United Kingdom (Brighton)**
EVENING ARGUS
Crowhurst Rd, Brighton, BN1 8AF, England,
44 127 354 4544; FAX 44 127 350 5703

Year founded: 1880.
Hours: Mon—Fri 8:30—430
Days Not Published: Christmas Day, Sunday
Resources: Reference books, maps, pamphlets. Microforms: roll. Newspaper index, Clippings.
Personnel
Librarian — Mary Peatfield, (595), AUKML

773 **United Kingdom (Cardiff)**
BBC WALES
Llandaf, Room LG102, Cardiff, CF5 2YQ, Wales,
222 222 572 500; FAX 222 222 572 798

Services: Research, Readers enquiries, Serials/periodicals.
Online Databases: FT Profile.
Personnel
Librarians — Huw Evans, (738), AUKML
Kate Lloyd Evans, AUKML
Sue Gress

774 **United Kingdom (Cardiff)**
S4C
Parc Ty Glas, Cardiff, CF5 4DU, Wales,
222 122 274 1209; FAX 222 122 275 4444

Services: Research, Readers' enquiries, Book ordering.
Personnel
Librarian — Jennifer Griffiths, (1209), AUKML

775 **United Kingdom (Cardiff)**
WESTERN MAIL & ECHO LTD.
Thomson House, Havelock St, Cardiff, CF1 1WR, Wales,
44 222 583 686; FAX 44 222 583 624

Year founded: Mail—1869; Echo—1884; Sunday—1988.
Newspaper Group: Thomson Newspapers
Hours: Mon—Fri 7:30am—10pm; Sat 7:30am—11am; Sun 2pm—10pm.

WESTERN MAIL & ECHO LTD. (cont'd)

Days Not Published: Christmas
The library works for the following titles: Western Mail, South Wales Echo, Wales on Sunday, Celtic Newspapers.

Services to Other News Libraries: Telephone reference. Sends copies of clips for fee. Requirements: for library access/research. Contact: Chief Librarian. Faxes clips.
Access: Open to other media for fee.
Resources: Photo files, reference books, maps. Microform: Jackets. Newspaper index, clippings, transparency files.
Special Collections: Welsh War Photos; Rugby Photos.
Personnel
Director — Anthony Woolway, (2930), AUKML

776 **United Kingdom (Coventry)**
COVENTRY NEWSPAPERS
Corporation St, Coventry, CV1 1FP, England,
44 120 363 3633; FAX 44 120 355 0869

Services: Research, Readers' enquiries, Serials/periodicals, Indexing, Cuttings.
Personnel
Librarian — June Fairbrother, AUKML

777 **United Kingdom (Darlington)**
NORTH OF ENGLAND NEWSPAPERS
Priestgate (PO Box 14), Darlington, DL1 1NF, England
44 132 538 1313; FAX 44 132 538 0539; Email: 100307.3313@compuserve.com

Services: Research, Statistical Research, Readers' enquiries, Book ordering, Serials/periodicals, Indexing.
Online Databases: Companies House; FT Profile.
Personnel
Librarians — Peter Chapman, AUKML
Jo Brudenell, AUKML
Stephen Thompson, AUKML
Jane Whitfield

778 **United Kingdom (Darlington)**
THE NORTHERN ECHO
PO Box 14, Priestgate, Darlington, DL1 1NF, England,
44 132 538 1313; FAX 44 132 538 0539

Personnel
Librarian — Nick Luft

779 **United Kingdom (Derby)**
DERBY EVENING TELEGRAPH
Northcliffe House, Meadow Rd, Derby, DE1 2DW, England,
44 133 229 1111; FAX 44 133 225 3027

Services: Research, Readers' enquiries, Book ordering, Indexing, Cuttings.
Personnel
Librarian — Chrissie Smith, (6800), AUKML

780 **United Kingdom (Dundee)**
D C THOMPSON & CO. LTD.
80 Kingsway E, Dundee, DD4 8SL, Scotland,
41 138 222 3131; FAX 41 138 245 4590

Services: Research, Readers' enquiries, Serials/periodicals.
Personnel
Librarians — Douglas Spence, (3219), AUKML
Joyce Lorimer, AUKML

781 **United Kingdom (Edinburgh)**
SCOTSMAN
20 North Bridge, Edinburgh, EH1 1YT, Scotland,
44 131 243 3363; FAX 44 131 226 7420

Services: Research, Readers' enquiries.
Online Databases: FT Profile; LEXIS/NEXIS; Glasgow Herald.
Personnel
Librarians — Peter Chapman
Moira Stevenson, AUKML

782 **United Kingdom (Glasgow)**
BBC SCOTLAND
Queen Margaret Dr, Glasgow G12 8DG, Scotland,
44 141 339 8844; FAX 44 141 334 0614

Services: Research, Serials/periodicals, Cuttings.
Online Databases: FT Profile.
Personnel
Librarian — Alexandra Gaffney, AUKML

783 **United Kingdom (Glasgow)**
CALEDONIAN NEWSPAPERS
195 Albion St, Glasgow, G1 1QP, Scotland,
41 141 552 6255; FAX 41 141 553 3587; Email: 100072.2732@compuserve.com

Services: Research, Readers' enquiries, Book ordering.
Online Databases: DIALOG; FT Profile; House of Commons.
Personnel
LIbrarians — Ian Watson, (3426), AUKML
Stroma Fraser, AUKML
Nisha Kharbanda, AUKML
Beverley Mercer, AUKML

784 **United Kingdom (Glasgow)**
HERALD
195 Albion St, Glasgow, G1 1QP, Scotland,
44 141 552 6255; FAX 44 141 553 1344

Morning, evening. Year founded: 1783.
Hours: Mon—Fri 8am—10pm; Sat 8am—2pm; Sun 10am—10pm.
Days Not Published: New Year's Day, Christmas, Sunday
News Databases: BASIS.
Electronic Clipping Files: Available through FT Profile, Reuters.
Resources: Photo files, negatives, reference books, pamphlets. Microforms: roll. Newspaper index, clippings.
Personnel
Librarian — David Ball
Editoria Librarian — Marie Campbell
Picture Librarian — Bill Doig

785 **United Kingdom (Glasgow)**
SCOTTISH DAILY RECORD
Anderson Quay, Glasgow, G3 8DA, Scotland,
44 141 242 3523; FAX 44 141 242 3527; Email: 100137.3304@compuserve.com

Services: Research, Statistical research, Readers' enquiries, Book ordering, Serials/periodicals.
Online Databases: DIALOG; Dow Jones; FT Profile; LEXIS/NEXIS.
Personnel
Librarian — Pat Baird, (3523), AUKML

786 **United Kingdom (Glasgow)**
UNIVERSITY OF STRATHCLYDE—Department of Information & Science
26 Richmond St, Glasgow, G1 1XH, Scotland,
41 141 552 4400; FAX 41 141 553 1393

Online Databases: DataStar; DIALOG; FT Profile.
Personnel
Librarian — Charles Oppenheim, (3911), AUKML

787 United Kingdom (Huddersfield)
HUDDERSFIELD NEWSPAPERS
Queen St S (PO Box 26), Huddersfield, HD1 2TD, England,
44 148 443 0000; FAX 44 148 442 3722

Services: Research, Readers' enquiries, Indexing, Cuttings.
Personnel
Librarian — Jan Holliday, (2301), AUKML

788 United Kingdom (Hull)
HULL DAILY MAIL
PO Box 34, Blundell's Corner, Beverly Rd, Hull, HU3 1XS, England,
44 482 27111; FAX 44 482 27111

Personnel
Librarian — Ruth Foster, (273)

789 United Kingdom (Leeds)
YORKSHIRE POST
Wellington St, Leeds, West Yorkshire LS1 1RF,
44 113 243 2701; FAX 44 113 238 8530

Services: Research, telephone reference.
Personnel
Librarians — Kathleen Rainford
Anne McQueen, (1327), AUKML

790 United Kingdom (Leicester)
LEICESTER MERCURY
St George St (PO Box 46), Leicester, LE1 9FQ, England,
44 116 251 2512; FAX 44 116 253 0645

Services: Research, Readers' enquiries, book ordering, indexing, cuttings.
Personnel
Librarian — Steve England, (2391), AUKML

791 United Kingdom (Liverpool)
LIVERPOOL DAILY POST
Old St, Liverpool, L69 3EB, England,
44 151 227 2000; FAX 44 151 236 4682

Services: Research, Readers' enquiries, Book ordering, Indexing, Cuttings.
Personnel
Librarian — Colin Hunt, (472 2484), AUKML

792 United Kingdom (London)
ASSOCIATED PRESS—
News Library
12 Norwich St, London, EC4A 1BP, England,

Personnel
Chief Librarian — Joan Fisher

793 United Kingdom (London)
ASSOCIATION OF UK MEDIA LIBRARIANS
c/o Kent House, Upper Ground, London, SE1 9LT, England,
44 171 261 3734

Personnel
Director — Michael Torner, (44 71 269 9693)
Secretary — Peter Chapman

794 United Kingdom (London)
BBC—
News/Research Library
Broadcasting House, Rm 513, London, W1A 1AA, England,
44 171 765 2807; FAX 44 171 765 3462

Online Databases: FT Profile.
Personnel
LIbrarians — Rosalyn Cook, (4602), AULML
Jenny Martin, (2807), AUKML

795 United Kingdom (London)
BBC—
Photograph Library
56 Wood La, London, W12 7SB, England,
44 181 743 8000; FAX 44 181 746 0353

Personnel
Librarian — Margaret Kirby, (62988), AUKML

796 United Kingdom (London)
BBC WORLD SERVICE
PO Box 76 Strand, London, WC2 B4H, England,
44 171 240 3456; FAX 44 171 379 6785

Online Databases: Dow Jones; FT Profile; LEXIS/NEXIS.
Personnel
Librarians — Declan Kelly, (2154), AUKML
Paul Richards, (2047), AUKML
Margaret Katny, AUKML

797 United Kingdom (London)
BBC—
Information Research Library
BBC Television Centre, Room B250, London, W12 7RJ, England,
44 181 225 8301; FAX 44 181 576 1768

Services: Research, Statistical research, Readers' enquiries, Book ordering, Serials/periodicals.
Online Databases: Blaise; Companies House; DataStar; DIALOG; FT Profile; House of Commons; LEXIS/NEXIS; UK Trademarks; CCN; Waterlows; Wilsonline; IMSMARQ; Jordans.
Personnel
Librarians — Graham Highley, (765 3462), AUKML
Michele Arnal, (576 1540), AUKML
Michelle Morgan, (8301; Michelle.Morgan@bbc.co.uk) AUKML
Linda Cockburn, (8313), AUKML

798 United Kingdom (London)
BRITISH FILM INSTITUTE
21 Stephen St, London, W1P 2LN, England,
44 171 255 1444; FAX 44 171 436 0165

Online Databases: FT Profile; DIALOG; Baseline.
Personnel
Librarian — Gillian Hartnoll, AUKML

799 United Kingdom (London)
BRITISH LIBRARY—
Newspaper Library
Colindale Ave, London, NW9 5HE, England,
44 171 323 7353; FAX 44 171 323 7379

Hours: Mon—Sat 10am—5pm.
Online Databases: Blaise; DIALOG; World Reporter; FT Profile.

BRITISH LIBRARY (cont'd)

Services: Copying, microfilming service.

The Newspaper Library contains nearly 600,000 volumes and parcels and over 220,000 reels of microfilm occupying approximately 18 miles of shelving. About 6,000 volumes are added to stock each year, together with about 11,000 reels of positive microfilm. The collections consist mainly of daily and weekly newspapers and periodicals, including London newspapers and journals from 1801 onward, English provincial, Welsh, Scottish and Irish newspapers from about 1700 onward, and large collections of Commonwealth and foreign newspapers.

The Newspaper Library aims to collect the principal newspapers in western and Slavonic languages from all countries. The United Kingdom collections are very comprehensive from about 1840 onward, apart from those volumes of English provincial and Irish newspapers which were destroyed in the war and cannot be replaced. United Kingdom newspapers are bound or microfilmed before they become available to readers. Because of this system, national newspapers for the last six months and other United Kingdom newspapers for the last two or three years are not usually available, though current files are maintained of The Times, The Observer, and the Sunday Times.

For historians interested in contemporary reports of events in the 17th and 18th centuries, and for the specialist historian of the British newspaper press, the collections of London newspapers housed in the main library at Bloomsbury must be considered as one of the richest resources of any library in the world.

Publications: Newsletter—Microfilm of Newspapers for Sale (Free)

Access: Call Information Officer (ext 7357). News photos (ext 7355).

Special Collections: In the early 19th century, the British Museum Library acquired the library of Dr. Charles Burney which was bought for its manuscripts and printed editions of the classics. More recently, the value of the 700 volumes of newspapers contained in the collections has been more fully appreciated. The Burney Collections is now normally made made available on microfilm; For the Civil War and Commonwealth period, the chief resource is the unequalled Thomason collection, which contains over 7,000 issues for years 1641-1663; The Oriental Collections in Store Street hold newspapers published in oriental scripts and take in the countries of the Near East, the Indian sub-continent and the Far East. Holdings also include some of the eastern Turkish provinces of the Soviet Union; The India Office Library holdings of South Asian newspapers in the English language in some cases complement those of the Newspaper Library, but many titles are unique to its collections.

Personnel

Librarians	Geoffrey Hamilton
	Jill Allbrooke, (7357), AUKML
	Pam Airey, (7354), AUKML
Head/Public Svcs	Geoff Smith, (7362), AUKML

Bloomsbury Humanities and Social Sciences Reading Rooms, Great Russell St, London WC1B 3DG (323 7676)

India Office Library, 197 Blackfriars Rd, London SE1 8NG (Open Mon-Fri 9:30am-6pm. Telephone: 928 9531)

Holborn Reading Room, 25 Southampton Buildings, London WC2A 1AW (Open Mon-Fri 9:30am-9pm. Telephone: 323 7494/

800 United Kingdom (London)
BUILDER GROUP
Builder House, 1 Millharbour, London, E14 9RA, England,
44 171 537 6044; FAX 44 171 537 6050

Services: Research, Readers' enquiries, Serials/periodicals, Book ordering.

Personnel

Librarian	Garret Mchon, AUKML

801 United Kingdom (London)
CABLE NEWS NETWORK
CNN House, 19-22 Rathbone Pl, London, W1P 1DF, England,
44 171 637 6838; FAX 44 171 637 6868

Online Databases: DIALOG; LEXIS/NEXIS.
Special Collections: Video and clipreels of news.

Personnel

Librarian	Mary Muller, AUKML

802 United Kingdom (London)
CONFEDERATION OF BRITISH INDUSTRIES—
Information Center
Centre Pt 103 New Oxford St, London, WC1A 1DU, England,
44 171 3797400; FAX 44 171 8361972

Personnel

Librarian	Jack A. Hyde, SLA

803 United Kingdom (London)
DAILY EXPRESS / SUNDAY EXPRESS
Ludgate House, 245 Blackfrairs Rd, London, SE1 94X, England,
44 171 928 8000; FAX 44 171 833 0244

Newspaper founded: Daily—1900; Sunday—1918.
Newspaper: Express Newspapers PLC

804 United Kingdom (London)
DAILY MAIL
Northcliffe House, 2 Derry St, Kensington, London, W8 5TT, England,
44 171 938 6000; FAX 44 171 938 4890

Founded: 1896.
Newspaper Group: Mail Newspapers
Online Databases: FT Profile.

Personnel

Librarians	George Johnson, (6303)
	Steve Torrington
	Paul Rossiter, AUKML

805 United Kingdom (London)
DAILY MIRROR / SUNDAY MIRROR
1 Canada Sq, Canary Wharf, London, E14 5AP, England,
44 171 510 3000; FAX 44 171 293 3000

Services: Research, Statistical research.
Online Databases: DataStar; DIALOG; FT Profile; Perfect Information.

Personnel

Librarians	Alan Hemple, (3884), AUKML
	John Ellard, (3112), AUKML

806 United Kingdom (London)
DAILY TELEGRAPH / SUNDAY TELEGRAPH
Canada Sq, Canary Wharf, London, E14 93R, England,
44 171 538 5000; FAX 44 171 538 3810

Founded: 1772.

DAILY TELEGRAPH / SUNDAY TELEGRAPH (cont'd)

Newspaper Group: Daily Telegraph
Personnel
Librarians — Alexandra Erskine, (6265), AUKML
Fiona Sanson, AUKML

807 **United Kingdom (London)**
ECONOMIST
25 St James's St, London, SW1A 1HB, England,
44 171 830 7000; FAX 44 171 839 2968

Services: Statistical research, Readers' enquiries, Serials/periodicals, Book ordering, Indexing, Cuttings.
Online Databases: DIALOG; FT Profile; House of Commons; LEXIS/NEXIS.
Personnel
Librarians — Carol Howard, (7067), AUKML
Andrew Bevan, (1376), AUKML

808 **United Kingdom (London)**
EVENING STANDARD
2 Derry St, Kensington, London, W5 5EF, England,
44 171 988 6000; FAX 44 171 873 3076

Newspaper Group: Evening Standard Co. Ltd.

809 **United Kingdom (London)**
EXPRESS NEWSPAPERS—
Picture Library
245 Blankfrairs Rd, London, SE1 94X, England, SE1 94X
44 171 922 7779; FAX 44 171 922 7791

Personnel
Librarians — Stuart D. Dempster, SLA
Paul Ross, AUKML

810 **United Kingdom (London)**
FINANCIAL TIMES
1 Southwalk Bridge, London, SE1 9HL, England,
44 171 873 3000; FAX 44 171 873 4854; Email: 1000751.3140@compuserve. com

Newspaper Group: Financial Times Ltd.
Home Page (URL): http://www.ft.com.
Services: Research, Statistical Research, Serials/periodicals, Book ordering, Cuttings
Online Databases: Companies House; DataStar; DIALOG; Dow Jones; FT Graphite; FT Profile; House of Commons; Maid; LEXIS/NEXIS.
Personnel
Librarians — Mary Batten, (4876), AUKML
Sara Margetts, (3920), AUKML
Peter Cheek, (3468), AUKML
David Snaddon, (3311), AUKML

811 **United Kingdom (London)**
THE GUARDIAN/OBSERVER
119 Farringdon Rd, London, EC1R 3ER, England,
44 171 239 9772; FAX 44 171 239 9532

Founded as the Manchester Guardian.
Newspaper Group: Media Corp. PLC
Hours: Mon—Fri 10am—8pm; Sat 10—6; Sun 1pm—8pm
Days Not Published: Boxing Day.
Access: Open to other media by appointment.
Electronic Clipping Files: Profile
Services: Research, Statistical Research, Readers' Enquiries, Serials, Periodicals, Book ordering, Cuttings.
Online Databases: LEXIS/NEXIS; FT Profile; Datastream; Context.
Personnel
Librarians — Helen Martin, (hmarti@guardian.co.uk), AUKML
Mick Turner, (9693), AUKML

812 **United Kingdom (London)**
IISS
23 Tavistock St, London, WC2E 7NQ, England,
44 171 379 7676; FAX 44 171 836 3108; Email: 10035.1461@compuserve.com

Services: Readers' enquiries, Serials/periodicals.
Online Databases: LEXIS/NEXIS.
Personnel
Librarian — Hilary Oakley, (232), AUKML

813 **United Kingdom (London)**
ILLUSTRATED LONDON NEWS—
Picture Library
20 Upper Ground, London, SE1 9LZ, England,
44 171 928 2111; FAX 44 171 928 8144

Services: Research, Readers' enquiries.
Personnel
Librarian — Elaine Hart, (4141), AUKML

814 **United Kingdom (London)**
THE INDEPENDENT
1 Canada Square, Canary Wharf, London, England, EC1Y 2DB
44 171 253 1222; FAX 44 171 01 608 1552

Newspaper Group: Newspaper Publishing PLC
Personnel
Librarians — Gertrud Erbach, (44 71 956 1424)
Justin Arundale

815 **United Kingdom (London)**
INDEPENDENT TELEVISION COMMISSION
33 Foley St, London, W1P 7LB, England,
44 171 306 7765; FAX 44 171 306 7750

Services: Research, Statistical Research, Readers' enquiries, Serials/periodicals, Book ordering, Indexing, Cuttings.
Online Databases: DIALOG; FT Profile.
Personnel
Librarians — Barrie McDonald, (7766), AUKML
Jan Kacperek, AUKML

816 **United Kingdom (London)**
IPC MAGAZINES
Stamford St, London, SE1 9LS, England,
44 171 261 6104; FAX 44 171 261 5347

Services: Research, Serials/periodicals, Indexing, Cuttings
Online Databases: FT Profile.
Personnel
Librarians — Jane Rogers, AUKML
Julia Kent, AUKML

817 **United Kingdom (London)**
LONDON NEWS NETWORK
London Television Centre, Upperground, London, SE1 9LT, England,
44 171 827 7784; FAX 44 171 827 7579

Services: Research.
Online Databases: FT Profile.
Personnel
Librarian — Peter Allen, (827 7558), AUKML

818 **United Kingdom (London)**
LONDON WEEKEND TELEVISION LIMITED—
Information Research Unit
South Bank Television Centre, London, SE1 9LT, England,
44 171 12 613 734; FAX 44 171 2 613 782

Services: Research, Book ordering.
Online Databases: Blaise; Companies House; DataStar; DIALOG; FT Profile; LEXIS/NEXIS.
Personnel

Librarians	Caroline White, (262 3386), AUKML
	Jill Tulip, (261 8077), AUKML
Reference	Sarah Adair, (3584/3386)

819 **United Kingdom (London)**
MORNING STAR
74 Luke St, London, England, EC2A 4PY
44 171 739 6166; FAX 44 171 739 5463

Newspaper founded 1827.
Newspaper Group: Associated Newspapers

820 **United Kingdom (London)**
REUTERS NEWS SERVICE
85 Fleet St, London, EC4P 4AJ, England,
44 171 250 1122; FAX 44 171 324 5311

Access: Not open to other media; open to public by appointment.
Online Databases: LEXIS/NEXIS.
Personnel

Senior Researcher	Ian Middleton, (542 7968)

New York Bureau: 199 Water St, 10th Fl, New York, NY 10038. 212-859-1610; FAX 212-859-1717.
UN Bureau: United Nations Room C316, New York, NY 10017. 212-355-7424. FAX: 212-355-0143.
Florida Bureau: 305-374-5014; 800-423-7327.

821 **United Kingdom (London)**
ROYAL INSTITUTE OF INTERNATIONAL AFFAIRS
Chatham House, 10 St James's Sq, London, SW1 4LE, England,
44 171 957 5700; FAX 44 171 957 5710; Email: riialibrary@gn.apc.org

Services: Readers' enquiries, Serials/periodicals, Indexing, Cuttings, Photocopying and FAXing service.
Online Databases: Blaise; Eurobases; FT Profile.
Personnel

Librarians	Susan Boyde, AUKML
	Mary Bone, AUKML
	Maureen Pinder, AUKML

822 **United Kingdom (London)**
THE STAR

Newspaper founded: 1978.
Newspaper Group: Express Newspapers PLC

823 **United Kingdom (London)**
THE SUN / NEWS OF THE WORLD
Virginia St, London, England, E1 9KJ
44 171 782 7000 / Library 44 171 782 6380; FAX 44 171 782 5605

Newspaper Group: News Group Newspapers Ltd.

824 **United Kingdom (London)**
TIME OUT MAGAZINE
Universal House, Tottenham Court Rd, London, W1A 1BZ, England,
44 171 813 6105; FAX 44 171 813 61291

Services: Research, Readers' enquiries, Serials/periodicals, Book ordering, Indexing, Cuttings.
Online Databases: FT Profile.
Personnel

Reference Libn	Fiona Tennyson, AUKML
Picture Libn	Naomi Lees, AUKML

825 **United Kingdom (London)**
THE TIMES / SUNDAY TIMES
Virginia St (PO Box 481), London, E1 9BD, England,
44 171 782 6378; FAX 44 171 782 6370

Newspaper Group: Times Newspapers Ltd.
Home Page (URL): http://www.the-times.co.uk.
Services: Research, Readers' enquiries, Serials/periodicals, Book ordering, Cuttings.
Online Databases: Companies House; DataStar; DIALOG; FT Profile; Maid; LEXIS/NEXIS; Reuters.
Personnel

Database Mgr	Richard Withey, (5029), AUKML
Librarians	Judith Dunn, (6319; judithdunn@delphi.com), AUKML
	Gertrud Erbach, (6378), AUKML

826 **United Kingdom (London)**
TIME—LIFE NEWS SERVICE
Brettenham House, Lancaster Pl, London, WC2E 7TL, England,
44 171 322 1070; FAX 44 171 322 1230

Services: Research, Statistical research, Readers' enquiries, Book ordering, Serials/periodicals, Cuttings.
Online Databases: Blaise; Companies House; FT Profile.
Personnel

Librarian	Mick Brunton, AUKML

827 **United Kingdom (London)**
UNITED STATES INFORMATION SERVICE
55/56 Upper Brook St, London, W1A 2LH, England,
44 171 499 5684; FAX 44 171 629 8288; Email: reflond@usia.gov

Services: Research, Readers' enquiries, Serials/periodicals.
Online Databases: DIALOG; FT Profile; LEXIS/NEXIS; LEGI-SLATE.
Personnel

Librarian	Kate Bateman, (5684), AUKML

828 **United Kingdom (London)**
VNU BUSINESS PUBLICATIONS
32-34 Broadwick St, London, W1A 2HG, England,
44 171 316 9000; FAX 44 171 316 9003

Services: Readers' enquiries, Serials/periodicals.
Online Databases: Maid; Reuters.
Personnel

Librarians	S.J. Beardsley, (9042), AUKML
	R.J. Gallehawk, (9043), AUKML

829 **United Kingdom (Manchester)**
MANCHESTER EVENING NEWS
164 Deansgate, Manchester, M60 2RR, England,
44 161 832 7200; FAX 44 161 834 3814

Services: Research, Statistical research, Readers' enquiries, Indexing, Cuttings
Personnel

Librarians	Judith Walker
	Judi McGhee, (2486), AUKML
	Alan Ormerod

830 **United Kingdom (Manchester)**
SPORT NEWSPAPERS
19 Great Ancoats St, Manchester, M60 4BT, England,
44 161 238 8175; FAX 44 161 236 4535

Services: Research, Readers' enquiries, Indexing, Cuttings.
Personnel
Librarian Bob Murray, AUKML

831 **United Kingdom (Middlesbrough)**
EVENING GAZETTE
Borough Rd, Middlesbrough, TS1 3AZ England,
44 164 224 5401 ext 239; FAX 44 164 221 0565

Services: Research, Readers' enquiries.
Personnel
Librarian Barbara Thompson, AUKML

832 **United Kingdom (Middlesbrough)**
EVENING GAZETTE
Borough Rd, Middlesbrough, TS1 3AZ England,
44 642 245 401; FAX 44 642 210 565

Services: Research, Readers' enquiries.
Personnel
Librarian Barbara Thompson, (239), AUKML

833 **United Kingdom (Norwich)**
ANGLIA TELEVISION
Anglia House, Norwich, NR1 3JG, England,
44 1603 615151; FAX 44 1603 615494

Access: Open to other media by appointment.
Services: Research.
Personnel
Librarian Belinda Fisher, (2225), AUKML

834 **United Kingdom (Plymouth)**
WESTERN MORNING/EVENING NEWS CO.
Derriford Business Park, 17 Brest Rd, Plymouth, Devon, 65AA, England,
44 175 276 5500; FAX 44 175 276 5543

Services: Research, telephone reference, cuttings.
Personnel
Librarian Jenny Parker, AUKML

835 **United Kingdom (Portsmouth)**
PORTSMOUTH PUBLISHING AND PRINTING
The News Centre, Hilsea, Portsmouth, PO2 9SX, England,
44 1705 664 488; FAX 44 1705 673 363

Services: Readers' enquiries.
Personnel
Librarian Brenda Jacobs, (2020), AUKML

836 **United Kingdom (Preston)**
UNIVERSITY OF CENTRAL LANCASHIRE
Centre for Resource & Information Management
Preston, PR1 2HE, England,
44 177 289 2299; FAX 44 177 289 2937; Email: cerlim@uk.ac.uclan

Services: Research.
Online Databases: DIALOG; FT Profile; LEXIS/NEXIS.
Personnel
Librarian Ann Irving, AUKML

837 **United Kingdom (Southampton)**
SOUTHERN NEWSPAPERS
45 Above Bar, Southampton, SO9 7BA, England,
44 170 363 4134; FAX 44 170 372 7357

Services: Research, Readers' enquiries.
Personnel
Librarian Peter Ashton, AUKML

838 **United Kingdom (Sunderland)**
SUNDERLAND ECHO
Pennywell Industrial Estate, Sunderland, SR4 9ER, England,
44 191 522 7761

Services: Research, Readers' enquiries.
Personnel
Librarian Elizabeth Weightman, (534 3011), AUKML

839 **United Kingdom (Swansea)**
SOUTH WALES EVENING POST
Adelaide St, Swansea, SA1 1QT, Wales,
44 792 650841; FAX 44 792 644008

Year founded: 1861.
Newspaper Group: Northcliffe Newspapers
Hours: Mon—Fri 8:30—4:30; Sat 8:30—12n.
Days Not Published: Christmas, Sunday.
Services to Other News Libraries: Telephone reference. Sends copies of clips. Contact: Philip Sebury.
Resources: Photo files, reference books, maps, pamphlets. Microform: roll. Newspaper index, clippings.
Personnel
Director Philip L. Sebury, (5320)
Library Assts Claire Trethewy
Gill Godfrey

840 **United Kingdom (Swindon)**
MEDIA IN WESSEX
Newspaper House, 100 Victoria Rd, Swindon, SN1 3BE, England,
44 1793 528 144; FAX 44 1793 542 434

Services: Research, Readers' enquiries, Cuttings.
Personnel
Librarian Indranee DeSilva, (253), AUKML

841 **United Kingdom (Wolverhampton)**
EXPRESS & STAR LTD.
51-53 Queen St, Wolverhampton WV1 3BU, England,
44 190 231 9438; FAX 44 190 231 9721

Personnel
Librarian Frances Cartwright

842 **United Kingdom (Wolverhampton)**
WOLVERHAMPTON EXPRESS & STAR
Queen St, Wolverhampton WV1 3BU, England,
44 902 319438; FAX 44 902 319721

Services: Research, Telephone Reference, Indexing, Cuttings.
Personnel
Librarian Frances Cartwright, AUKML

843 **United Kingdom (York)**
YORK & COUNTY PRESS
PO Box 29, 76-86 Walmgate, York, YO1 1YN, England
44 190 465 3051; FAX 44 190 462 6388; Email: 100307.3313@compuserve.com

Online Databases: FT Profile; Northern Echo.
Services: Research, book ordering, cuttings.
Personnel
Librarians Sue Matthews, AUKML
Peter Chapman, AUKML

844 **United Kingtom (Poole)**
UNIVERSITY OF BOURNEMOUTH—
Dorset House Library
Talbot Campus, Fern Barrow, Poole, BH12 5BB, England,
44 120 259 5460; FAX 44 120 259 5044

Services: Research, Readers' enquiries, Serials/periodicals, Book ordering.
Online Databases: DataStar; DIALOG; FT Profile.
Personnel
Librarian — Matt Holland, (5460), AUKML

Archival Systems

AP Preserver
The Arizona Republic / The Phoenix Gazette
Baltimore Sun
Chicago Tribune
The Columbus Dispatch
Contra Costa Times
Newport News Daily Press
Post and Courier
La Repubblica (Rome)
St. Petersburg Times
San Francisco Chronicle
Spokesman—Review
Star Tribune Newspaper of the Twin Cities
USA Today

ATEX
Jerusalem Post

Autologic
Fayetteville Observer—Times

AXS
Sacramento Bee
San Francisco Chronicle

Baseview Library System
La Repubblica (Rome)

Basis
Fort Worth Star—Telegram
Newsday, Inc.
San Diego Union—Tribune
San Francisco Chronicle
Telegram & Gazette, Sunday Telegram
The Washington Post

BRS
Los Angeles Times

Digital Link Gateway
Charlotte Observer
Newport News Daily Press
La Repubblica (Rome)

EyeQ Publisher
Fort Worth Star—Telegram

Fetch
Atlanta Journal and Atlanta Constitution
The Bradenton Herald
The Commercial Appeal
Deseret News
Detroit Free Press
Edmonton Sun
Greensboro News & Record
Kenosha News
Newport News Daily Press
The Oregonian
The Palm Beach Post
Post and Courier
San Francisco Examiner
San Jose Mercury News
Star—Ledger
The Times Leader
Wisconsin State Journal

Gannett Archivist
Bellingham Herald

Image Central
La Repubblica (Rome)

ImageSpeed
Atlanta Journal and Atlanta Constitution

Iron Mike Photogrid
Detroit Free Press

KARDEX
Gainesville Sun

Kudo Image Browser
Bellingham Herald

LASR
Bend Bulletin
The Home News & Tribune
The Huntsville Times
Milwaukee Journal Sentinel
Nashville Banner
Post and Courier
Sacramento Bee

Linotronic
Parade Publications, Inc.

MacArchive
Austin American—Statesman
Bend Bulletin
The Bradenton Herald
The Commercial Appeal

MediaSphere
Newsday, Inc.

Merlin
Boston Globe
Kitchener—Waterloo Record
Montreal Gazette
New York Times
The Province / Vancouver Sun
The Washington Post
Windsor Star

Multi-Ad Search
Southeast Missourian

NewsView
Asheville Citizen—Times
Austin American—Statesman
Chattanooga Times
Contra Costa Times
Herald—Sun
Journal—American
Lewiston Tribune
Montgomery Advertiser
Southeast Missourian
The Washington Post

PageSpeed
Gainesville Sun

PaperDesk
Nashville Banner
La Repubblica (Rome)

Photofile
La Repubblica (Rome)

PhotoView
Asheville Citizen—Times
Chattanooga Free Press
Chattanooga Times
Journal—American
Lewiston Tribune
Montgomery Advertiser
Salt Lake Tribune
Wilmington Morning Star/ Sunday Star—News

Presslink Explorer Archive
Philadelphia Newspapers
The State

SAVE
The Arizona Republic / The Phoenix Gazette
Boston Globe
Charlotte Observer
Chicago Tribune
Deseret News
Detroit Free Press
Greensboro News & Record
Journal of Commerce
Lexington Herald—Leader
The Morning Call
The News—Sentinel
The Oregonian
The Palm Beach Post
Philadelphia Newspapers
Portland Press Herald/Maine Sunday Telegram
Post—Tribune
The Roanoke Times
St. Louis Post—Dispatch
San Jose Mercury News
Spokesman—Review
The Sun Herald
The Sun News
Syracuse Herald Journal / Post—Standard / Herald American Post Standard
The Wichita Eagle
Wisconsin State Journal

Software Folio
Journal—American

Stauffer Gold
Brazosport Facts
Bremerton Sun
Columbia Daily Tribune
Corpus Christi Caller—Times
Delaware County Daily Times
The Patriot Ledger
The Times Leader
Tribune Chronicle
Winnipeg Free Press

TEXT and IMAGE ARCHIVES
Louisville Courier—Journal and Louisville Times
La Repubblica (Rome)

Ultra/Birmy
Jackson Citizen Patriot

News Databases

ATEX
- Mesa Tribune
- Moncton Times—Transcript
- U.S. News & World Report

BASIS
- Axel—Springer Publishing Corp.
- Bangor Daily News
- Daily Oklahoman / Oklahoma City Times
- Dallas Morning News
- Herald and Weekly Times
- Herald (Glasgow)
- Houston Chronicle
- The News Sun
- Newsday, Inc.
- Queensland Newspapers
- The State Journal Register
- Torrance Daily Breeze
- The Washington Post

Bibliographic-Minisis
- La Presse (Montreal)

BiblioTech
- U.S. News & World Report

Datatimes
- Boston Globe
- Des Moines Register
- Florida Times-Union
- Gannett Suburban Newspapers
- Gazette Telegraph
- Harrisburg Patriot and Evening News / Sunday Patriot
- Indianapolis Star / Indianapolis News
- Kansas City Star
- Lancaster New Era / Intelligencer Journal / Sunday News
- Mail Tribune
- Omaha World—Herald
- The Orange County Register
- The Orlando Sentinel
- The Pantagraph
- Reading Times / Eagle
- The Record (Hackensack)
- San Francisco Chronicle
- San Francisco Examiner
- Seattle Times
- Star Tribune Newspaper of the Twin Cities
- Tulsa World
- York Daily Record

DataTrek Professional Series
- CBS News (New York)

DIALOG
- Journal of Commerce
- Lexington Herald—Leader
- The Orlando Sentinel
- The Record (Hackensack)
- San Francisco Examiner

Digital Collections
- Louisville Courier—Journal and Louisville Times

Documaster
- Atlanta Journal and Atlanta Constitution
- Charleston Daily Mail
- Charleston Gazette and Sunday Gazette-Mail

Dow Jones
- Wall Street Journal (NY)

Folio Views
- Berkshire Eagle
- London Free Press
- Portsmouth Herald

IDI/Basis
- San Diego Union—Tribune

Image Speed
- Atlanta Journal and Atlanta Constitution

Info Globe
- Ottawa Citizen

Info-Ky
- Louisville Courier—Journal and Louisville Times

Infomart
- Calgary Herald
- Montreal Gazette
- Ottawa Citizen
- Toronto Sun
- Windsor Star

Information International Inc.
- The Journal—Gazette

ISYS
- The Bismarck Tribune

LASR
- Fresno Bee
- St. Petersburg Times
- Tampa Tribune
- Times—Union / Sunday Times Union

MacArchive
- The Palm Beach Post

NewsBank
- The Orange County Register

NewsLink
- Fairfax Editorial Library

Newstar
- WPLG TV Broadcast 10

NewsView
- Arkansas Democrat—Gazette
- Burlington Free Press
- Columbia Missourian
- Contra Costa Times
- Herald—Sun
- Lewiston Tribune
- Portsmouth Herald
- Telegraph Herald

NewsView *(cont'd)*
- Vancouver Columbian Newspaper

NEXIS
- ITAR—TASS News Agency (NY)
- Parade Publications, Inc.
- San Francisco Examiner

PhotoView
- Contra Costa Times
- Telegraph Herald

PLS
- USA Today

QL Systems
- Miami Herald
- Ottawa Citizen
- Providence Journal—Bulletin / Sunday Journal
- Times Journal Co.
- Toronto Star

SAVE
- Akron Beacon Journal
- American Banker / Bond Buyer
- Anchorage Daily News
- The Arizona Republic / The Phoenix Gazette
- Boston Globe
- The Bradenton Herald
- Buffalo News
- The Capital (Annapolis)
- Charlotte Observer
- Chicago Tribune
- The Columbus Dispatch
- The Commercial Appeal
- Daily Camera/Sunday Camera
- Daily News of Los Angeles
- Deseret News
- Flint Journal
- Grand Forks Herald
- Greensboro News & Record
- Greenville News
- Journal of Commerce
- The Kentucky Post
- Long Beach Press—Telegram
- Los Angeles Times
- Middletown Times Herald—Record/Sunday Record
- Modesto Bee
- Newport News Daily Press
- The Oregonian
- The Orlando Sentinel
- Ottawa Citizen
- The Palm Beach Post
- Philadelphia Newspapers
- Portland Press Herald/Maine Sunday Telegram
- Post—Tribune
- Richmond Times—Dispatch
- The Roanoke Times
- St. Louis Post—Dispatch
- St. Paul Pioneer Press
- San Jose Mercury News

SAVE ***(cont'd)***
- Seattle Post—Intelligencer
- The State
- Sun—Sentinel
- Syracuse Herald Journal / Post—Standard / Herald American Post Standard
- The Times—Picayune
- Toronto Sun
- Watertown Daily Times
- Wisconsin State Journal

SCS 800
- Tri—City Herald

SII
- Asbury Park Press
- Baltimore Sun
- The Beacon—News
- Bend Bulletin
- The Cincinnati Enquirer
- Fayetteville Observer—Times
- The Home News & Tribune

SII ***(cont'd)***
- The Huntsville Times
- Mobile Press Register
- Sacramento Bee
- San Francisco Examiner
- The Tennessean
- Verdens Gang
- The West Australian

Smarterm
- Ottawa Sun

Sonar Professional
- The Daily News (Longview)
- Hobbs Daily News-Sun
- The Sedalia Democrat

Stauffer Gold
- Albany Democrat—Herald
- Brunswick Times Record
- Hannibal Courier-Post
- Herald—Bulletin
- Longmont Daily Times—Call
- Missoulian

Stauffer Gold ***(cont'd)***
- The Patriot Ledger
- The Topeka Capital—Journal
- Tribune—Review
- Winnipeg Free Press

Symphony
- Ottawa Sun

TEQLIB
- Newport News Daily Press

Thunderstore
- Star—Ledger

VIEW
- Southeast Missourian

Newspaper Groups

A.M. Publications
Bellingham Herald

ABC/Capital Cities Inc.
The Times Leader

Alameda Newspapers Group
Hayward Daily Review
The Oakland Tribune

American Publishing
Big Spring Herald
Port Arthur News
The Transcript

Armadale Publishing
The Leader Post
Saskatoon Star—Phoenix

Associated Newspapers
Morning Star

Block Newspapers
The Blade
Pittsburgh Post—Gazette

Calkins Newspapers
Beaver County Times
Bucks County Courier Times
Burlington County Times
Doylestown Intelligencer/Record

Canadian Newspapers Co. Ltd.
Evening Telegram

Capital Cities Communications Inc.
The Belleville News Democrat
Fort Worth Star—Telegram
Kansas City Star

Carl A. Jones Enterprises
Johnson City Press

Central Newspapers, Inc.
The Arizona Republic / The Phoenix Gazette
Indianapolis Star / Indianapolis News
Muncie Star and Evening Press

Chicago Sun—Times, Inc.
Chicago Sun—Times

Chronicle Publishing Co.
The Pantagraph

Copley Newspapers
The Beacon—News
Joliet Herald-News
The News Sun
San Diego Union—Tribune
San Pedro News—Pilot
The State Journal Register
Torrance Daily Breeze

Cox Enterprises
Atlanta Journal and Atlanta Constitution
Austin American—Statesman
Dayton Daily News
Mesa Tribune
The Palm Beach Post

Cox Enterprises *(cont'd)*
Springfield News—Sun
Waco Tribune—Herald

Daily Telegraph
Daily Telegraph / Sunday Telegraph

Dear Newspapers
The Sedalia Democrat

Disney Company
Albany Democrat—Herald

Donrey Media Group
Denison Herald
Jacksonville Daily Progress
Las Vegas Sun / Las Vegas Review—Journal
Pine Bluff Commercial
Vallejo Times Herald
The Washington Times—Herald

Dow Jones & Co., Inc.
Wall Street Journal (NY)

Economist Group
Journal of Commerce

Evening Standard Co. Ltd.
Evening Standard

Express Newspapers PLC
Daily Express / Sunday Express
The Star (London)

Financial Times Ltd.
Financial Times (London)

Freedom Newspapers
The Gastonia Gazette
Gazette Telegraph
The Orange County Register
The Sun—Journal
Times—News
Turlock Journal

Frjals fjolmidlun Ltd.
Dagbladid-Visir

Gannett Newspapers
Battle Creek Enquirer
Burlington Free Press
Chronicle—Tribune (Marion)
The Cincinnati Enquirer
The Clarion Ledger
Commercial—News
Courier—News
Democrat and Chronicle / Times—Union
Detroit News
El Paso Times
Fort Collins Coloradoan
Fort Myers News-Press
Gannett Suburban Newspapers
Green Bay Press-Gazette
Hattiesburg American
Honolulu Advertiser
Huntington Herald-Dispatch
Idaho Statesman
The Ithaca Journal

Gannett Newspapers *(cont'd)*
Journal & Courier
Lansing State Journal
Louisville Courier—Journal and Louisville Times
Marin Independent Journal
Montgomery Advertiser
Muskogee Daily Phoenix and Times—Democrat
The News Journal
The News—Leader
Niagara Gazette
Norwich Bulletin
Pensacola News—Journal
Poughkeepsie Journal
Press & Sun—Bulletin
Reno Gazette—Journal
Rockford Register Star
The Rockland Journal—News
Salem Statesman—Journal
San Bernardino County Sun
The Saratogian
Star—Gazette
The Tennessean
The Times (Gainesville)
The Times (Shreveport)
Tucson Citizen
USA Today
Valley News Dispatch
Wausau Daily Herald

Garden State Newspapers
Yakima Herald-Republic

Gray Communications Systems Inc.
Herald (Albany, GA)

Groupe Quebecor Inc.
The Winnipeg Sun

Guy Gannett Communications
Portland Press Herald/Maine Sunday Telegram

Hagadone Newspapers
Sioux City Journal

Harte-Hanks Communications, Inc.
Abilene Reporter—News
Anderson Independent—Mail
Corpus Christi Caller—Times
Middlesex News
San Angelo Standard—Times
Wichita Falls Times Record News

Hearst Newspapers
Houston Chronicle
San Antonio Express—News
San Francisco Examiner
Seattle Post—Intelligencer
Times—Union / Sunday Times Union

Home News Enterprises
The Republic

Horwitz Newspapers
Journal—American
Peninsula Daily News

Howard Publications
The Times (Hammond)
Waterloo—Cedar Falls Courier

Independent Newspapers Ltd.
Auckland Star Limited
The Dominion / Dominion Sunday Times

Ingersoll Publications Co.
The News—Herald

Jefferson-Pilot Publications, Inc.
Beaumont Enterprise

John P. Scripps Newspapers Group
Bremerton Sun
Ventura County Star

Journal Communications
Milwaukee Journal Sentinel

Journal Register
Herald News
Trentonian

Knight-Ridder Newspapers Inc.
Akron Beacon Journal
The Bradenton Herald
Columbus Ledger—Enquirer
Contra Costa Times
Daily Camera/Sunday Camera
Detroit Free Press
Duluth News—Tribune
Grand Forks Herald
Lexington Herald—Leader
Long Beach Press—Telegram
The Macon Telegraph
Miami Herald
The News—Sentinel
Philadelphia Newspapers
Post—Tribune
St. Paul Pioneer Press
San Jose Mercury News
The State
The Sun Herald
The Sun News
Tallahassee Democrat
The Wichita Eagle

Landmark Communications, Inc.
Carroll County Times
Greensboro News & Record
The Roanoke Times
Virginian—Pilot and Ledger—Star

Lee Newspapers
The Bismarck Tribune
La Crosse Tribune
Globe-Gazette / Sunday Globe
Herald and Review
Journal—Times
Lincoln Journal Star
Rapid City Journal
Wisconsin State Journal

Lehman Newspapers
Longmont Daily Times—Call
Loveland Daily Reporter-Herald

Liberty Newspapers L.P.
Honolulu Star—Bulletin

Maclean-Hunter Telecommunications
Maclean's Magazine

Mail Newspapers
Daily Mail

McClatchy Newspapers
Anchorage Daily News
Fresno Bee
Modesto Bee
The News Tribune
Sacramento Bee
Tri—City Herald

Media Corp. PLC
The Guardian/Observer

Media General, Inc.
Richmond Times—Dispatch
Tampa Tribune
Winston—Salem Journal

Media News Group
Denver Post
Fairbanks Daily News Miner
Gloucester County Times

Moffitt Newspapers
Welch Daily News

Morgan Murphy Newspapers
Superior Evening Telegram

Morris Communications Corp.
Amarillo Daily News / Globe Times
Florida Times-Union
Lubbock Avalanche Journal
The Topeka Capital—Journal

Morris Enterprises
Hannibal Courier-Post

Multimedia Newspapers
Asheville Citizen—Times
Clarksville Leaf—Chronicle

NB Publishing Co. Ltd.
Evening Times—Globe—Telegraph—Journal

New England Newspapers
Berkshire Eagle

New York Times Co.
Florence Times Daily
Gainesville Sun
The Ledger
New York Times
Sarasota Herald—Tribune
Wilmington Morning Star/Sunday Star—News

Newhouse Newspapers
Ann Arbor News
The Bay City Times
Birmingham News
Flint Journal
Harrisburg Patriot and Evening News / Sunday Patriot
The Huntsville Times
Jackson Citizen Patriot
Jersey Journal
Kalamazoo Gazette
The Mississippi Press
Mobile Press Register
Muskegon Chronicle
The Oregonian
The Plain Dealer
Saginaw News
Star—Ledger

Newhouse Newspapers *(cont'd)*
Staten Island Advance
Syracuse Herald Journal / Post—Standard / Herald American Post Standard
The Times (Trenton)
The Times—Picayune
Union—News / Sunday Republican

News Corporation
Herald and Weekly Times

News Group Newspapers Ltd.
The Sun / News of the World

News Limited
Queensland Newspapers

Newspaper Publishing PLC
The Independent

Newspapers of New England, Inc.
Concord Monitor

Nixon Newspapers
Michigan City News-Dispatch
Peru Daily Tribune

Northcliffe Newspapers
South Wales Evening Post

October Press Ltd.
Corriere Canadese

Ogden Newspapers
Parkersburg News and Sentinel
Post—Journal
Wheeling Intelligencer and News Register

Omaha World Herald
Record

Ottaway Newspapers, Inc.
Cape Cod Times
The Daily Star
Free Press
Joplin Globe
Mail Tribune
Middletown Times Herald—Record/Sunday Record
The News—Times
Pocono Record
Santa Cruz Sentinel
Standard—Times
Traverse City Record-Eagle

Park Communications, Inc.
The Journal—Register

Piedmont Newspaper Group of Gannett Co., Inc.
Greenville News

PJS Enterprises
Journal Star

Post Corp. Newspapers
Appleton Post-Crescent

Power Corp.
Le Nouvelliste

Pulitzer Publishing Co.
Arizona Daily Star
St. Louis Post—Dispatch

Ray Barnes Newspapers, Inc.
The Daily Chief—Union

Robinson-Blackmore Printing & Publishing Ltd.
The Daily News (Halifax)

Sandusky Newspapers
Standard—Examiner

Sandusky-Norwalk Newspapers
Kingsport Times—News
Sandusky Register

Sanhoma Corp.
Ilta-Sanomat

Schibsted-Gruppen
Verdens Gang

Scripps-Howard
Birmingham Post-Herald
The Cincinnati Post
The Commercial Appeal
El Paso Herald—Post
The Evansville Courier
The Kentucky Post
Knoxville News—Sentinel
The Monterey County Herald
Rocky Mountain News

Shearman Newspapers
Lake Charles American Press

Sherry Communications
South Bend Tribune

Small Newspapers
The Dispatch
The La Porte Herald—Argus
Post—Bulletin

Southam
Calgary Herald
The Edmonton Journal
Montreal Gazette
News
The North Bay Nugget
Ottawa Citizen
The Province / Vancouver Sun
Sault Star
The Spectator
Windsor Star

Southeastern Newspapers Corp.
Savannah Morning News and Evening Press

Southern Newspapers, Inc.
Brazosport Facts

Summit Publishing Ltd.
The Daily Gleaner

Sun Publishing Co. Ltd.
The Brandon Sun

Swift-Pioneer Newspapers
Roseburg News—Review

Thompson Newspapers
Express Times
Star—News

Thomson Newspapers
Charleston Daily Mail
Daily News (Vernon)
The Daily News (Whittier)
The Daily Nonpareil
The Daily Press
Del Rio News—Herald
Express
Florence Morning News
Kokomo Tribune
Mansfield News Journal
Niagara Falls Review
Portsmouth Herald
Repository
San Gabriel Valley Daily Tribune
Toronto Globe and Mail
Waukesha Freeman
Western Mail & Echo Ltd.
Winnipeg Free Press

Times Mirror Co.
The Advocate (Stamford)
Baltimore Sun
Hartford Courant
Los Angeles Times
The Morning Call
Newsday, Inc.

Times Newspapers Ltd.
The Times / Sunday Times (London)

Toronto Sun Corp.
Edmonton Sun
The Financial Post
Ottawa Sun
Toronto Sun

Tower Media
Daily News of Los Angeles

Trans-Canada
La Presse (Montreal)

Tribune Company Owned Newspapers
Chicago Tribune
Sun—Sentinel
Times—Advocate

Uni Media, Inc.
Le Soleil

United Communications Corp.
Kenosha News

Walls Newspapers
Cleveland Daily Banner

Washington Post Co.
The Herald (Everett)

Wilson and Horton Ltd.
Christchurch Star

World Newspapers
Carlsbad Current—Argus

Worrell Newspapers, Inc.
Las Cruces Sun—News
The News and Daily Advance

Online Databases

Agri Data Network
Chicago Tribune

AirPac
The Palm Beach Post

Alis
Boersen

AMA Net
The Washington Post

AOL
ABC News Research Center
Akron Beacon Journal
The Arizona Republic / The Phoenix Gazette
Charlotte Observer
Daytona Beach News and Journal
Forbes Inc.
Lexington Herald—Leader
Modesto Bee
Newsday, Inc.
The Palm Beach Post
Post—Tribune
Vancouver Columbian Newspaper

AP
Edmonton Sun

Artikelbasen
Boersen

ASKsam
Investigative Reporters and Editors (IRE)

Ausinet
The Age/Sunday Age

Avisdata
Boersen

AZNET
Modesto Bee

Baseline
ABC News Research Center
British Film Institute
Forbes Inc.
National Broadcasting Co. (NY)
Time Warner
U.S. News & World Report

BASIS
Seattle Times

BC Online
The Province / Vancouver Sun

Biosis
Queensland Newspapers

Blaise
BBC/Information Research Library
British Library
London Weekend Television Limited
Royal Institute of International Affairs
Time—Life News Service
University of Wales

Blood Stock
Newsday, Inc.

Bloomberg
Time Warner

Broadcast News
ABC News Research Center

BRS
The Age/Sunday Age
Miami Herald
U.S. News & World Report

Burrelle's
ABC News Research Center
The Arizona Republic / The Phoenix Gazette
Associated Press (New York)
Kansas City Star
National Broadcasting Co. (NY)
New York Times
USA Today

C-Text
Winnipeg Free Press

Canadian Press
Canadian Broadcasting Corp.
Edmonton Sun
Montreal Gazette
Ottawa Citizen
The Washington Post
Windsor Star

CCN
BBC/Information Research Library

CDA Spectrum
Forbes Inc.

CDB Infotek
ABC News Research Center
The Arizona Republic / The Phoenix Gazette
The Commercial Appeal
National Broadcasting Co. (NY)
Newsday, Inc.
The Orange County Register
The Palm Beach Post
San Francisco Chronicle

Citadel
US Smithsonian Institution

Companies House
BBC/Information Research Library
Financial Times (London)
London Weekend Television Limited
North of England Newspapers
Time—Life News Service
The Times / Sunday Times (London)

CompuServe
ABC News Research Center
The Advocate (Baton Rouge)
Baltimore Sun
The Bradenton Herald
Charlotte Observer
The Commercial Appeal
Daytona Beach News and Journal
Forbes Inc.
Kansas City Star
Louisville Courier—Journal and Louisville Times
Modesto Bee
Newsday, Inc.
The Oregonian
The Orlando Sentinel
The Palm Beach Post
St. Petersburg Times
San Jose Mercury News
Sun—Sentinel
Tampa Tribune
WPLG TV Broadcast 10

Context
The Guardian/Observer

Copley Database
The Beacon—News

CQ Washington Alert
Los Angeles Times
National Broadcasting Co. (NY)
National Press Club and News Information Center
St. Petersburg Times
Time Warner
U.S. News & World Report
The Washington Post

DAMAR
The Orange County Register

Data Resources, Inc.
Los Angeles Times

Database Technologies
The Palm Beach Post

DataQuick
The Arizona Republic / The Phoenix Gazette
The Orange County Register
Sacramento Bee
San Francisco Chronicle

DataStar
- Aalborg Stiftstidende
- ABC News Research Center
- BBC/Information Research Library
- Boersen
- Daily Mirror / Sunday Mirror
- Financial Times (London)
- Forbes Inc.
- London Weekend Television Limited
- Politiken Newspapers
- The Times / Sunday Times (London)
- U.S. News & World Report
- University of Bournemouth
- University of Strathclyde
- University of Wales

Datastream
- The Guardian/Observer

Datatimes
- ABC News Research Center
- The Advocate (Baton Rouge)
- The Age/Sunday Age
- Akron Beacon Journal
- American Banker / Bond Buyer
- Anchorage Daily News
- Arizona Daily Star
- The Arizona Republic / The Phoenix Gazette
- Associated Press (New York)
- Atlanta Journal and Atlanta Constitution
- Austin American—Statesman
- Baltimore Sun
- Bangor Daily News
- Boston Globe
- Boston Herald
- Buffalo News
- Canadian Broadcasting Corp.
- CBS News (New York)
- Charlotte Observer
- Chicago Sun—Times
- Chicago Tribune
- The Christian Science Monitor
- The Cincinnati Enquirer
- The Cincinnati Post
- The Columbus Dispatch
- The Commercial Appeal
- Contra Costa Times
- Daily News of Los Angeles
- Daily Oklahoman / Oklahoma City Times
- Daily Reporter
- Dallas Morning News
- Dayton Daily News
- Democrat and Chronicle / Times—Union
- Denver Post
- Des Moines Register
- Detroit Free Press
- Detroit News
- The Evansville Courier
- Forbes Inc.
- Fort Worth Star—Telegram
- Fresno Bee
- Gannett Suburban Newspapers
- Gazette Telegraph
- The Grand Rapids Press
- Greensboro News & Record
- Harrisburg Patriot and Evening News / Sunday Patriot

Datatimes *(cont'd)*
- Hartford Courant
- Herald—Sun
- Houston Chronicle
- Idaho Statesman
- Indianapolis Star / Indianapolis News
- International Herald Tribune (Paris)
- Journal Star
- Kansas City Star
- Knoxville News—Sentinel
- Lancaster New Era / Intelligencer Journal / Sunday News
- Las Vegas Sun / Las Vegas Review—Journal
- Lexington Herald—Leader
- Los Angeles Times
- Louisville Courier—Journal and Louisville Times
- Maclean's Magazine
- Miami Herald
- Milwaukee Journal Sentinel
- Mobile Press Register
- Montreal Gazette
- The Morning Call
- Muskegon Chronicle
- Nashville Banner
- National Association of Broadcasters
- National Broadcasting Co. (NY)
- National Geographic Society
- National Press Club and News Information Center
- National Public Radio / Broadcast Library
- National Public Radio / Reference Library
- New York Times
- New York Times Regional Newspaper Group
- The News & Observer
- The News Tribune
- Newsday, Inc.
- Newsweek Magazine
- The Oakland Tribune
- Omaha World—Herald
- The Orange County Register
- The Oregonian
- The Orlando Sentinel
- Ottawa Citizen
- The Palm Beach Post
- The Pantagraph
- The Patriot Ledger
- Philadelphia Newspapers
- Pittsburgh Post—Gazette
- The Plain Dealer
- Politiken Newspapers
- Portland Press Herald/Maine Sunday Telegram
- The Press—Enterprise
- Providence Journal—Bulletin / Sunday Journal
- The Province / Vancouver Sun
- Reading Times / Eagle
- The Record (Hackensack)
- Richmond Times—Dispatch
- The Roanoke Times
- Rocky Mountain News
- Sacramento Bee
- St. Louis Post—Dispatch

Datatimes *(cont'd)*
- St. Paul Pioneer Press
- St. Petersburg Times
- Salt Lake Tribune
- San Antonio Express—News
- San Diego Union—Tribune
- San Francisco Chronicle
- San Francisco Examiner
- San Jose Mercury News
- Seattle Post—Intelligencer
- Seattle Times
- Southern Progress Corporation
- Spokesman—Review
- Star Tribune Newspaper of the Twin Cities
- Star—Ledger
- The State
- The State Journal Register
- Sun—Sentinel
- Syracuse Herald Journal / Post—Standard / Herald American Post Standard
- Telegram & Gazette, Sunday Telegram
- The Tennessean
- Thirteen/WNET
- Time Warner
- The Times—Picayune
- Times—Union / Sunday Times Union
- Torrance Daily Breeze
- Tucson Citizen
- Tulsa World
- U.S. News & World Report
- USA Today
- Vancouver Columbian Newspaper
- The Village Voice
- Virginian—Pilot and Ledger—Star
- Wall Street Journal (NY)
- The Washington Post
- The Washington Times
- The Wichita Eagle
- Wilmington Morning Star/ Sunday Star—News
- Wisconsin State Journal
- York Daily Record

DBT
- Star—Ledger
- WPLG TV Broadcast 10

DIALOG
- Aalborg Stiftstidende
- ABC News Research Center
- The Advocate (Baton Rouge)
- The Age/Sunday Age
- Akron Beacon Journal
- American Banker / Bond Buyer
- Anchorage Daily News
- The Arizona Republic / The Phoenix Gazette
- Associated Press (New York)
- Atlanta Journal and Atlanta Constitution
- Baltimore Sun
- BBC/Information Research Library
- Boersen
- Boston Globe
- The Bradenton Herald
- British Film Institute
- British Library

DIALOG ***(cont'd)***
Buffalo News
Cable News Network
Caledonian Newspapers
Canadian Broadcasting Corp.
CBS News (New York)
Charlotte Observer
Chicago Sun—Times
Chicago Tribune
The Christian Science Monitor
The Cincinnati Post
The Columbus Dispatch
The Commercial Appeal
Congressional Research Service
Contra Costa Times
Daily Mirror / Sunday Mirror
Daily News of Los Angeles
Daily Oklahoman / Oklahoma City Times
Dallas Morning News
Dayton Daily News
Democrat and Chronicle / Times—Union
Detroit Free Press
Economist/London
Economist/New York Bureau
Financial Times (London)
Forbes Inc.
Fresno Bee
Gannett Suburban Newspapers
Gazette Telegraph
Herald—Sun
Houston Chronicle
Idaho Statesman
Independent Television Commission
John Fairfax Group
Kansas City Star
Lexington Herald—Leader
London Free Press
London Weekend Television Limited
Los Angeles Times
Louisville Courier—Journal and Louisville Times
Maclean's Magazine
Miami Herald
The Morning Call
National Association of Broadcasters
National Broadcasting Co. (NY)
National Geographic Society
National Press Club and News Information Center
National Public Radio / Broadcast Library
National Public Radio / Reference Library
New York Daily News
New York Times
New York Times Regional Newspaper Group
Newport News Daily Press
Newsday, Inc.
Newsweek Magazine
The Orange County Register
The Oregonian
The Orlando Sentinel
Ottawa Citizen
The Palm Beach Post
The Patriot Ledger
Philadelphia Newspapers

DIALOG ***(cont'd)***
The Plain Dealer
Politiken Newspapers
Providence Journal—Bulletin / Sunday Journal
The Record (Hackensack)
Richmond Times—Dispatch
Rocky Mountain News
Sacramento Bee
St. Louis Post—Dispatch
St. Paul Pioneer Press
St. Petersburg Times
San Diego Union—Tribune
San Francisco Chronicle
San Francisco Examiner
San Jose Mercury News
Scholastic Inc.
Scottish Daily Record
Seattle Post—Intelligencer
Seattle Times
Southern Progress Corporation
Star Tribune Newspaper of the Twin Cities
The State
The Sun News
Sun—Sentinel
Syracuse Herald Journal / Post—Standard / Herald American Post Standard
Tampa Tribune
Thirteen/WNET
Time Warner
The Times / Sunday Times (London)
The Times—Picayune
Times—Union / Sunday Times Union
Toronto Star
Toronto Sun
Torrance Daily Breeze
United States Information Service
U.S. News & World Report
US Smithsonian Institution
University of Bournemouth
University of Central Lancashire
University of Strathclyde
University of Wales
USA Today
Virginian—Pilot and Ledger—Star
Wall Street Journal (NY)
The Washington Post
The Washington Times
Waterloo—Cedar Falls Courier
Watertown Daily Times
The Wichita Eagle
Wilmington Morning Star/ Sunday Star—News
Wisconsin State Journal
WPLG TV Broadcast 10

DMV Database
Gannett Suburban Newspapers

Dow Jones
ABC News Research Center
Akron Beacon Journal
Anchorage Daily News
The Arizona Republic / The Phoenix Gazette
Associated Press (New York)
Atlanta Journal and Atlanta Constitution

Dow Jones ***(cont'd)***
Baltimore Sun
BBC World Service
Boston Globe
Canadian Broadcasting Corp.
CBS News (New York)
Chicago Tribune
The Christian Science Monitor
The Columbus Dispatch
The Commercial Appeal
Dallas Morning News
Dayton Daily News
Detroit Free Press
Economist/New York Bureau
Financial Times (London)
Forbes Inc.
Fort Worth Star—Telegram
Kansas City Star
Lexington Herald—Leader
Los Angeles Times
Maclean's Magazine
Miami Herald
The Morning Call
National Broadcasting Co. (NY)
National Public Radio / Broadcast Library
National Public Radio / Reference Library
New York Times
New York Times Regional Newspaper Group
Newsday, Inc.
Newsweek Magazine
Omaha World—Herald
The Orange County Register
The Palm Beach Post
The Patriot Ledger
Philadelphia Newspapers
Providence Journal—Bulletin / Sunday Journal
The Province / Vancouver Sun
The Record (Hackensack)
Richmond Times—Dispatch
The Roanoke Times
Rocky Mountain News
St. Paul Pioneer Press
San Diego Union—Tribune
San Francisco Chronicle
Scholastic Inc.
Scottish Daily Record
Star Tribune Newspaper of the Twin Cities
Star—Ledger
Telegram & Gazette, Sunday Telegram
Time Warner
Toronto Globe and Mail
U.S. News & World Report
The Village Voice
Wall Street Journal (NY)
The Washington Post

Dun & Bradstreet
San Francisco Chronicle
San Francisco Examiner

Economic Bulletin Board
Time Warner

EPIC
CBS News (New York)
US Smithsonian Institution

Eurobases
Royal Institute of International Affairs

Federal Election Commission (FEC)
New York Times
Newsday, Inc.
The Washington Post

Financial Post Online
Reader's Digest Magazines Ltd.

First Search
US Smithsonian Institution

FT Graphite
Financial Times (London)

FT Profile
Aalborg Stiftstidende
ABC News Research Center
BBC
BBC Scotland
BBC Wales
BBC World Service
BBC/Information Research Library
Birmingham Post and Mail
Boersen
British Film Institute
British Library
Caledonian Newspapers
Central Broadcasting
Daily Mail
Daily Mirror / Sunday Mirror
Economist/London
Financial Times (London)
The Guardian/Observer
Independent Television Commission
IPC Magazines
John Fairfax Group
London News Network
London Weekend Television Limited
North of England Newspapers
Politiken Newspapers
Royal Institute of International Affairs
Scotsman
Scottish Daily Record
Time Out Magazine
Time—Life News Service
The Times / Sunday Times (London)
United States Information Service
University of Bournemouth
University of Central Lancashire
University of Strathclyde
York & County Press

G.N.A.S.
Niagara Gazette

Genios
Politiken Newspapers

Glasgow Herald
Scotsman

Globe Information Services
The Province / Vancouver Sun

Grateful Med
Burlington Free Press

Haver Analytics
Newsday, Inc.

House of Commons
BBC/Information Research Library
Caledonian Newspapers
Economist/London
Financial Times (London)

IMSMARQ
BBC/Information Research Library

Info Globe
ABC News Research Center
Calgary Herald
Canadian Broadcasting Corp.
Chicago Tribune
Forbes Inc.
Maclean's Magazine
Montreal Gazette
National Broadcasting Co. (NY)
Ottawa Citizen
Ottawa Sun
Reader's Digest Magazines Ltd.
The Spectator
Toronto Globe and Mail
Toronto Star
Toronto Sun
The Washington Post
Windsor Star

Infodex
Montreal Gazette

Infomart
Calgary Herald
Canadian Broadcasting Corp.
Kitchener—Waterloo Record
Maclean's Magazine
Montreal Gazette
Ottawa Citizen
Ottawa Sun
The Province / Vancouver Sun
Reader's Digest Magazines Ltd.
The Spectator
Toronto Globe and Mail
Toronto Star
Toronto Sun
Windsor Star

Information America
Atlanta Journal and Atlanta Constitution
National Broadcasting Co. (NY)
New York Times
The Palm Beach Post
San Francisco Chronicle
San Francisco Examiner
Wall Street Journal (NY)

Internet
Anchorage Daily News
Chicago Tribune
Detroit Free Press
Gazette Telegraph
The Palm Beach Post
Sioux City Journal
Vancouver Columbian Newspaper

Investext
Time Warner

IRSC
National Broadcasting Co. (NY)
The Orange County Register
San Francisco Examiner

ISC
The Palm Beach Post

Jordans
BBC/Information Research Library

Kentucky Economic Information System
Lexington Herald—Leader

Kompass/Affars-Data
Boersen

LEGI-SLATE
ABC News Research Center
United States Information Service

LegiTech
The Orange County Register
San Francisco Chronicle

LEXIS
The Arizona Republic / The Phoenix Gazette
Daily News of Los Angeles
New York Times
The Orange County Register
Sacramento Bee
San Francisco Chronicle
Wilmington Morning Star/ Sunday Star—News

LEXIS/NEXIS
ABC News Research Center
The Age/Sunday Age
Arkansas Democrat—Gazette
Associated Press (New York)
Austin American—Statesman
BBC World Service
BBC/Information Research Library
Boston Globe
Burlington Free Press
Cable News Network
The Capital (Annapolis)
Chicago Tribune
The Cincinnati Enquirer
The Commercial Appeal
Dallas Morning News
Dayton Daily News
Economist/London
Financial Times (London)
Forbes Inc.
Gannett Suburban Newspapers
Gazette Telegraph
The Guardian/Observer
Herald—Sun
IISS
International Herald Tribune (Paris)
John Fairfax Group
Kansas City Star
London Weekend Television Limited
Los Angeles Times
Maclean's Magazine
Miami Herald
Nashville Banner
National Broadcasting Co. (NY)
National Press Club and News Information Center
New York Times Regional Newspaper Group
Newsday, Inc.
Omaha World—Herald

LEXIS/NEXIS *(cont'd)*
The Palm Beach Post
Philadelphia Newspapers
Politiken Newspapers
Providence Journal—Bulletin / Sunday Journal
The Province / Vancouver Sun
Reader's Digest Magazines Ltd.
Reuters News Service
Rocky Mountain News
St. Louis Post—Dispatch
St. Petersburg Times
San Antonio Express—News
Scholastic Inc.
Scotsman
Scottish Daily Record
Star—Ledger
Syracuse Herald Journal / Post—Standard / Herald American Post Standard
The Tennessean
Time Warner
The Times / Sunday Times (London)
Toronto Globe and Mail
Toronto Star
United States Information Service
US Information Agency
University of Central Lancashire
Vancouver Columbian Newspaper
The Village Voice
The Washington Post
The Washington Times

Livedgar
Newsday, Inc.

Lusknet
The Washington Post

Maid
Financial Times (London)
The Times / Sunday Times (London)
VNU Business Publications

Maryland Legislature
The Washington Post

MEDLARS
The Advocate (Baton Rouge)
Los Angeles Times

Minitel
International Herald Tribune (Paris)

Netscape
The Province / Vancouver Sun

New York State Department of Motor Vehicles (NYS DMV)
Newsday, Inc.

NewsBank
Arizona Daily Star
Denver Post
Fort Worth Star—Telegram
St. Louis Post—Dispatch
San Diego Union—Tribune

NewsNet
ABC News Research Center
The Arizona Republic / The Phoenix Gazette
Associated Press (New York)
Chicago Tribune
Houston Chronicle
National Association of Broadcasters
Newsday, Inc.
Time Warner

NEWSTEX
The Canadian Press
Montreal Gazette

NEXIS
The Advocate (Baton Rouge)
American Banker / Bond Buyer
The Arizona Republic / The Phoenix Gazette
Asheville Citizen—Times
Atlanta Journal and Atlanta Constitution
Baltimore Sun
Bangor Daily News
Bend Bulletin
Boston Herald
Buffalo News
Calgary Herald
Canadian Broadcasting Corp.
CBS News (New York)
Charleston Daily Mail
Charleston Gazette and Sunday Gazette-Mail
Charlotte Observer
Chicago Sun—Times
The Christian Science Monitor
The Columbus Dispatch
Congressional Research Service
Contra Costa Times
Daily News of Los Angeles
Democrat and Chronicle / Times—Union
Denver Post
Detroit Free Press
Detroit News
Economist/New York Bureau
Fresno Bee
Greensboro News & Record
Hartford Courant
Honolulu Advertiser
Honolulu Star—Bulletin
Houston Chronicle
Idaho Statesman
Indianapolis Star / Indianapolis News
ITAR—TASS News Agency (NY)
Lewiston Tribune
Lexington Herald—Leader
Louisville Courier—Journal and Louisville Times
Marin Independent Journal
Milwaukee Journal Sentinel
Montgomery Advertiser
Montreal Gazette
The Morning Call
National Geographic Society
National Public Radio / Broadcast Library
National Public Radio / Reference Library
New York Daily News
New York Times

NEXIS *(cont'd)*
Newsweek Magazine
The Orange County Register
The Orlando Sentinel
Ottawa Citizen
Pittsburgh Post—Gazette
The Plain Dealer
Portland Press Herald/Maine Sunday Telegram
Post and Courier
Post—Tribune
The Press—Enterprise
The Record (Hackensack)
The Roanoke Times
Sacramento Bee
St. Paul Pioneer Press
Salt Lake Tribune
San Diego Union—Tribune
San Francisco Chronicle
San Francisco Examiner
San Jose Mercury News
Seattle Times
Star Tribune Newspaper of the Twin Cities
The State Journal Register
Sun—Sentinel
Tampa Tribune
Thirteen/WNET
The Times—Picayune
Times—Union / Sunday Times Union
Toronto Sun
Torrance Daily Breeze
U.S. News & World Report
USA Today
Virginian—Pilot and Ledger—Star
Wall Street Journal (NY)
The Wichita Eagle
Wilmington Morning Star/ Sunday Star—News
Wisconsin State Journal

Northern Echo
York & County Press

OCLC
Los Angeles Times
Louisville Courier—Journal and Louisville Times
National Geographic Society

Oregon State Library
The Oregonian

Ovid
National Broadcasting Co. (NY)

PACER
Newsday, Inc.
The Palm Beach Post

Perfect Information
Daily Mirror / Sunday Mirror

Periscope
ABC News Research Center
National Broadcasting Co. (NY)
New York Times
Time Warner

Polinfo
Boersen
Politiken Newspapers

PostHaste
The Washington Post

Presscom
The Age/Sunday Age

Prodigy
Gannett Suburban Newspapers
Providence Journal—Bulletin / Sunday Journal

Profile
Boersen
Maclean's Magazine
Toronto Globe and Mail
The Washington Post

Publicom
Boersen

QL Law
Toronto Star

QL Systems
Calgary Herald
Canadian Broadcasting Corp.
Maclean's Magazine

QNIS
The Age/Sunday Age

QuickLaw
The Province / Vancouver Sun
Reader's Digest Magazines Ltd.

Retsinformation
Boersen

Reuters
ABC News Research Center
The Age/Sunday Age
Time Warner
The Times / Sunday Times (London)
VNU Business Publications

Rex
Boersen

RLIN
Forbes Inc.

SAVE
Akron Beacon Journal
Boston Globe
Calgary Herald
Canadian Broadcasting Corp.
Charlotte Observer
Chicago Sun—Times
Chicago Tribune
The Columbus Dispatch

SAVE *(cont'd)*
Daily News of Los Angeles
Deseret News
Detroit Free Press
Lexington Herald—Leader
Miami Herald
Middletown Times Herald—Record/Sunday Record
Montreal Gazette
National Association of Broadcasters
National Enquirer
Newport News Daily Press
The News—Sentinel
The Oregonian
The Orlando Sentinel
Ottawa Citizen
Philadelphia Newspapers
Post—Tribune
Richmond Times—Dispatch
Rocky Mountain News
Sacramento Bee
Seattle Post—Intelligencer
Seattle Times
Star—Ledger
The State
The Sun News
Thirteen/WNET
Times—Union / Sunday Times Union
Toronto Sun
The Washington Post
Waterloo—Cedar Falls Courier
The Wichita Eagle

SCIPIO
Congressional Research Service

SmartLine BBS
Austin American—Statesman

Southam News Service
Windsor Star

Sovset
Time Warner

Spectrum
Newsday, Inc.

Teleboersen
Boersen

Textline
Toronto Globe and Mail

Toronto Sun Database
Ottawa Sun

UK Trademarks
BBC/Information Research Library

USNI Military Database
U.S. News & World Report
The Washington Post

Virginia Legislature
The Washington Post

VU/TEXT ***see SAVE***

Warner Computer Systems
Time Warner

Washington Alert
ABC News Research Center
The Advocate (Baton Rouge)
Newsday, Inc.
San Francisco Chronicle
USA Today

Waterlows
BBC/Information Research Library

WDIA
Newsday, Inc.
The Palm Beach Post

WESTLAW
The Columbus Dispatch
Forbes Inc.
Newsday, Inc.
The Palm Beach Post
USA Today

Wilsonline
ABC News Research Center
BBC/Information Research Library
Lexington Herald—Leader
Miami Herald
National Broadcasting Co. (NY)
Thirteen/WNET
Time Warner

World Reporter
British Library

Special Collections

Advertising
Newspaper Association of America (NAA)

African-American—Newspapers
Daily Challenge

Airships
Akron Beacon Journal

Alberta—Government Publications
Red Deer Advocate

Almanacs
Providence Journal—Bulletin / Sunday Journal

American Civil Liberties Union (ACLU)
American Civil Liberties Union Library (ACLU)

Antarctic Regions
National Geographic Society

Architecture
Chicago Tribune

Architecture, South Carolina
Post and Courier

Archives
National Press Club and News Information Center
The Newspaper Guild

Archives, Newspaper Division (SLA)
Newspaper Association of America (NAA)

Arizona Project
Investigative Reporters and Editors (IRE)

Arizona—History—1870-
The Arizona Republic / The Phoenix Gazette

Audiotapes, Speakers—Collections
National Press Club and News Information Center

Authors—Missouri
St. Louis Post—Dispatch

Automobiles—Collectors and Collecting
American Automobile Manufacturers Association

Automobiles—History
American Automobile Manufacturers Association
Flint Journal

Bird, Piasa
The Telegraph

Bromhead Cartoons
Auckland Star Limited

Brooklyn Citizen (Newspaper)
Brooklyn Public Library

Brooklyn Daily Eagle (Newspaper)
Brooklyn Public Library

Brooklyn Daily Times (Newspaper)
Brooklyn Public Library

Brooklyn Eagle
Brooklyn Public Library

Brooklyn Tablet (Newspaper)
Brooklyn Public Library

Brooklyn—History
Brooklyn Public Library

Burney Collection of Newspapers 1603—1800
British Library

California—History
San Francisco Examiner

Canada History—Korean War
The Canadian Press

Canada—Government Publications
Red Deer Advocate

Canadian Press Diary
The Canadian Press

Caricatures and Cartoons—Collections
National Press Club and News Information Center

Cartography
National Geographic Society

Cartoons
Auckland Star Limited

Chicago—History
Chicago Tribune

Civil Rights
American Civil Liberties Union Library (ACLU)

Commonwealth Games 1978
Edmonton Sun

Cumulus Image Archive
Modesto Bee

Daily Long Island Democrat (Newspaper)
Brooklyn Public Library

Directories
National Enquirer

Discovery and Exploration
National Geographic Society

Eastman, George
Democrat and Chronicle / Times—Union

Edmonton Eskimos
Edmonton Sun

Edmonton Oilers
Edmonton Sun

Family Life
The Oregonian

Finance
Boersen

Florida—History
St. Petersburg Times

Freedom of Information
Chicago Tribune

Geneology—Collections
Boston Globe

Geography
National Geographic Society

Geology
National Geographic Society

Golden Gate Bridge
Marin Independent Journal

Government Documents
Florence Times Daily
U.S. News & World Report

Graphic Arts
Modesto Bee

Graphs—Collections
St. Petersburg Times

Gretzky, Wayne
Edmonton Sun

Hartford Courant
Hartford Courant

Harvard University
Boston Globe

Hawaiiana
Honolulu Advertiser
Honolulu Star—Bulletin

Hemingway, Ernest
Toronto Star

Historic Houses
Rocky Mountain News

Hockey Players
Edmonton Sun

Indiana—History
Indianapolis Star / Indianapolis News
Kokomo Tribune

Indians of North America
Chicago Tribune

Iran-Contra Affair
The Washington Post

Journalism
Newspaper Association of America (NAA)

Kent State University Incident, 1970
Akron Beacon Journal

Kodak
Democrat and Chronicle / Times—Union

Korean War—Canada
The Canadian Press

Law, Canada
Red Deer Advocate

Life Magazine
Democrat and Chronicle / Times—Union

Local History
Baltimore Sun
Bellingham Herald
The Bradenton Herald
Chicago Tribune
Columbia Missourian
Dayton Daily News
Elyria Chronicle—Telegram
The Herald (New Britain)
Newsday, Inc.
The News—Sentinel
The Oregonian
The Plain Dealer
Post and Courier
Post—Tribune
Providence Journal—Bulletin / Sunday Journal
The Record (Troy)
Rocky Mountain News
St. Petersburg Times
San Francisco Examiner
Santa Barbara News—Press
Santa Cruz Sentinel
Torrance Daily Breeze

Long Islander (Newspaper)
Brooklyn Public Library

Lovejoy, Elijah
The Telegraph

Magazines—Collections
Investigative Reporters and Editors (IRE)

Maine Register
Portland Press Herald/Maine Sunday Telegram

Maine—History
Portland Press Herald/Maine Sunday Telegram

Maps and Atlases—Collections
St. Petersburg Times

Marx Brothers
Freedonia Gazette

Maryland—History
Baltimore Sun

Massachusetts—History
Boston Globe

Mencken, H. L.
Baltimore Sun

Michigan—History
Flint Journal

Motion Picture Almanacs
Democrat and Chronicle / Times—Union

Motion Picture Industry—History
Des Moines Register

Music, Rock—Festival
Middletown Times Herald—Record/Sunday Record

National Geographic Magazine
National Geographic Society

Natural History
National Geographic Society

Negatives—Collections
The Province / Vancouver Sun

New Britain Herald (Bound Volumes) 1885-
The Herald (New Britain)

New York (State)—History
Watertown Daily Times

Newspapers, Asian
British Library

Newspapers, Historical
The Advocate (Stamford)
Brooklyn Public Library
Burlington County Times
Norwich Bulletin
The Times (Shreveport)

Newspapers, International—Collections
British Library
Inca-Fiej Research Association
New York Public Library

Newspapers, Irish
British Library

Newspapers, London (England)
British Library

Newspapers, Near East
Boersen
Jerusalem Post

Newspapers, Scottish
British Library

Newspapers, Slavic
British Library

Newspapers, South Asian
British Library

Newspapers, United Kingdom 1840—
British Library

Newspapers, Welsh
British Library

Newspapers—Collections
American Antiquarian Society
British Library
Brooklyn Public Library
The Herald (New Britain)
Investigative Reporters and Editors (IRE)
The Palm Beach Post
Tucson Citizen
Turlock Journal

Ohio—History
The Plain Dealer

Oklahoma City (OK) Bombing
Daily Oklahoman / Oklahoma City Times

Pamphlets—Collections
U.S. News & World Report

Papers of Raymond V. Ingersoll
Brooklyn Public Library

Paul Gapp Library of Architecture and Urban Affairs
Chicago Tribune

Periodicals, Santa Barbara (CA)
Santa Barbara News—Press

Photographs—Collections
Associated Press
Elyria Chronicle—Telegram
National Press Club and News Information Center
The Province / Vancouver Sun

Photographs—Near East
Jerusalem Post

Presidents—U.S.
The Washington Post

Public Opinion Polls
Louis Harris and Associates, Inc.

Publishers and Publishing
Newspaper Association of America (NAA)

Quayle, Dan
The News—Sentinel

Radio Journalists
ABC News Research Center

Radio News Broadcasts
CBS News (New York)

Radio News—Collections
ABC News Research Center

Radio Scripts
CBS News (New York)

Reader's Digest—Collections
Reader's Digest Association Inc.

Registers of Birth
Portland Press Herald/Maine Sunday Telegram

Rhode Island—History
Providence Journal—Bulletin / Sunday Journal

Richard M. Nixon
The Washington Post

Rubber Industry and Trade
Akron Beacon Journal

Rugby—Photographs—Collections
Western Mail & Echo Ltd.

Space Flight and Technology
The Huntsville Times

Special Libraries Association—Newspaper Division
Newspaper Association of America (NAA)

Spoleto Festival
Post and Courier

Spot Color Maps
St. Petersburg Times

Starkweather, Charles
Lincoln Journal Star

Sullivan Brothers
Waterloo—Cedar Falls Courier

Tampa Bay Photographs—Collections
Tampa Tribune

Tampa Times—Clippings
Tampa Tribune

Tampa—History
Tampa Tribune

Telecommunications
Newspaper Association of America (NAA)
Telephone Directories
The News Journal
Telephone Directories—Portland
Portland Press Herald/Maine Sunday Telegram
Television Journalism
ABC News Research Center
Canadian Broadcasting Corp/TV News Library
CBS News (New York)
National Public Radio / Broadcast Library
Television News—Collections
ABC News Research Center
Canadian Broadcasting Corp/TV News Library
CBS News (New York)
National Public Radio / Broadcast Library
Television Programs—Guides
Thirteen/WNET
Tennessee Valley Authority
Florence Times Daily
Texana Collection
Dallas Morning News
Texas—History
Dallas Morning News
Theatre World
Democrat and Chronicle / Times—Union
Thomason, George Collection 1641—1663
British Library
Toronto Telegram
Toronto Sun
Travel
National Geographic Society
U.S. Congress
The Washington Post
U.S.—Politics and Government
The Washington Post
Universiade
Edmonton Sun
Uplink
Investigative Reporters and Editors (IRE)
Urban Affairs
Chicago Tribune
Video (News)—Collections
Cable News Network
Wadlow, Robert
The Telegraph
Watergate Affair
The Washington Post
Welsh War—Photographs—Collections
Western Mail & Echo Ltd.
Wernher von Braun
The Huntsville Times
Williamsburg Daily Times (Newspaper)
Brooklyn Public Library
Woodstock (New York) Festival
Middletown Times Herald—Record/Sunday Record
World War I
Chicago Tribune
La Presse (Montreal)
World War II
Des Moines Register
The European Stars and Stripes
La Presse (Montreal)
World War II—Canada
The Canadian Press
Xerox
Democrat and Chronicle / Times—Union

Personnel

A

277 Abbott, Greg
588 Abbott, Kathryn
493 Absher, Kim
818 Adair, Sarah
255 Adams, Eleanor S.
279 Adams, Ethel
517 Adams, Sherry
799 Airey, Pam
593 Aitken, Eliza
520 Alexander, Ruth
753 Alhamidi, Abdulrahman
426 Allaire, Robert
300 Allard, Steve
799 Allbrooke, Jill
817 Allen, Peter
687 Alnaes, Ingvild
14 Alteri, Sandra
337 Altman, Nancy
156 Alzofon, Sammy
374 Amster, Linda
694 Andersen, Gunhild Leth
374 Anderson, Donna
152 Anderson, Laurie
574 Anderson, Peggy A.
684 Andreasen, Aase
26 Andrew, Robert
639 Andrews, David
476 Angell, Bill
374 Annan, Marilyn
187 Apple, Barbara
569 Arkens, Michelle M.
750 Arkivar, Hilde Flaten
290 Armao, Rosemary
797 Arnal, Michele
579 Arndt, Roseann
273 Arnold, Allison
224 Arnold, Jill
814 Arundale, Justin
323 Arzapalo, DeeDee
837 Ashton, Peter
616 Ashurst, Carol
364 Atwood, Allan
383 Azzolino, Angela

B

630 Bachand, Michelle
308 Bachhuber, Leslie
347 Bacon, Janet
741 Bacsa, Margot
160 Bade, Debra K.
249 Baily, Gail
313 Baird, Christine
52 Baird, Morna
785 Baird, Pat
751 Bakken, Dagfinn
784 Ball, David
550 Ball, Donna
62 Ballard, Monica
349 Bankes, Cryder
427 Banks, Marie M.
396 Barger, Timothy K.
333 Barnard, Catherine A.
604 Barrett, Allison
558 Barta, Linda
641 Bartholomaeus, John
489 Bartosch, Julie
538 Basnight, Clara P.
43 Basofin, Pete
827 Bateman, Kate
810 Batten, Mary
263 Baulch, Vivian
695 Baun, Gertrud
642 Bayliss, Helen
382 Bealer, Jane
409 Beall, Robert L.
828 Beardsley, S.J.
20 Beauers, Sharon
433 Beaver, Anita
89 Belcher, Vicki
315 Belknap, Lisa
768 Bell, Kathleen
134 Belton, Jennifer
18 Bemis, Monte
752 Benjaminsen, Karin
152 Bennett, Kitty
639 Bennett, Tracey
110 Benson, Ann
324 Berg, Donna R.
142 Bergwall, Shauna
341 Bernard, Suzanne
807 Bevan, Andrew
660 Bex, Jan
223 Bidwell, Sharon
539 Bilinski, Suzanne
499 Binford, Tammy
691 Bjernemose, Helle
310 Blair, Donna
77 Blanchfield, Virginia
673 Blenner, Hanne
533 Blodgett, Gini
100 Blodgett, Goni
463 Boal, Denise
383 Bolch, Jonathan
412 Bollten, Renee
82 Bologna, Anita
52 Bolvin, Debbie
383 Bonardi, AnnMarie
821 Bone, Mary
211 Booker, Ray
642 Bopf, Frank
491 Borner, Barbara
527 Bosche, Edith
67 Boss, Janet
463 Bowers, Alletta
504 Bowles, Renay
43 Boyd, Rebecca
443 Boyd, Suzanne
821 Boyde, Susan
553 Boyer, Tom
177 Boylan, Victoria
444 Bradford, Mary
145 Bravon, Thelma
636 Breingan, Brian
640 Breingan, Brian
678 Brejnholm, Gertrud
351 Brennan, Elizabeth
377 Brennan-Green, Sarah
110 Briscoe, Ellen
555 Britton, Pilaivan H.
377 Britton, Robert P.
131 Brockett, Anne
3 Broglie, Lisa
91 Bromley, Marilyn M.
383 Brooks, Pamela
394 Brower, Eleanor M.
294 Brown, Gerald D.
533 Brown, Jeanette
492 Brown, Phyllis J.
777 Brudenell, Jo
826 Brunton, Mick
404 Bryant, Ann
693 Buchmann, Mette Charis
174 Buckles, Mildred
466 Budgick, Barbara
345 Buell, Hal
242 Buentello, Sandy
549 Buker, Lori
760 Bulak, Peter
163 Bulloch, Linda
304 Burch, Lisa
769 Burke, Anna
771 Burke, Anna
255 Burkett, Nancy H.
3 Burnett, Jason
49 Burns, Rotimi
449 Burns, Ruth
227 Burris, Nancy I.
619 Burton, Donna M.
617 Butcher, Theresa M.
426 Butler, Nina
231 Butler, Susan
511 Byington, Teena

C

292 Caldwell, Bill
280 Callies, Teresa M.
342 Callinan, Mary L.
127 Calvert, Karin H.
379 Calvo-Platero, Mario
663 Camarso, Susana H.
286 Cambell, Judy
439 Campbell, Carol A.
784 Campbell, Marie
533 Campbell, Teresa
100 Campbell, Theresa
229 Campo, Charles A.
110 Canby, Susan Fifer
50 Canter, Judy
376 Cappelson, Sharon
725 Caraffa, Vittorio
281 Carlson, Lisa
84 Carlson, Melinda S.
344 Carlson, Steve
312 Carney, Louise
412 Carpenter, James
399 Carr-Bourcy, Lisa
38 Carter, Gayle
494 Carter, Shirley
536 Carter, Sue
841 Cartwright, Frances
842 Cartwright, Frances
136 Caster, Sandra
344 Cataldo, Mary Ann
352 Cathcart, Cynthia A.
402 Cathey, Pat
140 Cauvel, Robert
41 Chamberlain, Jacqueline S.
155 Chambers, Jerry
48 Chan, Stella W.
281 Chang, Yee
252 Chapman, Linda
223 Chapman, Pat
777 Chapman, Peter
781 Chapman, Peter
793 Chapman, Peter
843 Chapman, Peter
629 Charlebois, Pierre
662 Charles, Deborah A.
397 Chasney, Susan
810 Cheek, Peter
112 Chen, Denise
156 Chen, Xiao Kai
383 Cherry, Brenda
729 Chisaki, Watanabe
194 Chisholm, Carol
349 Choy, Nori
623 Chuk, Denise
366 Church, Alice
759 Ciernikova, Jana
70 Cisneros, Juanita
425 Clark, Beth
383 Clark, Patricia
555 Clark, Stephanie
518 Claus, Kathryn I.
562 Clay, Patty
405 Clements, Mary
590 Cochrane, Betty
797 Cockburn, Linda
533 Coffelt, Tristan
504 Coffey, Jennifer
547 Coffin, Jenetta Rose
424 Cofta, Mary Ann
341 Cohen, Madeline
375 Cohen, Madeline
159 Colburn, Lauren
723 Cole, Christine
769 Cole, Christine
771 Cole, Christine
368 Cole, Nancy
15 Colletta, Donna
557 Collins, Janet G.
170 Collins, Phyllis
521 Collins, Voletta
28 Coloma, Kent
164 Comer, Harriet
644 Condous, Crystal
703 Conrod-Magnian, Daniel
533 Constantinides, Lynette
488 Cook, Mary
794 Cook, Rosalyn
509 Copeland, Carmela
655 Corbisier, Genevieve
476 Cordin, Betty
347 Cornish, Paul
94 Cosgrove, Alexandra
131 Costello, Lisa
477 Cote, Marie
248 Couture, Gail
282 Cowan, Vincent
504 Craigie, Lois
271 Crawford, Karen
529 Croft, Dave
237 Cronin, John
581 Crosby, Karen
313 Crowley, M.J.
358 Crystal, Cynthia
618 Culbert, Maryjane
263 Culpepper, Linda
383 Cunningham, Evelyn
769 Curley, Jackie
771 Curley, Jackie
526 Curran, Colleen
383 Cyrus, Dianne

D

217 Dahlgren, Teresa E.
463 Daley, Joe
607 Dallaire, Sylvie
470 Dalman, Janice
600 Danciu, Tammie
383 Danehy, Mary
399 Daniels, Esther
530 Daraban, Anna
291 Darr, Beverly
278 Date, Sandy
50 David, Rebecca
134 Davis, Cassandra
302 Davis, Merry Anne
65 Davis, Pulaski O.
15 Dawson, Joanne
359 Dawson, Victoria A.
657 De Bock, Anne
54 De Lapa, Sue
740 de Waard, Ineke
720 Deamer, Bryn
412 DeBase, Charles
124 Deegan, Eileen G.
513 DeLaCruz, Sandra
514 DeLaCruz, Sandra
399 Delaney, Patricia
655 Delanoy, Lut
510 Delgado, Rosa
49 Dellapa, June
215 Delperdang, Judy L.
809 Dempster, Stuart D.
738 Dengerink, Thea
226 Derise, Ivy
190 Derk, Roseann
840 DeSilva, Indranee
72 dHamilton, Marva
155 Diamandis, Alyce
156 Diaz, Holly
481 Dickerson, Amy
482 Dickerson, Amy
475 Diehl, Cathy
412 Dillner, Becky
582 Dilts, Kathryn M.
451 DiSante, Linda B.

460 Ditterline, Susan Y.
6 Dixon, Diane
156 Dixon, Mary
784 Doig, Bill
390 Dolan, Lynne
383 Dombek, Lynn
463 Donahue, Frank
553 Donaldson, Cathy
449 Doncevic, Lois A.
620 Donnelly, Celia
237 Donnelly, Chris
293 Donovan, Derek
146 Donovan, Elizabeth
390 Doremus, Susan
609 Dorse, Joan
509 Doss, T. Alan
28 Douglas, Margaret
635 Doyle, Sharon
450 Doyle, Tim
159 Drewkes, Kathy
266 Dryer, Ruth
383 DuBois, Nan
770 Duerden, Margaret
398 Dufresne, Deborah L.
622 Dugas, Susan
255 Dunlap, Ellen S.
825 Dunn, Judith
11 Durrett, Rachel
261 Dusman, Peggy

E

610 Earls, Leone
613 Earls, Leone
209 Easton, Marilyn
484 Edds, Carolyn
28 Edelson, Daniel
745 Edmonds, Carol
337 Effrat, Eileen
281 Ehmcke, Ruth
67 Ehresman, Paula
38 Eisenberg, Pam
752 Eliassen, Tone
494 Elkins, Anna L.
805 Ellard, John
463 Elliott, Jenny
463 Elliott, Steve
161 Eltzroth, Lee
790 England, Steve
814 Erbach, Gertrud
825 Erbach, Gertrud
74 Erickson, Donald K.
49 Errihard, Scott
806 Erskine, Alexandra
319 Ethier, Sally
773 Evans, Huw
773 Evans, Kate Lloyd
525 Evans, Ruth
712 Everett, Richard
159 Everett, Virginia
769 Evetts, Mike
771 Evetts, Mike

F

776 Fairbrother, June
440 Farley, Austin G.
32 Farrand, Carol
222 Farrar, Lu-An Dunn
656 Farrell, Noel
515 Fennell, Janice C.
79 Ferdula, Tami Jo
310 Fersch, Dorothy
708 Finkler, Susanne
355 Finn, Philip
581 Firkys, Jacci
833 Fisher, Belinda
792 Fisher, Joan
414 Fisher, Nancy
452 Fitting, Joan
367 Fitzgerald, Carol
196 Fitzgerald, Sandra E.
159 Flagg-Davis, Vivian
606 Flegg, Catherine
390 Fleury, Rosanne M.
554 Flint, Angie
159 Flynn, Kathleen
533 Fogle, Ruth
523 Foley, Kathy
430 Follett, Irma
141 Ford, Peter W.
631 Forgues, Andre
131 Forsyth, Kate
752 Foss, Bjorg Saether
438 Foster, Pauline
788 Foster, Ruth
700 Foutrier, Sylvie
468 Fox, Frank
601 Fox, Michael
49 Francis, Lynette
783 Fraser, Stroma
157 Frier, Susan
382 Frohlinger, Margery
208 Fromme, Mary Lou
326 Fry, Kathy
504 Fudala, Cathy

G

782 Gaffney, Alexandra
631 Gagnon, Claudine
347 Gale, Margaret
28 Gallay, Vicki
828 Gallehawk, R.J.
154 Galloway, Debra
304 Gammon, Claudette A.
341 Ganeles, Judith
467 Gannon, Margaret
711 Ganzmann, E.
38 Gao, Wen
284 Garcia, Susan
284 Gardner, Mary
376 Gardner, Roberta J.
411 Garris, Ivy Louise
128 Garvin, Margaret A.
506 Garza, Gina
711 Gasterich, Franz-Josef
269 Gawronski, Pamela
153 Gehle, Janice
49 Geiger, Richard
685 Gemzoe, Suzan
549 Gennotti, Patricia
327 George, Nancy L.
676 Gether, Birgitte
390 Giangrande, Laura
556 Gibson, Diane
152 Giglio, Claire
647 Gijsbrechts, Luc
50 Gilbreath, Marvin
234 Gildersleeve, Larkie
206 Ginter, Kathy
289 Glazer, Rhonda
58 Gnerre, Samuel J.
159 Gnewikow, Kevin
622 Goddard, Jillian
839 Godfrey, Gill
15 Goebel, Heather
610 Goldberg, Louise
114 Goldborough, Marjorie
342 Goldman, Viki
112 Goldstein, Robert
176 Golembiewski, Terry Marie
51 Gomez, C.C.
156 Gonzalez, Manny
89 Goodfriend, David
390 Goralske, Edward
356 Gordon, George
52 Gordon, Marcia
376 Goss, Anita
52 Gott, Janis
381 Gottlieb, Melinda
626 Gouin, Christiane
586 Goulet, Patricia
463 Graham, Jennie
306 Graham, Mollie F.
337 Granat, Pearl
584 Grant, Bruce
274 Grant, Suzanne
206 Grauel, Rusty
424 Graziano, Patti A.
744 Grebenar, Catherine M.
500 Green, Lisa
416 Green, Marcus L.
374 Greenfeld, Judy
773 Gress, Sue
383 Gretes, Francis
65 Greto, Victor
465 Gretsky, Joanne
774 Griffiths, Jennifer
149 Grimsley, Judy L.
315 Groden, Diana
497 Gross, Linda P.
337 Guadagno, Dorothy
618 Guinane, Basil
300 Gullett, Michelle
160 Gunderson, Dina S.
517 Gutierrez, Jo
659 Gybels, Paul

H

192 Habayeb, Jody S.
533 Hagarty, Joe
50 Hagen, Arthur
423 Hahn, Robert C.
689 Hald, Pia
364 Hale, Brian
418 Halgrimson, Andrea H.
244 Hallaren, Nancy B.
159 Hallman, Richard
799 Hamilton, Geoffrey
129 Hamilton, Regina M.
39 Hammes, Linda
282 Hamrick, Rhonda
80 Hanes, Barbara
22 Hansen, Patricia
172 Hard, Patricia
412 Hardesty, Christopher
743 Harding, Anna
152 Hardnett, Carolyn
530 Hardy, Linda
45 Hardy, Peggy
338 Harling, Lynne
482 Harlow, Barbara
541 Harris, Belinda J.
4 Harris, Franklin
373 Harris, Ilona G.
303 Harris, Judy
371 Harris, Laura
813 Hart, Elaine
798 Hartnoll, Gillian
87 Hartz, Mary Katherine
83 Haslam, Anne
399 Hatch, Elizabeth
62 Hatfield, Mona
300 Hauser, Jeanne
375 Hausler, Judith
416 Hauswald, Virginia D.
341 Hayden, Carlton B.
439 Hayer, Melissa
410 Hayes, Howard
495 Hayslett, Teri
487 Hazard, Jim
56 Head, Alison J.
419 Headrick, Ann
158 Hedrich, Beth
188 Heiny, Anita
655 Heiremans, Iris
480 Hemphill, Lee
805 Hemple, Alan
255 Hench, John B.
476 Henderson, Linda
344 Herschaft, Randy R.
623 Hertel, Ute
417 Herzberg-Bender, Barbara
221 Herzog, Barbara
713 Hess, M.
595 Hickman, Claire
322 Hicks, Bonnie
533 Hicks, Raymond
797 Highley, Graham
152 Hijek, Barbara
575 Hildebrand, Janice
420 Hill, Norma
108 Hill, Susan M.
468 Hines, William
735 Hinojosa, Rogelio
736 Hinojosa, Rogelio
1 Hobbs, Ann
530 Hodges, Becky
502 Holland, Anne
844 Holland, Matt
787 Holliday, Jan
671 Holmer, Elsa
281 Holt, David
50 Hom, Melissa
415 Hord, Kim; PKimPhord$wilmington.net)
622 Hornby, Julie
483 Horner, Barbara
761 Horvathova, Luba
383 Horymski, Chris
448 House, David
642 Houston, Cathy
278 Hovde, Roberta
112 Howard, Beth
807 Howard, Carol
571 Howard, Donna
182 Howard, Judy
127 Howe, Robert H.
503 Hudson, Kim
425 Hughes, Diana
756 Hui, Lee Meow
159 Hulshof, Kathryn
513 Humble, Leslie Trich
514 Humble, Leslie Trich
791 Hunt, Colin
412 Hunt, Jean
624 Hunt, Patrick J.
425 Hunter, James J.
175 Huss, Judith L.
310 Hutchinson, Margaret
802 Hyde, Jack A.

I

245 Iannalfo, Linda M.
31 Ingebretsen, Dorothy
836 Irving, Ann
140 Isaacs, Bob
167 Iwamoto, Margaret
168 Iwamoto, Margaret

J

412 Jack, Ron
159 Jackson, John
519 Jackson, Pat
835 Jacobs, Brenda
739 Jacobs, Ruud
681 Jacobsen, Susanne
83 James, Cecilia
344 James, Susan
591 Jamieson, Marjorie
383 Jamison, Sandra
49 Jampol, Gerald
278 Jansen, Robert
177 Jansson, John
209 Janus, Bridget
766 Jaun, Hans-Peter
533 Jelks, Clarencetta
633 Jenkins, Eric
492 Jennings, Lynn
683 Jensen, Mette
572 Jensen, Rosemary
50 Jermyn, Lois
426 Jesse, Michael
623 Jessop, Deborah J.
17 Jett, Jeannie
684 Johansen, Johs. Chr.
337 Johnson, Angela
538 Johnson, Ann Kinken
804 Johnson, George
148 Johnson, Gerald
247 Johnson, Judy
288 Johnson, Nina
51 Johnson, Rene
194 Johnson, Valerie
622 Johnston, Bob
219 Johnston, Tricia
537 Joines, Elizabeth
454 Joint, Penny
651 Jonckheere, Jan
652 Jonckheere, Jan
421 Jones, Annie
426 Jones, Charlotte
358 Jones, Clarita
268 Jones, June
649 Jones, Linda
642 Jones, Simon
270 Joseph, Gina

K

815 Kacperek, Jan
185 Kamler, Clarence
680 Kampmann, Dorrit
464 Kane, Angelika R.
349 Kapnick, Laura B.
41 Kapper, Nadine S.
365 Karpevych, Christine
45 Kaschube, Anita
67 Kasel, Carol L.
796 Katny, Margaret
167 Kaya, Beatrice
168 Kaya, Beatrice
743 Kaye, Marshar
531 Keeler, Susan
426 Keenan, Yevetta

310 Keller, Deborah
425 Kelley, Susan
796 Kelly, Declan
17 Kenan, Charlotte
152 Kenney, Cary
495 Kent, Carolyn
816 Kent, Julia
721 Keren-David, Nina
614 Khan, Asma S.
783 Kharbanda, Nisha
337 Kiely, Theresa
472 Kier, Kathe
763 Kilner, Susanne
298 Kimble, Kathleen R.
384 Kin, Kan
769 Kinchin-Sevier, Teresa
771 Kinchin-Sevier, Teresa
453 King, Carol
795 Kirby, Margaret
261 Kirchner, Dan
86 Kirks, Jo
104 Kirks, Jo
605 Kirkup, Lois
622 Kirsh, Julie
91 Kitchell, Catherine
615 Kitchener, Ron
404 Klemmer, Sara Gesler
664 Klimova, Alena
144 Kline, Sandy
66 Klute, Karen
449 Knauss, Dianne
109 Kohrs, Charlotte
426 Koolbeck, Dean
611 Kopak, Jeannette
374 Korbut, Lora
281 Korent, Kim
436 Kovacic, Kathi A.
383 Kramer, Susan
198 Kreag, Mark
412 Krueger, Sperry
192 Kump, Cindy
640 Kunst, Rosemary

L

539 LaBarbera, Belida
256 Labonte, George H.
568 Laes, Diane
52 Laffranchi, Lorene
130 Laing, William E.
374 Lake, Linda
416 Lamb, Diane A.
534 Lamb, Mary
321 Lambright, Theresa
345 Lamos, Grant
383 Lampach, Charles
52 Lance, Gary
228 Landry, Dot
667 Langballe Madsen, Ann
704 Lange, Eckard
503 Langood, Kristi
672 Larsen, Jorgen
668 Larsen, Lise
571 Larson, Ronald
265 Larzelere, David
473 Latinski-Cadden, Ann
655 Laurent, Nadine
685 Laursen, Jesper
539 LaVallee, Katherine
262 Lavey, Shelley
37 Lavoie, Steven A.
31 Lawrence, William
296 Lawson, Maudie
297 Lawson, Maudie A.
274 Lea, Lorri D.
425 Leach, Matt
312 Leahy, Mary
824 Lees, Naomi
533 Leevy-Washington, Lisa
512 Lehman, Julie
594 Leidemer, Frederick
178 Leisch, Janet
156 Leming, Mary Kate
123 Lenz-Commerford, Pamela J.
125 Lenz-Commerford, Pamela J.
762 Leon, Michelle
412 Leonard, Teresa G.
376 Leventhal, Louis
93 Leveque, Anne
584 Levesque, Kathy
368 Levinson, Debra
383 Levinstein, Joan
233 Levy, Sandra
68 Lewis, Kathleen M.
341 Lichstein, Shulamis
350 Lile, Grace
479 Liles, Pam
385 Lindberg, Lottie
620 Lindegger, Sonja
554 Lindgren, Sara
238 Lindsay, Joan
63 Lindsey, Kathy
254 Linn, Marilyn
49 Littlefield, Barbara Jo
40 Locker, Connie
383 Loflin, Glenn
412 Loggains, Tonya
174 Logsdon, Diane
463 Loielo, Gene
524 Lopez, Mary
750 Lorentzen, Anniken
780 Lorimer, Joyce
615 Losiggio, Tina
412 Lothery, Todd
555 Love, Lisa
38 Love, Penny
233 LoVullo, Lisa
778 Luft, Nick
31 Lutgen, Thomas M.
233 Lyon, Dee
532 Lyons, Phyllis
159 Lyons, Valerie

M

415 MacCallum, Mary
263 Mack, Anita
401 MacKenzie, Holly
434 Mackzum, Mary F.
446 Macomber, Sandra L.
231 MacVane, Marcia
231 Madsen, Linda
47 Magill, Anne
66 Makings, Victoria L.
49 Malarkey, Charles
113 Malesky, Kee
362 Malkin, Lawrence
152 Maloney, Eileen
310 Mammone, David
335 Mancini, Romy
479 Manning, Mary S.
517 Mantel, Melissa
583 Mantua, Elaine
632 Marchand, Robert
682 Marcussen, Lisbeth
810 Margetts, Sara
581 Marr, Norma
661 Marshall, Frances K.
811 Martin, Helen
794 Martin, Jenny
152 Martin, John
504 Mask, Jalyn
601 Masterman, Christine
302 Mateo, Rosita
696 Mathiesen, Kirsten
697 Mathiesen, Kirsten
174 Mathis-Kull, Carlene
228 Matlock, Martha
490 Matthews, Mary
843 Matthews, Sue
23 Matthews, Vera
326 Matturro, Richard
325 Maturro, Richard
195 Matuska, Karen
533 Maxwell, Barbara
406 Maxwell, Daisy D.
368 Mayer, Vera
469 Mazur, Victoria P.
213 McAuliff, Stephen
602 McCallum, Anita
233 McCardell, Paul
471 McCleary, Louise
461 McConnell, Jill
571 McCormick, Dennis
383 McCree, Karen
231 McCue, Julia
815 McDonald, Barrie
554 McDonald, Jeanette
383 McDonald, Lany W.
150 McDowell, Christine
627 McFarlane, Agnes
829 McGhee, Judi
656 McGlynn, Mary
800 Mchon, Garret
474 McInnis, Joan M.
478 McIntosh, Willie
8 McKay, Emily
75 McKula, Kathleen
412 McLeod, Tiffany
251 McMahon, Grace
581 McMillan, Pauletta
238 McMillin, Joyce
347 McNally, Peter
451 McNaughton, Marlene
162 McNeill, Valerie
789 McQueen, Anne
225 Meaux, Cassie
767 Medhurst, Jamie
585 Mehrer, Peter
140 Meiners, Michael
2 Melcher, Kay
437 Mello, Fran
337 Mendell, Donna
383 Mendelson, Margaret
432 Menker, Bill
610 Mercer, Anne
783 Mercer, Beverley
279 Meredith, Gretchen
78 Mesing, Wilbur
81 Michels, Leigh
341 Middleton, Gerard
820 Middleton, Ian
743 Millar, Andrea J.
173 Miller, Deborah
49 Miller, Johnny
214 Mills, Amy
642 Mills, Brigette
456 Mills, Deanna S.
588 Millward, Debra
222 Minch, Linda
358 Mintz, Anne P.
533 Mitchell, George
299 Mitchell, Kris
295 Mittelhauser, Milene
145 Moffett, Martha
691 Moldrup, Lis R.
20 Molen, Sandra
684 Moller, Lise
697 Moller, Steve Vinther
679 Moller, Tine Hauge
628 Monette, Gerard
375 Mooney, Aidan
447 Moore, Capra
435 Moore, Dolores
293 Moore, Felicia
496 Moore, Lillie
334 Moore, Nancy C.
8 Moore, Rebecca L.
290 Moores, Bruce
499 Moran, Sally
520 Morelle, Bobbie
389 Morgan, Melody
797 Morgan, Michelle
670 Mork, Niels
544 Morris, Carole Teshima
500 Morrison, Annette
179 Morrison, Lisa
674 Mose Mortensen, Margrethe
230 Mosqueda, Laura
50 Moss, C.L.
374 Motyka, John
223 Moulton, Patty
709 Mounier, Angela
95 Mulhollan, Daniel P.
166 Muller, Julia C.
801 Muller, Mary
554 Mulvihill, Susan W.
231 Murphy, Elizabeth
180 Murphy, Patra
745 Murphy, Pauline
830 Murray, Bob
556 Murray, Dareth
24 Murray, Saundra L.
210 Myers, Helen
533 Mzil, JoAnn

N

727 Nakamichi, Keiko
3 Nathews, Ann
383 Neering, Patricia
425 Neitch, Linda
495 Nelms, Rosemary W.
183 Nelson, Judy
622 Nelson, Katherine Webb
146 Nemeti, Gaye
724 Nespolesi, Stefano
674 Nestelso, Lise
508 Neu, Margaret Jane
707 Neuwiller, Charlene
743 Niccol, Barbara
710 Niedermeier, M.
666 Nielsen, Peter Steen
621 Noble, Sonja
263 Nolan, Jennifer
3 Noll, Ruthanne
670 Normand, Birgitte
588 Norris, Deanna
707 Nossinski, Ortwin
281 Nygren, Debra

O

812 Oakley, Hilary
533 O'Brian, Susan
382 Obus, Harriet
786 Oppenheim, Charles
829 Ormerod, Alan
328 Ormsby, Rita J.
677 Ornager, Fagleder Susanne
169 Orvis, Althea
38 Ostmann, Sharon
49 O'Sullivan, Niamh
675 Otterstrom, Jette
606 Overall, Dale
19 Owen, Vickie
199 Owens, Rita L.

P

233 Packard, Jean
301 Pai, Padmini
376 Paksons, John
237 Pakule, Elizabeth
152 Palmer, Suzanne
12 Palmisano, Sharon
463 Panzer, Michael
495 Paraham, Gregory J.
625 Pare, Gilles
207 Park, Mary Alice
317 Parker, Annette
834 Parker, Jenny
181 Parmley, JoAnn
184 Parmley, JoAnn
349 Parnes, Carole
397 Parsons, Jill M.
383 Paton, Robert
50 Patterson, Melvin
623 Patterson, Susan
151 Paul, Nora M.
712 Pauluth-Cassel, Beate
404 Paynter, Marion
189 Peabody, Jane
772 Peatfield, Mary
672 Pedersen, Nils Ulrik
320 Pence, Judy
416 Pennington, Melinda Currie
262 Pepper, Alice
62 Perkins, Laura
528 Perrin, Kim
140 Perry, Dean
479 Perry, Lathornia
522 Perry, Suzanne M.
203 Peterka, Marybeth
152 Peters, Deborah
567 Peterson, Dale A.
576 Peyton, Michel
463 Pickett, Constance
821 Pinder, Maureen
344 Pine, Donald
651 Plottier, Armand
112 Plumb, Katherine
594 Poirier, Bob
243 Poirier, Diane
463 Porter, Michael
476 Pothier, Patricia
383 Power, Ed
383 Pradt, Mary
637 Prain, Frank
358 Prall, Naomi S.
15 Prendergast, Peg
412 Prescott, Jonathan
587 Preston, Colin
533 Priestland, Mary
261 Primack, Diane
85 Projent, Colette

6 Pruitt, Angel
487 Punneo, Jackie
258 Puravs, Grace L.

Q

341 Quade, Nancy
337 Quigley, Iris
156 Quigley, Michelle

R

213 Rabe, Rob
339 Racine, Patricia
340 Racine, Patricia
16 Raines, Elaine Y.
789 Rainford, Kathleen
530 Ramirez, Antonio
23 Ramirez, Nancy
383 Ramos, Andi
60 Ramos, Connie
529 Randall, Colleen
699 Ranta, Janne
412 Raynor, David
702 Reasor, Daniel
241 Rebello, Judy
743 Reed, Jennifer
216 Reed, Ranae
47 Reeves, Sharon Stewart
349 Register, Sam
757 Rehakova, Drahoslava
52 Reifer, Joe
412 Reu, Norman
49 Rhodes, Kathleen
250 Rhodes, Nancy
507 Rice, Margaret R.
457 Rice, Ruth
281 Rich, Paulette
480 Richards, Dargan A.
796 Richards, Paul
65 Richardson, Tess
623 Ricketts, Mike
332 Ridosh, Margaret
400 Riley, Frances Henry
638 Ritchie, Vickie
283 Robards, Paul E
412 Roberts, Colline
35 Roberts, Elizabeth
34 Roberts, Kate
12 Robinson, Michael
113 Robinson, Rob
33 Rocha, Rosie
383 Rodriguez, Elias
737 Roestenburg, Wil
816 Rogers, Jane
73 Rogers, Virginia
380 Ronan, Linda
684 Ronberg, Gitte
38 Rose, Jan
264 Rose, Lori
27 Rosen, Karen
405 Rosen, Michelle
684 Rosendal, Michaela
533 Rosenstein, Bruce
369 Rosenthal, Faigi
38 Rosentreter, Mike
395 Ross, Bonnie L.
426 Ross, David
809 Ross, Paul
10 Ross, Peggy
804 Rossiter, Paul
197 Rother, Elizabeth
177 Rott, Richard
513 Royer, Liz
514 Royer, Liz
605 Ruberry, Charlene
390 Rubino, Cynthia C.
213 Ruby, Helen
407 Rucker, Virginia
276 Rudd, June M.
672 Rude, Mette Marie
592 Ruff, Denette
692 Rungsoe, Lisette
383 Rusin, Annette
348 Russell, Jamie B.
149 Russo, Ric
383 Ryan, Amy
637 Ryan, Catherine
281 Rysgaard, Kathy

S

509 Sall, Judy
405 Sammons, Janet
287 Sanders, Sharon K.
806 Sanson, Fiona
376 Santiago, Edgar
554 Santrop, Tracy
455 Saul, Ann
540 Saunders, Charles
260 Sauve, Ann
52 Savin, Jessica
378 Schachter, Bert
588 Schachter, Deborah
647 Schauvaerts, Marc
126 Scheeder, Donna W.
605 Scheer, Jim
278 Scheiman, Linda
5 Scherer, Valeria
709 Schmid, Helga
713 Schmidt, Hella
277 Schmierbach, Edie
571 Schmitt, Carol
708 Schmockel, Heike
262 Schmuckal, Christine
31 Schneider, Cary
639 Schokman, David
577 Scholzen, Kathleen A.
310 Schulman, Paul
690 Schwensen, Hanne
383 Scroggs, Justin
409 Scullion, Gail
239 Seaberg, Guy P.
235 Sealover, Robin
839 Sebury, Philip L.
522 Sedeno, Edna A.
375 Seiffer, Lynn
330 Seigel, Lesley
309 Selingo, Betty
618 Selz, Robin
403 Semonche, Barbara P.
706 Sendker, Sabine
618 Serhijczuk, George
412 Sese, Donna
156 Sessoms, Marion
316 Shanahan, Patricia
156 Shapiro, Barbara G.
331 Shapiro, Elliot
240 Sharp, Steven
769 Sharpe, Alison
771 Sharpe, Alison
494 Shaver, Julia
769 Shaw, Gill
771 Shaw, Gill
159 Shea, Dorothy
137 Shealy, M.K.
529 Shelline, Stewart
192 Shepherd, Michelle
139 Sheppard, Cheryl
310 Shoobs, Adrian
412 Shu, Hilary
578 Siburt, Debra
598 Sidney, Katrina
445 Sieg, Pamela S.
680 Siersback, Poul
305 Silver, Robin
69 Silvers, Shirley Jean
412 Simmons, Peggy
463 Simmons, Sandy
262 Simon, Lorraine
682 Simonsen, Majbrit
537 Simpson, Melissa
31 Simpson, Mildred
509 Sims, Jerome
149 Simser, Jill
584 Sinclair, John M.
368 Singer, Stan
559 Sinsel, Donean
341 Skaggs, Tony
314 Skerritt, Elizabeth
337 Skinner, Mary Ann
684 Skovmand, Solveig
747 Slatter, Mary
299 Sloan, Patricia
752 Smeby, Ellen Anette
13 Smetzer, Mary Beth
132 Smith, Barbara
779 Smith, Chrissie
545 Smith, Deb
429 Smith, Ellen C.
799 Smith, Geoff
495 Smith, Janet D.
608 Smith, Kirsten J.
552 Smith, Lytton E.
132 Smith, Martin
222 Smith-Niemi, Linda
64 Smokler, Charlotte
810 Snaddon, David
386 Sokolowski, David
670 Sorensen, Birgit Farbol
52 Spain, Mark
390 Spano, Karen
780 Spence, Douglas
766 Spitzenpfeil, Ruth
71 Spitzer, Helene
485 Sponder, Sheri
191 Sprepski, Ellen
353 Sprules, Marcia L.
702 Spurgeon, Bradford
419 Stadstas, Jenelle
15 Stanley, John
426 Stanley, Sasha
769 Stanton, Tim
771 Stanton, Tim
535 Staples, Gloria
9 Stearns, Debra
299 Steider, Susan
425 Stephenson, Dave
500 Steptoe, Chantay
503 Sterling, Tanya
143 Sterzel, Maryann P.
171 Stetson, Charlotte
647 Stevens, Hans
15 Stevens, Paula
349 Stevenson, Jean
781 Stevenson, Moira
546 Stewart, Linda
533 Stewart-Stern, Arabella
52 Stickler, Diana
49 Stillwell, Otis
185 Stilson, Jan
358 Stinson, Linda
459 Stiver, Wendy
200 Stodghill, Darla
610 Strachan, Gail
428 Strachan, Jane
57 Strom, Thai
612 Struthers, Laura
341 Stuart, Candace
38 Stuart, Lois
533 Sudlow, Jean
416 Sugden, Bonnie Toenniessen
155 Suits, Sherry
441 Suklis, Glenda
763 Svensson, Lars
449 Swartz, Patrice
218 Swearingen, JoAnn
337 Sweeney, Kathy
486 Sykes, Allene
412 Sykes, Joyce
495 Sykes, Shirley
135 Szadkowski, Joseph

T

223 Taflinger, Mark
233 Tag, Charlene
58 Takata, Steve
734 Tan, Cecilia Chun Huang
220 Tanner, Allan
622 Tapscott, Glenna
449 Tauber, Eugene
370 Taylor, Susy
341 Tenenbaum, Ruth
824 Tennyson, Fiona
336 Terry, Sandra
707 Tesh, Debra
223 Tharp, Leonard
237 Thibeault, Alan
18 Thomas, Alfred M.
364 Thomas, Brett
831 Thompson, Barbara
832 Thompson, Barbara
409 Thompson, Jim
272 Thompson, Linda
777 Thompson, Stephen
149 Thompson, Susan
383 Thornton, Angela
281 Thraen, Pat
162 Thrower, Patricia F.
420 Tierney, Catherine M.
285 Tike, Beverly
344 Tishman, Jeffrey
533 Titone, Angela
639 Todd, Peter
614 Tom, Perry
793 Torner, Michael
311 Torres, Olga
804 Torrington, Steve
599 Treble, Patricia A.
839 Trethewy, Claire
131 Trimble, Kathleen
194 Tucker, Louise K.
236 Tuite, Elisabeth
818 Tulip, Jill
50 Tuller, Michael
605 Tuominen, Liisa
76 Turdin, Lynne
262 Turk, Victoria
811 Turner, Mick
112 Tuszynski, Tom
605 Tysick, Ronald P.

U

731 Ueno, Tomoko
504 Uhlaender, Scott
541 Urquhart, Steven
152 Usberghi, Sue

V

330 Vairamides, Sharon
699 Valiaho, Ratva
543 Valois, Renee
620 Valpy, Amanda
655 Van Beneden, Anna
742 van der Linden, M.
131 Van Fleet, Xi
647 Van Hamme, Franky
15 Van Leeuwen, Nancy
49 Van Niekerken, Bill
358 Van Voris, Velma
175 Vance, Carolyn J.
186 Vance, Sandra L.
657 Vandelois, Christian
111 Vandergrift, Barbara P.
658 Vantournhout, Ann
400 Varner, Zana
52 Vaughn, Sharon
764 Vaverka, Ronald D.
28 Velasquez, Miriam
390 Villen, Nancy
113 Vinh, Alphonse
431 VonThron, Deborah
463 Voves, Ed
665 Vozobule, Jaroslav

W

223 Wadlington, Judy
622 Wagler, Joyce
570 Walden, Marilyn R.
669 Waldorf, Grethe
83 Walker, Charlotte J.
829 Walker, Judith
408 Wallace, Dot
451 Wallace, Gladys
337 Wallace, Loretta
505 Walls, Jeanne
114 Walsh, Barclay
329 Walsh, Judith
115 Walters, Donna
524 Walters, Steve
500 Washam, Glenda
54 Wasielewski, Fran
233 Waters, Susan
55 Watson, Christine
783 Watson, Ian
49 Webb, Mary Jo
267 Weible, Susanne M.
31 Weigel, Judith
838 Weightman, Elizabeth
383 Weil, Carol
246 Weisberg, Samuel
532 Wells, Christine
533 Wells, Tish
741 Werst, Anne
275 Wertz, Briget
462 Wesolowski, Paul G.
564 West, Brenda
193 Weston, Laura L.
383 Whatford, Helen
392 Wheeler, Virginia
637 Whelan, Jude
622 White, Barbara
818 White, Caroline
205 White, Faye

542 White-Williams, Patricia
777 Whitfield, Jane
146 Whiting, Bill
516 Whitner, Calvin
310 Wilder, Paul T.
344 Wilkinson, Arnold
118 Williams, Colleen
330 Williams, Loren
326 Williams, Margaret
623 Williams, Maureen
318 Williams, Sharon
591 Williamson, Joan
134 Williems, Margot
156 Willis, Derek
259 Willison, Linda
458 Wilson, Edward G.
23 Wilson, Mabel
177 Wilson, Mary
383 Wilson, Pamela
38 Wilson, Scott
825 Withey, Richard
61 Woessner, Wanda
401 Wolfe, Jill
212 Wolfe, Phyllis
232 Wolod, Janice C.
349 Wolozin, Sara
642 Woolley, Kathryn
643 Woolley, Kathy
775 Woolway, Anthony
539 Wray, Sharon
147 Wright, Joseph F.
166 Wright, Sara
201 Wright, Wende
204 Wysong, Breena
476 Wyss, Albert

Y

548 Yardley, Donna
53 Yasuda, Midori
385 Yeh, Elizabeth
726 Yoshikio, Nori

Z

257 Zaborey, Paula
156 Zaborski, Jackie
263 Zacharias, Patricia
383 Zack, Carol
309 Zagariello, Winifred
551 Zanone, Geri
523 Zipp, Judith
345 Zoeller, Chuck
422 Zwick, Ray

Birmingham Post-Herald

MIDLAND
INDEPENDENT NEWSPAPERS LIMITED

Alabama (Birmingham)

THE DECATUR DAILY

Alabama (Decatur)

TimesDaily

Alabama (Florence)

The Huntsville Times

Huntsville News

Alabama (Huntsville)

Anchorage Daily News

Alaska (Anchorage)

The Arizona Republic
The Phoenix Gazette

Arizona (Phoenix)

The Arizona Daily Star
Tucson Citizen

Arizona (Tucson)

Arkansas Gazette.
Arkansas Democrat

Arkansas (Little Rock)

Specials

The Bakersfield Californian

California (Bakersfield)

TIMES ADVOCATE

California (Escondido)

INDEPENDENT PRESS-TELEGRAM

California (Long Beach)

The Daily Review

California (Hayward)

Marin Independent Journal

California (Ignacio)

Los Angeles Times

LOS ANGELES
Herald Examiner

Daily News
LOS ANGELES

California (Los Angeles)

MONTEREY COUNTY
The Herald
MONTEREY COUNTY'S LARGEST NEWSPAPER

California (Monterey)

Independent Journal

California (Novato)

The Oakland Tribune.

California (Oakland)

Niagara Falls Review

California (Ontario)

Times Tribune

California (Palo Alto)

The Sacramento Bee

The Sacramento Union

California (Sacramento)

SAN BERNARDINO COUNTY
The Sun

399 N. "D" Street, San Bernardino, CA 92401

California (San Bernardino)

The San Diego
Union-Tribune.

Since 1886

San Diego Daily Transcript

California (San Diego)

San Francisco Examiner

San Francisco Chronicle

California (San Francisco)

San Jose Mercury News

California (San Jose)

THE ORANGE COUNTY
Register

California (Santa Ana)

SANTA BARBARA NEWS-PRESS

California (Santa Barbara)

Santa Cruz Sentinel

California (Santa Cruz)

Stockton Record

California (Stockton)

Daily Breeze

California (Torrance)

Turlock Journal

California (Turlock)

Ventura County
STAR ☆ Free Press

Contra Costa Times
California (Walnut Creek)

Daily Camera
Colorado (Boulder)

Colorado Springs Sun
The Morning Newspaper SATURDAY 25¢

COLORADO SPRINGS
GAZETTE TELEGRAPH
Colorado (Colorado Springs)

Rocky Mountain News

THE DENVER POST
Colorado (Denver)

FORT COLLINS
COLORADOAN
Colorado (Fort Collins)

Loveland Daily
Reporter-Herald
Colorado (Loveland)

The News-Times™
Connecticut (Danbury)

The Hartford Courant
Connecticut (Hartford)

THE HERALD
Connecticut (New Britain)

The Day

Connecticut (New London)

THE ADVOCATE

Connecticut (Stamford)

Record-Journal

Connecticut (Meriden-Wallingford)

USA TODAY

U.S.News & WORLD REPORT

National Geographic Society Library

The Washington Times

The Washington Post

District of Columbia

The Bradenton Herald

Florida (Bradenton)

FORT MYERS NEWS-PRESS

Florida (Fort Myers)

Gainesville Sun

Florida (Gainesville)

The Florida Times-Union

Florida (Jacksonville)

The Ledger

Florida (Lakeland)

el Nuevo Herald

The Miami Herald

The Miami News

The Miami Herald

Florida (Miami)

The Orlando Sentinel

Florida (Orlando)

Naples Daily News

Florida (Naples)

St. Petersburg Times

Evening Independent

Florida (St. Petersburg)

THE TAMPA TRIBUNE

Making a difference in our community

Sun-Sentinel

Florida (Tampa)

THE ALBANY

Sunday Herald

Georgia (Albany)

The Atlanta Journal

THE ATLANTA CONSTITUTION

Georgia (Atlanta)

The Augusta Chronicle

The South's Oldest Newspaper-Established 1785

Georgia (Augusta)

The Macon Telegraph

Georgia (Macon)

Savannah Morning News
SAVANNAH EVENING PRESS
111 WEST BAY STREET, P.O. BOX 1088
SAVANNAH, GEORGIA 31402-1088

Georgia (Savannah)

The Idaho
Statesman

Idaho (Boise)

ALTON TELEGRAPH PRINTING CO.

Illinois (Alton)

The Beacon-News

Illinois (Aurora)

The Belleville
News-Democrat

Illinois (Belleville)

The Pantagraph

Illinois (Bloomington)

The News-Gazette

Illinois (Champaign)

Chicago Tribune

CHICAGO
Sun-Times

Illinois (Chicago)

Herald & Review

Copyright 1989 Decatur, Illinois Newsstand: 50 cents • Home delivery: 28 cents

Illinois (Decatur)

THE DISPATCH

Illinois (Moline)

THE ROCK ISLAND
ARGUS

Illinois (Rock Island)

The State Journal-Register

Illinois (Springfield)

The News-Sun

Illinois (Waukegan)

Anderson Daily Bulletin
THE ANDERSON HERALD

Indiana (Anderson)

The Evansville Press

Indiana (Evansville)

The Journal-Gazette

Indiana (Fort Wayne)

The News-Sentinel

Indiana (Fort Wayne)

Post-Tribune

Indiana (Gary)

THE TIMES

Indiana (Hammond)

KOKOMO kt TRIBUNE

Indiana (Kokomo)

Wed., March 21, '84
REPORTER

Indiana (Martinsville)

The News-Dispatch

Indiana (Michigan City)

SOUTH BEND
Tribune

Indiana (South Bend)

The Gazette

Iowa (Cedar Rapids)

Waterloo Courier

Iowa (Waterloo)

Abilene
Reporter-News

The Kentucky Post

Kentucky (Covington)

The Wichita Eagle

Kansas (Wichita)

LEXINGTON HERALD-LEADER

Kentucky (Lexington)

The Courier-Journal

Kentucky (Louisville)

MORNING ADVOCATE
STATE TIMES

Louisiana (Baton Rouge)

THE DAILY IBERIAN

Louisiana (New Iberia)

The Times-Picayune
The States-Item

Louisiana (New Orleans)

Bangor Daily News

Maine (Bangor)

Portland Press Herald
Maine Sunday Telegram

EVENING EXPRESS

Maine (Portland)

The Capital

Maryland (Annapolis)

THE SUN
The Evening Sun

Maryland (Baltimore)

The Boston Globe

Massachusetts (Boston)

The Boston Herald

Massachusetts (Boston)

THE CHRISTIAN SCIENCE MONITOR

Massachusetts (Boston)

The Enterprise

Massachusetts (Falmouth)

Cape Cod Times

Massachusetts (Hyannis-Cape Cod)

Lawrence Eagle-Tribune

Massachusetts (Lawrence)

Daily Evening Item

Massachusetts (Lynn)

The Transcript

Massachusetts (North Adams)

The Berkshire Eagle

Massachusetts (Pittsfield)

The Morning Union

Massachusetts (Springfield)

TELEGRAM & GAZETTE

SUNDAY TELEGRAM

Massachusetts (Worchester)

THE ANN ARBOR NEWS

Michigan (Ann Arbor)

The Detroit News

Michigan (Detroit)

Detroit Free Press

Michigan (Detroit)

THE FLINT JOURNAL

Michigan (Flint)

The Grand Rapids Press

Michigan (Grand Rapids)

THE JACKSON Citizen Patriot

Michigan (Jackson)

Times Herald

Michigan (Port Huron)

The Saginaw ***NEWS***

Michigan (Saginaw)

TRAVERSE CITY Record-Eagle

Michigan (Traverse City)

Duluth News-Tribune

The Northland's Newspaper

Minnesota (Duluth)

St. Paul Pioneer Press

Minnesota (St. Paul)

THE SUN HERALD

Mississippi (Biloxi-Gulfport)

Hattiesburg AMERICAN

Mississippi (Hattiesburg)

The Clarion-Ledger

Mississippi (Jackson)

The Mississippi Press

Mississippi (Pascagoula)

SOUTHEAST MISSOURIAN

Missouri (Cape Girardeau)

Columbia Daily **Tribune**

Missouri (Columbia)

Columbia **Missourian**

The Joplin Globe

Missouri (Joplin)

THE KANSAS CITY STAR.

The Kansas City Times

Missouri (Kansas City)

ST. LOUIS POST-DISPATCH

Missouri (St. Louis)

Journal and Star

Nebraska (Lincoln)

Omaha World-Herald

Nebraska (Omaha)

Reno Gazette-Journal

Nevada (Reno)

NEW HAMPSHIRE SUNDAY NEWS

The Union Leader

New Hampshire (Manchester)

The Courier-News

New Jersey (Bridgewater)

The Daily Journal

New Jersey (Elizabeth)

The Record

New Jersey (Hackensack)

THE HOME NEWS & TRIBUNE

New Jersey (New Brunswick)

The Herald-News

New Jersey (Passaic)

Burlington County Times

New Jersey (Willingboro)

The Gloucester County Times

New Jersey (Woodbury)

Newsday

New York (Long Island)

The Times Herald RECORD

New York (Middletown)

ABCNEWS

AMERICAN BANKER

AP Associated Press

DAILY NEWS

America's Largest Newspaper

The Journal of Commerce

Medical Tribune

NBC NEWS

NEW YORK POST

The New York Times

New York City Tribune

PARADE

THE WALL STREET JOURNAL.

TASS
Telegraph Agency of the U.S.S.R.

Thirteen · wnet

356 West 58th Street
New York NY 10019

Time Inc.
A TIME WARNER COMPANY

New York (New York)

NIAGARA GAZETTE

New York (Niagara Falls)

the Saratogian

New York (Saratoga Springs)

THE POST-STANDARD
Morning
Herald American
Sunday
SYRACUSE
HERALD-JOURNAL
Evening

New York (Syracuse)

The Times Herald
RECORD
New York (Troy)

Watertown Daily Times

New York (Watertown)

The Reporter Dispatch

New York (White Plains)

ASHEVILLE
CITIZEN-TIMES
VOICE OF THE MOUNTAINS

North Carolina (Asheville)

The Charlotte Observer

North Carolina (Charlotte)

the chapel hill Herald

The Herald-Sun

THE DURHAM SUN

North Carolina (Durham)

Fayetteville Observer-Times

A Great Way To Start Your Day

North Carolina (Fayetteville)

NEWS & RECORD

North Carolina (Greensboro)

THE NEWS & OBSERVER

North Carolina (Raleigh)

WINSTON-SALEM JOURNAL

North Carolina (Winston-Salem)

THE BISMARCK TRIBUNE

North Dakota (Bismarck)

Akron Beacon Journal

Ohio's Complete Newspaper.

Ohio (Akron)

THE CINCINNATI ENQUIRER

Ohio (Cincinnati)

THE PLAIN DEALER

Ohio (Cleveland)

The Columbus Dispatch

Ohio (Columbus)

DAYTON DAILY NEWS

Ohio (Dayton)

THE CHRONICLE-TELEGRAM

Ohio (Elyria)

NEWS JOURNAL

Ohio (Mansfield)

Tribune Chronicle

THE DAILY OKLAHOMAN
OKLAHOMA CITY TIMES

Oklahoma (Oklahoma City)

THE PONCA CITY NEWS
"Your Hometown Newspaper"

Oklahoma (Ponca City)

THE BULLETIN

Oregon (Bend)

Medford Mail Tribune

Oregon (Medford)

The Oregonian

Oregon (Portland)

SUNDAY CALL-CHRONICLE

THE MORNING CALL

Pennsylvania (Allentown)

Beaver County Times

Pennsylvania (Beaver)

THE EXPRESS

Pennsylvania (Easton)

Intelligencer Journal

Pennsylvania (Lancaster)

The Inquirer
IT'S YOUR LIFE

PHILADELPHIA DAILY NEWS
THE PEOPLE PAPER

Pennsylvania (Philadelphia)

POTTSVILLE REPUBLICAN

Pennsylvania (Pottsville)

DELAWARE COUNTY
DAILY and SUNDAY TIMES

Pennsylvania (Primos)

The Scranton Times

Pennsylvania (Scranton)

CENTRE DAILY TIMES

Pennsylvania (State College)

Valley News Dispatch

Pennsylvania (Tarentum)

The Times Leader

Pennsylvania (Wilkes-Barre)

The Providence Journal

The Evening Bulletin

Rhode Island (Providence)

The Call

Rhode Island (Woonsocket)

The Post and Courier

South Carolina (Charleston)

The State

South Carolina (Columbia)

The Greenville News
— and —
GREENVILLE PIEDMONT

South Carolina (Greenville)

The Chattanooga Times

Tennessee (Chattanooga)

Johnson City Press
The A.M. Authority©

THE KNOXVILLE
JOURNAL

Tennessee (Knoxville)

THE COMMERCIAL APPEAL

Tennessee (Memphis)

Nashville Banner

Tennessee (Nashville)

Abilene Reporter-News

Texas (Abilene)

Austin American-Statesman

Texas (Austin)

Brazosport
The Facts

Texas (Clute)

Corpus Christi Caller-Times

Texas (Corpus Christi)

The Dallas Morning News

Texas (Dallas)

Del Rio News-Herald

Texas (Del Rio)

Houston Chronicle

The Houston Post

Texas (Houston)

TEMPLE DAILY TELEGRAM

Texas (Temple)

DESERET NEWS

The Salt Lake Tribune

Utah (Salt Lake City)

THE ALEXANDRIA Journal

Virginia (Alexandria)

THE ARLINGTON Journal

Virginia (Arlington)

THE PRINCE GEORGE'S Journal

Virginia (Prince George)

MONTGOMERY
THE Journal

Virginia (Montgomery)

Daily Press

Virginia (Newport News)

The Virginian-Pilot
AND
THE LEDGER-STAR

Virginia (Norfolk)

N

Virginia (Reston)

Roanoke Times & World-News

Virginia (Roanoke)

THE Journal

Army Times

Air Force Times

FEDERAL TIMES

NAVY TIMES

Virginia (Springfield)

THE BELLINGHAM HERALD

Washington (Bellingham)

THE DAILY NEWS

Washington (Longview)

The Seattle Times

Seattle Post-Intelligencer

Washington (Seattle)

THE SPOKESMAN-REVIEW
Spokane Chronicle

Washington (Spokane)

The Morning
News Tribune

Washington (Tacoma)

The COLUMBIAN

Washington (Vancouver)

The Herald-Dispatch

West Virginia (Huntington)

THE WELCH DAILY NEWS

West Virginia (Welch)

KENOSHA NEWS

Wisconsin (Kenosha)

Milwaukee
THE JOURNAL

Milwaukee
Sentinel

Wisconsin (Milwaukee)

the Journal Times

Wisconsin (Racine)

Wisconsin
State Journal

Wisconsin (Madison)

The Sheboygan Press

Wisconsin (Sheboygan)

Calgary Herald

Canada (Alberta - Calgary)

THE EDMONTON SUN

Canada (Alberta - Edmonton)

The Advocate
CENTRAL ALBERTA'S DAILY NEWSPAPER

Canada (Alberta - Red Deer)

THE Province

The Vancouver Sun

Canada (British Columbia - Vancouver)

Winnipeg Free Press

Canada (Manitoba - Winnipeg)

The Times-Transcript

Canada (New Brunswick - Moncton)

The London Free Press

Canada (Ontario - London)

The Hamilton Spectator

Canada (Ontario-Hamilton)

THE OTTAWA Citizen

Canada (Ontario - Ottawa)

CANADA'S NATIONAL NEWSPAPER

THE GLOBE AND MAIL

CANADA'S WEEKLY NEWSMAGAZINE

Maclean's

Canada (Ontario)

SUN

Canada (Ontario - Toronto)

THE TORONTO STAR

Canada (Ontario - Toronto)

The Windsor Star

Canada (Ontario - Windsor)

THE OTTAWA SUN 25¢

LE DEVOIR

Canada (Quebec - Montreal)

The Gazette

Canada (Quebec-Montreal)

La Presse

Canada (Quebec-Montreal)

LE SOLEIL

Canada (Quebec - Quebec)

LeaderPost

Canada (Saskatchewan)

BANNERS / International

The Courier-Mail

Australia (Queensland-Brisbane)

Børsen

Denmark (Copenhagen)

THE JERUSALEM POST

Israel (Jerusalem)

International Herald Tribune

Published With The New York Times and The Washington Post

LE FIG-ECO

LE FIGARO

Le Monde

France (Paris)

LA NAZIONE

Italy (Florence)

LA GAZZETTA DEL MEZZOGIORNO

Italy (Puglia)

CORRIERE DELLA SERA

Italy (Milano)

la Repubblica

Italy (Rome)

LA SICILIA

Italy (Sicily)

朝日新聞

Japan

Luxemburger Wort

LUXEMBOURG

NATIONAL BUSINESS REVIEW

N.Z.'s NATIONAL DAILY • Auckland (09) 371-287 (Advert) 371-629 (Ed) • Wellington 732-610 • Christchurch 556-438 • Circ. (09) 521-1945 •

Auckland STAR LIMITED

New Zealand (Auckland)

CHRISTCHURCH STAR

New Zealand (Christchurch)

THE DOMINION

New Zealand (Wellington)

DV Frjalst ohað dagblað

VG

Norway (Oslo)

the IRISH NEWS

Belfast

South Wales Evening Post

Daily Mail

30p

THE TIMES

The Guardian

THE OBSERVER

United Kingdom (London)